# THE ANCIENT EGYPTIAN
# BOOK OF THE DEAD

# THE ANCIENT EGYPTIAN
# BOOK
# OF THE
# DEAD

Translated by
Raymond O. Faulkner

Edited by Carol Andrews

University of Texas Press, Austin
Published in Co-operation with
British Museum Publications

**Front cover** *Scene showing the Opening of the Mouth ceremony carried out on the mummy of Hunefer. See Spell 23.* 9901/5

**Half-title page** *Ani and his wife adore Thoth, the god of wisdom and learning. See Spell 175.* 10470/29

**Title page** *The hippopotamus-goddess Opet, wearing horns and a disc, and the cow-goddess of the West, Hathor. See Spell 186.* 10470/37

International Standard Book Number 0-292-70425-9
Library of Congress Catalog Card Number 90-70343
© 1972 The Limited Editions Club, New York
Revised edition 1985. Photographs and additional material
© The Trustees of the British Museum
All rights reserved

First University of Texas Press Edition, 1990

Requests for permission to reproduce material from this work
should be sent to Permissions, University of Texas Press,
Box 7819, Austin, Texas, 78713-7819.

Designed by Grahame Dudley.
Typeset in Linotype Garamond
by Peter MacDonald, Hampton.
Illustrations originated in Spain
by Grijelmo S.A., Bilbao.
Printed in Great Britain by
BPCC Hazell Books
Aylesbury, Bucks, England
Member of BPCC Ltd.

# Contents

# PREFACE

The translations contained in this volume are made from that corpus of funerary texts known as the *Book of the Dead*. They are accompanied by reproductions of new colour and black and white photographs mostly taken especially for this edition from the rich collection of Egyptian funerary papyri in the British Museum.

Dr R.O. Faulkner, the translator of this English version, was the leading modern British authority on the progressive stages of funerary texts developed in antiquity for use successively by kings, nobles and less highly placed Egyptians. His translations of the *Pyramid Texts* appeared in 1969 and of the *Coffin Texts* between 1973 and 1978. He was in the meanwhile invited to prepare a translation of the *Book of the Dead* for the Limited Editions Club of New York to accompany a splendid coloured photographic facsimile of a large part of the Papyrus of Ani, one of the finest illustrated texts of the *Book of the Dead* in the British Museum. The sumptuous publication of 1972 has since been acknowledged as containing the most reliable translation of this fascinating, but perplexing, compilation of spells, prayers and incantations. It is, sadly, not easily available, and students and others interested in the texts are unable to read or consult it without difficulty. To remedy this position and to ease the frustration of potential users, the Limited Editions Club have, with exceptional generosity, given permission for Dr Faulkner's work to be reproduced in this present edition. The British Museum is profoundly grateful to Mr Sidney Schiff, President of the Limited Editions Club, and his associates, for recognising so clearly the need to make Faulkner's translation more widely accessible, and for responding so handsomely to the request that it might be reprinted with new illustrations.

Dr Faulkner explained in his Foreword that the great majority of spells making up the ancient compilation were represented in his translation. He omitted a few spells at the request of his original publisher because

they duplicate, or virtually duplicate the spells which are translated, and a few others, or parts of spells which are too corrupt or obscure to yield intelligible translation. Of those omitted by Faulkner because they were composed at a far later date than the painted papyri of the Theban Recension on which his version was based, the whole of Spell 162, and the titles and rubrics of Spells 163 to 165 have been newly translated for the present edition, and are illustrated by interesting vignettes from Late Period papyri. As in Faulkner's original edition, four texts, two of them quite short, have been left out because, as he rightly said, 'they lack interest except to the professional scholar.' Faulkner also pointed out 'that a few spells were numbered twice over by the scholars of the nineteenth century, and in such cases the texts in question have been allotted here the numbers by which they are generally known.'

In explaining the basis of his translation, Dr Faulkner had the following remarks to make on sources and on the presentation of his version:

With one exception, all the spells in this book have been translated afresh by the present writer, but due acknowledgement must be paid to P. Barguet, *Livre des Morts,* Paris, 1967, a valuable work which has been held in constant consultation. The one exception is Spell 78; here, by permission of the Egypt Exploration Society, I have used, with only very minor modifications, the admirable translation published by the late Professor A. de Buck in the *Journal of Egyptian Archaeology,* vol.35. It is, of course, clear that in a publication such as the present, which is addressed to the educated layman and not to the professional scholar, the textual and philological commentaries which normally would accompany translations such as these, so as to justify the renderings, would be entirely out of place. Likewise at the publisher's request, the bracketed query-mark has been omitted after words and sentences where there is possible doubt as to the meaning. Passages printed in italic type represent the use of red ink on the original papyrus; three dots (...) signify that words have been lost or omitted or are untranslatable; while on occasion

*Vignette incorrectly termed Spell 16: above an animated djed-pillar representing Osiris, which carries a crook and flail and is flanked by his sister-goddesses Isis and Nephthys, stands the newly risen sun-god as a falcon wearing a sun-disc and adored by dancing baboons. 9901/1*

round brackets ( ) enclose either a word obviously omitted by the ancient copyist or an English word added to make the sense of a passage clearer.

The editorial work required to prepare Faulkner's original translation for the present publication has been skilfully carried out by Miss Carol A. R. Andrews, Research Assistant in the Department of Egyptian Antiquities. She has translated those spells and parts of spells omitted by Faulkner, which are mentioned above, and she has also made a few other small emendations based on alternative versions and the findings of recent scholarship. In addition, she has selected the illustrations used here, which will give this edition particular interest.

The photographs have mostly been taken by Mr Peter Hayman of the Photographic Service of the British Museum. Miss Andrews has also revised and enlarged the Glossary, and provided a new introduction to the translation, including information on the various important papyri in the British Museum, and other details of history and textual development which were not appropriate for the original publication.

December 1984

T. G. H. James
Keeper of Egyptian Antiquities
British Museum

# Sources of the Illustrations

The illustrations to this edition are taken from the British Museum papyri listed below. The numbers in the captions refer, in each case, to the British Museum registration number, followed by the number of the sheet on which the particular vignette is found.

BM**9900** Hieroglyphic funerary papyrus of the Copiest of the Temple of Ptah, and of the Temples of Upper and Lower Egypt, Draughtsman in the Sculptors' Workshop, Child of the Royal Nursery, Nebseny son of the Draughtsman Tjena and the Lady Mutreshti.
Memphis. Eighteenth Dynasty, *c*.1400 BC   BC

BM**9901** Hieroglyphic funerary papyrus of the Royal Scribe and Steward of King Sety I, Overseer of Royal Cattle and Scribe of Divine Offerings, Hunefer.
Memphis (?). Nineteenth Dynasty, *c*.1310 BC

BM**9911** Hieroglyphic funerary papyrus of Kerquny son of Abt-Wesir and Gernubit.
Ptolemaic Period, *c*.250 –150 BC

BM**9946** Hieroglyphic funerary papyrus of the Offerer of Incense (?) in the Temple of Amun, Ankh-Hap son of Pashermin and Iutetenast.
Thebes. Ptolemaic Period, *c*.300 –200 BC

BM**9949** Hieroglyphic funerary papyrus of the Wesay, Khary.
Memphis (?). Eighteenth–Nineteenth Dynasties, *c*.1350–1300 BC

BM**9951** Hieroglyphic funerary papyrus of the Sistrum-player, Mutirdais.
Thebes (?). Ptolemaic Period, *c*.300 BC

BM**9964** Hieroglyphic funerary papyrus of the Accounting Scribe for Royal Silver and Gold, Scribe of the Royal Treasury in Pernefer, Overseer of the Dockyard of Amun in the Southern City, the Steward, Nebamun son of the Judge, Scribe and Overseer of Royal Land (?) Inyotef and the Lady Tetishat.
Thebes. Eighteenth Dynasty, *c*.1400 BC

BM**9995** Hieratic funerary papyrus of the Hereditary Count and Noble, Kerasher, born of Tasent.
Ptolemaic–Roman Periods, 1st Century BC

BM**10009** Hieroglyphic funerary papyrus of the Scribe, Userhat.
Eighteenth Dynasty, *c*.1400 BC

BM**10010** Hieroglyphic funerary papyrus of the Chantress of Amun, Muthetepti.
Thebes. Twenty-first Dynasty, *c*.1050 BC

BM**10039** Hieratic funerary papyrus of Astwert daughter of Tanahebu.
Ptolemaic Period, *c*.250 –150 BC

BM**10086** Hieratic funerary papyrus of Ta-Amen-iw daughter of Neshorpakhered.
Ptolemaic Period, *c*.250 –150 BC

BM**10088** Hieratic funerary papyrus of Tint-Djehuty daughter of Tadineferhotep.
Ptolemaic Period, *c*.250 –150 BC

BM**10098** Hieratic funerary papyrus in which the space left for the owner's name has been filled with the word 'so-and-so' written in demotic.
Memphis (?). Ptolemaic Period, 1st–2nd Centuries BC

BM**10253** Hieratic funerary papyrus of Padiamennebnesutawy, born to Neshor.
Ptolemaic Period, *c*.300 BC

BM**10257** Hieratic funerary papyrus of the God's Father Horemheb, born to Ta-di-ipt-wert.
Ptolemaic Period, *c*.300 –200 BC

BM**10470** Hieroglyphic funerary papyrus of the Royal Scribe, Accounting Scribe for Divine Offerings of all the gods, Overseer of the Granaries of the Lords of Tawer, Ani.
Nineteenth Dynasty, *c*.1250 BC

BM**10471** Hieroglyphic funerary papyrus of the Royal Scribe and Chief Military Officer, Nakht.
Eighteenth–Nineteenth Dynasties, *c*.1350 –1300 BC

BM**10472** Hieroglyphic funerary papyrus of the Chief of the Concubines of Osiris, Chief of the Concubines of Nebtu and Khnum, Chantress of Amun, Anhai.
Twentieth Dynasty, *c*.1100 BC

BM**10477** Hieroglyphic funerary papyrus of the Steward of the Chief Treasurer, Nu son of the Steward of the Chief Treasurer, Amenhotep and the Lady Sensenb.
Eighteenth Dynasty, *c*.1400 BC

BM**10478** Hieroglyphic funerary papyrus made for a Scribe and Priest whose name has been erased but ended with the elements -en-Mut.
Nineteenth Dynasty, *c*.1300 –1250 BC

BM**10479** Hieroglyphic funerary papyrus of the *Sma*-priest and Scribe of the Oracle, Hor son of the *Sma*-priest Djedhor and the Lady Sebat.
Akhmim. Ptolemaic Period, *c*.300 BC

BM**10554** Hieratic funerary papyrus of the First Chief of the Concubines of Amun, Prophetess of Mut, of Anhur-Shu, of Min, Horus and Isis at Akhmim, of Osiris, Horus and Isis at Abydos, of Horus of Djufy, of Amun at Iurudj, Nestaneb-tasheru daughter of the High Priest of Amun Pinudjem II and Nesikhons.
Thebes. Twenty-first Dynasty, *c*.950 BC

BM**10558** Hieratic funerary papyrus of Ankhwahibre.
Ptolemaic Period, *c*.300 BC

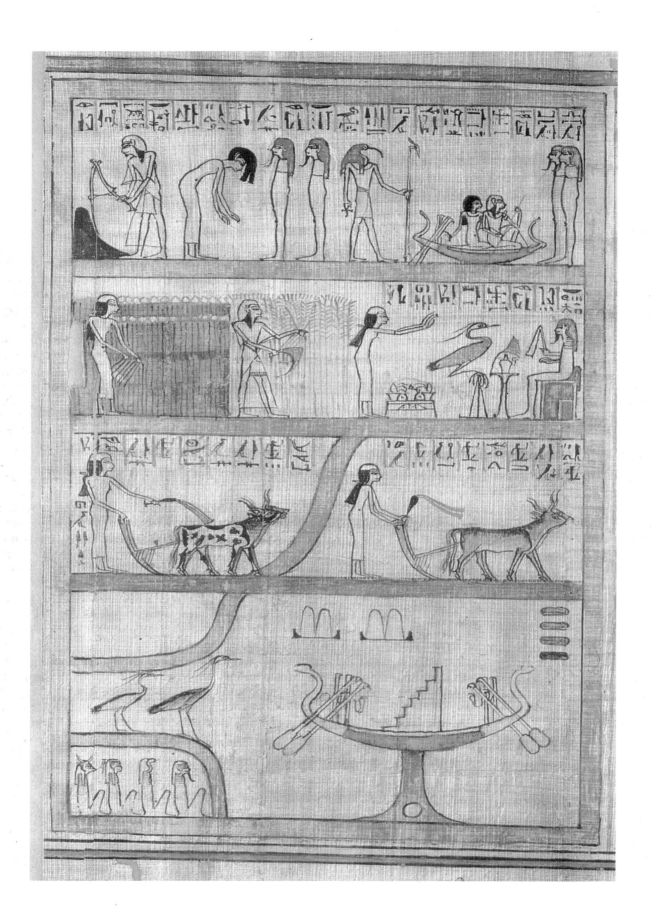

# —Introduction—

The *Book of the Dead* is the name now given to sheets of papyrus covered with magical texts and accompanying illustrations called vignettes which the ancient Egyptians placed with their dead in order to help them pass through the dangers of the Underworld and attain an afterlife of bliss in the Field of Reeds, the Egyptian heaven. Some of the texts and vignettes are also found on the walls of tombs and on coffins or written on linen or vellum rather than on papyrus. The very rare examples of *Books of the Dead* written on leather (for example BM10281) were probably master copies, used by scribes who were commissioned to reproduce their contents.

The term *Book of the Dead* was chosen by modern Egyptologists because the texts on funerary papyri are divided into individual spells, or chapters, nearly two hundred in number, although no one papyrus contains all of them. These chapters formed a repertoire from which selection was made. If the prospective owner of a *Book of the Dead* was wealthy and his death not untimely he would commission an expert scribe to write the text for him and it would consist of his own personal choice of chapters. An expert draughtsman scribe would be employed to provide the illustrative vignettes. Others, less fortunate, had to make do with a ready written text in which spaces had been left for the insertion of the name and titles of the buyer. In one instance, in a funerary papyrus of Ptolemaic date (about 200 BC) written in the hieratic script (BM10098), instead of leaving a space for the prospective owner's name the scribe has written on each occasion in demotic, the script in current use for everyday documents, the word *men* meaning 'so-and-so'. Presumably the papyrus had never been bought.

The earliest *Book of the Dead* papyri date to the mid-fifteenth century BC, but the ritual utterances and in-

*Spell 110 Anhai and her husband undertake various activities in the Field of Rushes including hacking up the earth, pulling flax, reaping grain, ploughing with two teams and paddling across the Lake of Offerings. Four members of the Great Ennead sit on an island, the Heron of Abundance and a god of the Underworld are adored and the bark of Wennefer is shown moored at the end of a waterway. 10472/5*

cantations they contain have a history which can be traced back more than a thousand years earlier. Some of the spells in the *Book of the Dead* originated in the *Pyramid Texts* which first appeared carved in hieroglyphs on the walls of the burial chamber and anteroom of the pyramid of King Wenis, last ruler of the Fifth Dynasty, about 2345 BC. Although this is their first written appearance it is clear from their content that many of these utterances had been in existence for centuries. One *Pyramid Text* (Spell 662) tells the dead king to cast the sand from his face, a clear allusion to burial in the desert sand which was especially common during the Predynastic Period, before 3100 BC. Another utterance (Spell 355) says that bricks have been removed from the great tomb, a reference to mud-brick mastaba tombs of the type discarded by royalty since the early Third Dynasty, about 2680 BC. Some of the *Pyramid Text* utterances are hymns and addresses to various gods or magical recitations to assure the royal resurrection and protection from malign influences. Others are concerned with the Opening of the Mouth ceremony which was performed on the mummy and tomb statues during the funeral rites and with the Offering Ritual which was carried out after the burial.

The *Pyramid Texts* also reflect a belief in an astral afterlife among the circumpolar stars which predates the ideas of the pyramid-builders who believed in a solar afterlife spent in the company of the sun-god. The tone of the *Pyramid Texts* is often threatening: the king almost bullies the gods into allowing him to enter heaven. There is little evidence that he expected to become one of their number automatically. It is possibly of significance that none of the kings of the Fourth Dynasty or the other kings of the Fifth Dynasty felt the need to have these texts carved within their tombs. The rulers who could command the building of the pyramids at Giza and sun-temples at Abu Gurab presumably had no doubt of their entry into heaven to join their fellow gods. Once they had made their appearance, the *Pyramid Texts* continued to be carved inside the pyramids of kings and queens of the Sixth Dynasty and early First Intermediate Period for another two hundred years.

The Middle Kingdom (about 2040–1786 BC) was a

time when funerary beliefs and practices were democratised, when a guaranteed afterlife, which before had been restricted to royalty and great noblemen, became open to all who could afford to acquire the relevant equipment. Now to the Utterances of the *Pyramid Texts* were added many more spells, and this new repertoire was written not in hieroglyphs but in the cursive script called hieratic, in closely crowded vertical columns within the wooden coffins of commoners. Because of their new location the spells are now known as *Coffin Texts*, and it is they which are the direct predecessors of the texts written in *Book of the Dead* papyri of the New Kingdom and later.

A new development in the *Coffin Texts* is that· the sun-god is no longer supreme: Osiris is the king under whom the blessed dead hope to spend eternity, the god with whom the dead became assimilated as 'the Osiris so-and-so'. Indeed, from now on the term 'the Osiris so-and-so' means little more than 'the late' or 'the deceased'. This new importance of Osiris in the afterlife is best illustrated by his assumption of the role of judge of the dead. During the Old Kingdom (about 2686–2181 BC) when only the great nobility, apart from the king, were assured of an afterlife, living one's earthly life according to a strict moral code was considered sufficient to secure eternal bliss. But the breakdown of order during the political troubles of the First Intermediate Period, which led to tomb-robbery and the desecration of cemeteries, shattered this belief. So, in an attempt to deter such wrong-doing, the idea was encouraged that judgement would be passed on the dead for the actions they had committed on earth. At first it was an anonymous Great God who passed sentence, but once Osiris became pre-eminent as god of the dead during the Middle Kingdom, it was only natural that he should be the god before whom the trial took place. Chapter 125 of the *Book of the Dead* is entirely devoted to the judgement of the dead and the various vignettes depicting the Weighing of the Heart, by which it was ascertained whether the deceased was worthy to enter the kingdom of Osiris, are among some of the best-known scenes from funerary papyri.

Another new concept appearing in the *Coffin Texts* is a belief in an afterlife spent in the Field of Reeds where agricultural tasks would have to be carried out by the deceased for all eternity. Since Egypt was an agricultural community with an annual need for ploughing, sowing, harvesting, maintenance of irrigation works and remarking of boundaries after the inundation, the Other World was envisaged as an identical environment requiring the same hard labour. Hence the shabti-formula makes its first appearance, a spell to relieve the dead of all hard work in the afterlife by providing a magical substitute worker, a shabti figurine. One of the very first noted occurrences of the shabti-formula (Spell 472) is inside the outer wooden coffin from el-Bersha of a physician called Gua (BM 30839). From the New Kingdom onwards shabtis inscribed with Chapter 6 of the *Book of the Dead* and carrying agricultural implements become one of the commonest elements of Egyptian funerary equipment. The Field of Reeds with its waterways, islands and divine inhabitants, and the ploughing, sowing and reaping required of the dead, is regularly depicted in the vignette of Chapter 110 of the *Book of the Dead*.

Thus the chapters of the *Book of the Dead* papyri of the New Kingdom and later incorporate at least three quite separate traditions: there are traces of the earliest beliefs in an astral afterlife, spells in which the sun-god with his associated gods is supreme, and others in which Osiris is all-important. The Egyptians saw no incongruity in such a situation. In Egyptian religion old beliefs were rarely discarded, new ideas and concepts were merely tacked on, even when in direct contradiction to existing views. That is why the Egyptians could believe in an afterlife in which the deceased would spend eternity in the company of the circumpolar stars as an akh, at the same time as being restricted to the burial chamber and offering chapel of the tomb as a ka, but also visiting the world of the living, inhabiting the Elysian Fields and travelling across the sky and through the Underworld with the sun-god as a ba. It is hardly surprising, therefore, that the Egyptians themselves called the text of funerary papyri the *Book of Coming Forth by Day*, for it concerned to so great an extent the freedom granted to the spirit forms which survived death to come and go as they pleased in the afterlife.

Some of the earliest *Book of the Dead* papyri, such as those of Nu (BM 10477), Userhat (BM 10009), Kha (Turin Museum) and Yuya (Cairo Museum) contain a surprisingly small number of chapters and are further distinguished by having few vignettes. During the course of the New Kingdom, however, the repertoire of chapters grew steadily and vignettes became more prominent. Indeed, during the Third Intermediate Period (about 1085–715 BC) many funerary papyri consisted of almost nothing but illustrations. Moreover, there are some chapters which always existed only in vignette form, for example Chapters 16 and 143. Illustrations are usually restricted to a narrow frieze above the text except for occasional examples which run the whole height of the papyrus. When the text is written in horizontal lines rather than in vertical columns full-height vignettes are usually evenly spaced between sections of text. In funerary papyri of the Late Period (after about 600 BC) small vignettes are frequently set in the midst of the text itself. *Books of the Dead* with large sections of text, not necessarily accurately copied, must always have cost more than those in which vignettes predominated.

***Vignette of Ani and his wife*** *Ani stands with his arms raised in adoration behind a tray on two stands which is heaped with offerings and topped by a bowl of burning incense. Behind him stands his wife Tutu shaking a sistrum in one hand and rattling a menat-collar in the other.* 10470/2

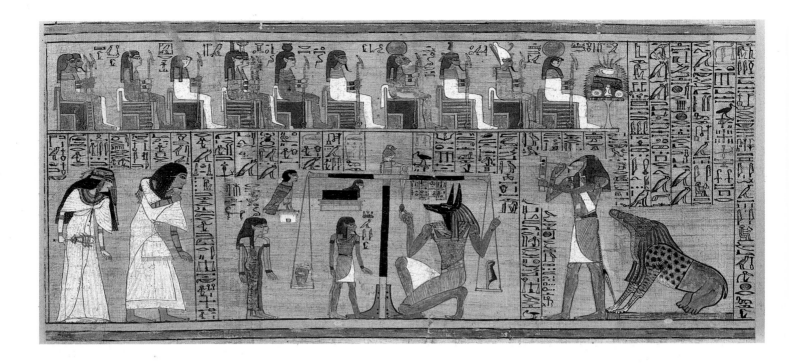

During the New Kingdom there was still little attempt to regularise the order in which selected chapters appeared. Often, too, variants of the same chapter appeared in different parts of the same papyrus. In other instances chapters were cut off in the middle of the text purely because the scribe had run out of space. Some papyri give proof that the text and illustrations were produced separately without regard to each other, for chapters and their vignettes do not coincide. In spite of this lack of order certain spells are found in every extant *Book of the Dead* papyrus: Chapter 1, which concerns the Coming Forth by Day after Burial, Chapter 17, which concerns the Coming Forth by Day Triumphant over all enemies, and Chapter 64, which concerns the Coming Forth by Day in various Transformations. Funerary papyri of the Twenty-sixth Dynasty and later (after about 600 BC) are characterised not only by a new style of vignette with subdued use of colour but by a regularising of the order of chapters and a fixing of their total number at 192. This unchanging text of Late Period funerary papyri is sometimes known as the Saite Recension to distinguish it from the more arbitrary contents of earlier *Books of the Dead*, which are said to embody the Theban Recension.

Some of the oldest chapters of the *Book of the Dead* can actually be traced back to the original Utterances in the *Pyramid Texts*, but without exception they have survived in so corrupt a form as to be virtually unintelligible. Chapters 174, 177 and 178 are examples of such survivals. Other spells also appear to be ancient, but examination often proves that they are relatively recent

Above: **Spell 125** *Ani and his wife Tutu watch as his heart is weighed against an ostrich feather representing Maat. Anubis checks the accuracy of the balance. Thoth stands ready to write down the result and Ammit, the hybrid monster, waits to gobble down any heart weighed down by sin. Ani's human-headed soul, his destiny and birth-goddesses and his fate look on. Twelve gods and goddesses holding was-sceptres are enthroned behind a heaped offering table as witnesses to the judgement. 10470/3.*

in composition. One of the most important spells concerned with the heart was Chapter 30B of the *Book of the Dead*, which was always to be inscribed 'on a scarab made from nephrite [a green stone], mounted in fine gold, with a silver suspension ring and placed at the throat of the deceased'. The spell was reputed to be very old, having been found 'in Hermopolis, under the feet of the Majesty of this god [that is, beneath a statue of the god Thoth]. It was written on a block of Upper Egyptian mineral in the writing of the god himself and was discovered in the time of the Majesty of the vindicated King of Upper and Lower Egypt Menkaure. It was the king's son Hordedef who found it while he was going around making an inspection of the temples.' Menkaure or Mycerinus, as Classical authors called him, was a pharaoh of the Fourth Dynasty who built the smallest of the three pyramids at Giza. Hordedef himself was revered throughout the pharaonic period for his reputation as a wise man, so any spell connected with him would be bound to have extra potency. Yet one of the earliest heart scarabs is that belonging to King Sobkemsaf II of the Seventeenth Dynasty, who reigned about 1590 BC, nine centuries after Mycerinus. It looks sus-

*A human-headed green jasper heart scarab set in a gold mount inscribed with a very early version of Spell 30B. Tomb robbers brought to trial in c.1125 BC confessed to stealing it from the mummy of King Sobkemsaf II. Thebes. Seventeenth Dynasty, c.1590 BC. EA 7876.*

piciously as though a false pedigree was created for Chapter 30B to make it look older than it really was: the spell was almost certainly only composed a very short time before it was first inscribed on a heart scarab. Hordedef was also linked with Chapter 137A concerning the four torches which would give light to the deceased. This spell was reputed to have been found by the prince 'written in the god's own hand in a secret chest in the temple of Wenut [a hare goddess]' at Hermopolis.

According to one version, the all-important Chapter 64 was found 'in the foundations of the One-who-is-in-the-Henu-bark [that is, beneath the temple of the funerary god Sokaris] by a Supervisor of Wall-builders in the time of the Majesty of the King of Upper and Lower Egypt, Semty, vindicated'. Semty or Khasty, the name cannot be read with certainty, is better known as Den, fifth king of the First Dynasty, who ruled about 2875 BC. Since writing only makes its appearance in Egypt with the beginning of the First Dynasty some two hundred years earlier the spell could scarcely claim to be more ancient. But it cannot be without significance that it appears to have no antecedent in the *Pyramid Texts*. So, like Chapters 30B and 137A, Chapter 64 was probably composed far more recently than would first appear to be the case. This would certainly help to explain the number of variant forms of this chapter: because it was a recent composition, the definitive version of the text had not yet been decided.

On the other hand, some of the versions of chapters which were incorporated into the repertoire at quite a late stage made no attempt to hide their recent composition. Some copies of Chapter 166 concerning the spell for the headrest state that the text was found 'at the neck of the mummy of King Usermaatre [that is, Ramesses II or Ramesses III] in the necropolis'. Some versions of Chapter 167 concerning the bringing of the udjat-eye relate how the text was found by prince Khaemwese, son of King Ramesses II, in the cemetery at Saqqara or else was composed by Amenhotep son of Hapu, Chief of building works under King Amenophis III. Significantly for the potency of this spell, both Khaemwese and Amenhotep son of Hapu were revered by the Egyptians for their wisdom.

At first *Book of the Dead* texts were written in a form of semi-cursive hieroglyphs known as linear hieroglyphs or *Book of the Dead* hieroglyphs. However, unlike hieratic (the cursive script which developed from hieroglyphs but whose signs soon became quite distinct from the original hieroglyphic signs on which they were based), the script employed in funerary papyri always remained visibly hieroglyphic. During the New Kingdom chapters were invariably written in vertical columns but they were often to be read in the opposite or retrograde direction to normal practice.

Although vignettes were frequently highly coloured only black ink was used for the text, except for the title of each spell or particularly important sections which were normally written in red to make them stand out. Because of their colouring these passages are usually known as rubrics. In rare instances yellow rather than red was used (see, for example, BM 9968). Funerary papyri of the Third Intermediate Period and later (after about 1085 BC) were often written in hieratic rather than in linear hieroglyphs and in that case the text was written in horizontal lines arranged in pages not in columns. Sometimes parts of a papyrus were written in hieratic and other parts in linear hieroglyphs. During the Graeco-Roman Period (after 305 BC), when hieratic survived only as the script of funerary papyri, a few *Books of the Dead* were written in demotic, the third script employed by the Egyptians which by then was in current use for documents of a non-funerary nature. Mention has already been made of the hieratic *Book of the Dead* of the Ptolemaic Period (BM 10098) in which the prospective owner is designated only as 'so-and-so' but written in demotic, a script with which the scribe was obviously better acquainted.

A *Book of the Dead* papyrus could be as long or as short as required. The Greenfield Papyrus (BM 10554) which is 41 metres in length, is one of the longest known. For practical purposes the height of any papyrus, funerary or otherwise, was rarely greater than 48 centimetres. On the other hand, some funerary papyri of the Third Intermediate Period are very narrow indeed.

Funerary papyri might be rolled up, tied with a strip of linen and sealed with a piece of stamped mud. They would then be placed on or in the coffin or inside a wooden statuette of the funerary god Ptah-Sokaris-Osiris or even inside the hollowed-out plinth on which the statuette stood. The papyrus of Anhai (BM 10472) was found inside just such a figure. Some papyri were inserted among the folds of the bandages which enveloped the mummy, either over the chest, beneath the arms or between the legs.

From the New Kingdom onwards a *Book of the Dead* papyrus became an essential part of the funerary equipment and every Egyptian who could afford to acquire a copy was buried with it close at hand for use in the afterlife. That is why so many and varied examples have survived and why so much has been learned about the text which has been called erroneously but very evocatively the Bible of Ancient Egypt.

Carol A. R. Andrews
Department of Egyptian Antiquities
British Museum

# —— THE SPELLS ——

# THE SPELLS

Illustrated above and below: ***Spell 1*** *Kerasher's mummy, attended by figures of Isis and Nephthys, lies on a boat-shaped bier which is drawn along by a priest, as is a shrine containing a divine figure. An incense-burner and standards are carried towards two miniature obelisks before which the lector priest reads from a papyrus. The mummy is held upright by a priest wearing a jackal's head while water is poured over it and Kerasher's widow grieves on her knees watched by an enthroned falcon-headed Re-Horakhty. In the lower register Anubis tends the mummy flanked by Isis and Nephthys, who kneel with a gesture of mourning. Behind are twelve of the twenty-one portals of the House of Osiris, each represented as an elaborate gateway behind which squats its guardian carrying a knife. 9995/3*

# INTRODUCTORY HYMN TO THE SUN-GOD RE

*Worship of Re when he rises in the eastern horizon of the sky by N*

He says: Hail to you, you having come as Khepri, even Khepri who is the creator of the gods. You rise and shine on the back of your mother (the sky), having appeared in glory as King of the gods. Your mother Nut shall use her arms on your behalf in making greeting. The Manu-mountain receives you in peace, Maat embraces you at all seasons. May you give power and might in vindication – and a coming forth as a living soul to see Horakhty – to the ka of N.

He says: O all you gods of the Soul-mansion who judge sky and earth in the balance, who give food and provisions; O Tatenen, Unique One, creator of mankind; O Southern, Northern, Western and Eastern Enneads, give praise to Re, Lord of the Sky, the Sovereign who made the gods. Worship him in his goodly shape when he appears in the Day-bark. May those who are above worship you, may those who are below worship you, may Thoth and Maat write to you daily; your serpent-foe has been given over to the fire and the rebel-serpent is fallen, his arms are bound, Re has taken away his movements, and the Children of Impotence are non-existent. The Mansion of the Prince is in festival, the noise of shouting is in the Great Place, the gods are in joy, when they see Re in his appearing, his rays flooding the lands. The Majesty of this noble god proceeds, he has entered the land of Manu, the land is bright at his daily birth, and he has attained his state of yesterday. May you be gracious to me when I see your beauty, having departed from upon earth. May I smite the Ass, may I drive off the rebel-serpent, may I destroy Apep when he acts, for I have seen the abdju-fish in its moment of being and the bulti-fish piloting the canoe on its waterway. I have seen Horus as helmsman, with Thoth and Maat beside him, I have taken hold of the bow-warp of the Night-bark and the stern-warp of the Day-bark. May he grant that I see the sun-disc and behold the moon unceasingly every day; may my soul go forth to travel to every place which it desires; may my name be called out, may it be found at the board of offerings; may there be given to me loaves in the Presence like the Followers of Horus, may a place be made for me in the solar bark on the day when the god ferries across, and may I be received into the presence of Osiris in the Land of Vindication.

For the ka of N.

*Vignette of Osiris In a shrine topped by an archaic falcon and a frieze of cobras stands Osiris carrying a crook, flail and was-sceptre. Before him is a lotus on which stand the Four Sons of Horus; behind him is Isis carrying an ankh. 10470/30.*

# INTRODUCTORY HYMN TO OSIRIS

WORSHIP of Osiris Wennefer, the Great God who dwells in the Thinite nome, King of Eternity, Lord of Everlasting, who passes millions of years in his lifetime first-born son of Nut, begotten of Geb, Heir, Lord of the Wereret-crown, whose White Crown is tall, Sovereign of gods and men. He has taken the crook and the flail and the office of his forefathers. May your heart which is in the desert land be glad, for your son Horus is firm on your throne, while you have appeared as Lord of Busiris, as the Ruler who is in Abydos. The Two Lands flourish in vindication because of you in the presence of the Lord of All. All that exists is ushered in to him in his name of 'Face to whom men are ushered'; the Two Lands are marshalled for him as leader in this his name of Sokar; his might is far-reaching, one greatly feared in this his name of Osiris; he passes over the length of eternity in his name of Wennefer.

Hail to you, King of Kings, Lord of Lords, Ruler of Rulers, who took possession of the Two Lands even in the womb of Nut; he rules the plains of the Silent Land, even he the golden of body, blue of head, on whose arms is turquoise. O Pillar of Myriads, broad of breast, kindly of countenance, who is in the Sacred Land: May you grant power in the sky, might on earth and vindication in the realm of the dead, a journeying downstream to Busiris as a living soul and a journeying upstream to Abydos as a heron; to go in and out without hindrance at all the gates of the Netherworld. May there be given to me bread from the House of Cool Water and a table of offerings from Heliopolis, my toes being firm-planted in the Field of Rushes. May the barley and emmer which are in it belong to the ka of the Osiris N.

# THE JUDGEMENT OF THE DEAD

THE HEART OF THE DEAD MAN IS WEIGHED IN THE SCALES OF THE BALANCE AGAINST THE FEATHER OF RIGHTEOUSNESS

## —— SPELL 30B ——
[illustrated pp.56,57]

O my heart which I had from my mother! O my heart which I had from my mother! O my heart of my different ages! Do not stand up as a witness against me, do not be opposed to me in the tribunal, do not be hostile to me in the presence of the Keeper of the Balance, for you are my ka which was in my body, the protector who made my members hale. Go forth to the happy place whereto we speed; do not make my name stink to the Entourage who make men. Do not tell lies about me in the presence of the god; it is indeed well that you should hear!

*Thus says* Thoth, judge of truth, to the Great Ennead which is in the presence of Osiris: Hear this word of very truth. I have judged the heart of the deceased, and his soul stands as a witness for him. His deeds are righteous in the great balance, and no sin has been found in him. He did not diminish the offerings in the temples, he did not destroy what had been made, he did not go about with deceitful speech while he was on earth.

*Thus says* the Great Ennead to Thoth who is in Hermopolis: This utterance of yours is true. The vindicated Osiris N is straightforward, he has no sin, there is no accusation against him before us, Ammit shall not be permitted to have power over him. Let there be given to him the offerings which are issued in the presence of Osiris, and may a grant of land be established in the Field of Offerings as for the Followers of Horus.

*Thus says* Horus son of Isis: I have come to you, O Wennefer, and I bring N to you. His heart is true, having gone forth from the balance, and he has not sinned against any god or any goddess. Thoth has judged him in writing which has been told to the Ennead, and Maat the great has witnessed. Let there be given to him bread and beer which have been issued in the presence of Osiris, and he will be for ever like the Followers of Horus.

*Thus says* N: Here I am in your presence, O Lord of the West. There is no wrong-doing in my body, I have not wittingly told lies, there has been no second fault. Grant that I may be like the favoured ones who are in your suite, O Osiris, one greatly favoured by the good god, one loved of the Lord of the Two Lands, N, vindicated before Osiris.

**Spell 125** *The Negative Confession. Within an elaborate shrine with open doors squat the Forty-two Assessors of the Dead. Each is addressed by name and to each Nakht denies having committed a specific sin. The confession is witnessed by the enthroned falcon-headed sun-god and the two Maats, all carrying was-sceptres, and by Thoth as a baboon wearing the moon on his head and holding a scribe's palette. 10471/11.*

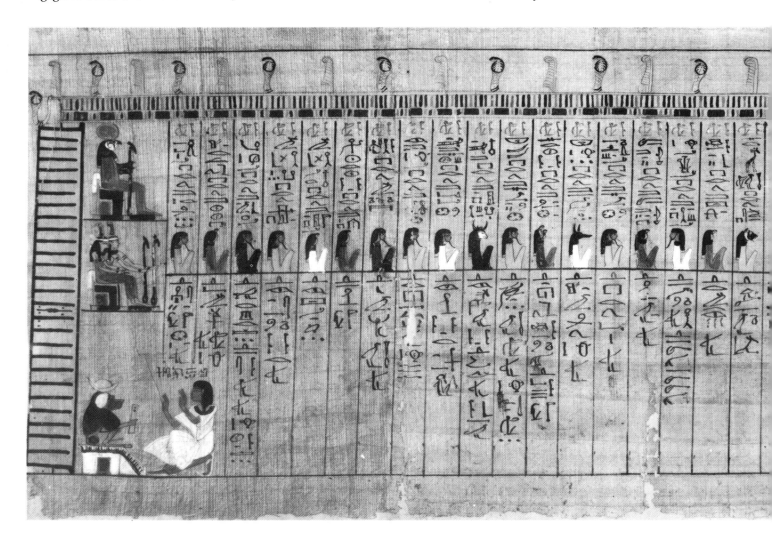

THIS SPELL IS INSERTED HERE RATHER THAN IN THE ACCEPTED NUMERICAL ORDER BECAUSE OF ITS OBVIOUS CONNECTION WITH THE JUDGEMENT. THERE IS NO MENTION OF THE WEIGHING OF THE HEART, BUT THE DECEASED DECLARES TO THE TRIBUNAL OF FORTY-TWO GODS THAT HE HAS NOT COMMITTED A SERIES OF SPECIFIED SINS, WHICH IN EGYPTIAN EYES APPARENTLY COVERED EVERY CONCEIVABLE KIND OF WRONGDOING. THE DECLARATION, LONG KNOWN BY THE SELF-CONTRADICTORY TITLE OF 'THE NEGATIVE CONFESSION,' IS BETTER NAMED 'THE DECLARATION OF INNOCENCE'.

### INTRODUCTION

*What should be said when arriving at this Hall of Justice, purging N of all the evil which he has done, and beholding the faces of the gods*

Hail to you, great god, Lord of Justice! I have come to you, my lord, that you may bring me so that I may see your beauty, for I know you and I know your name, and I know the names of the forty-two gods of those who are with you in this Hall of Justice, who live on those who cherish evil and who gulp down their blood on that day of the reckoning of characters in the presence of Wennefer. Behold the double son of the Songstresses; Lord of Truth is your name. Behold, I have come to you, I have brought you truth, I have repelled falsehood for you. I have not done falsehood against men, I have not impoverished my associates, I have done no wrong in the Place of Truth, I have not learnt that which is not, I have done no evil, I have not daily made labour in excess of what was due to be done for me, my name has not reached the offices of those who control slaves, I have not deprived the orphan of his property, I have not done what the gods detest, I have not calumniated a servant to his master, I have not caused pain, I have not made hungry, I have not made to weep, I have not killed, I have not commanded to kill, I have not made suffering

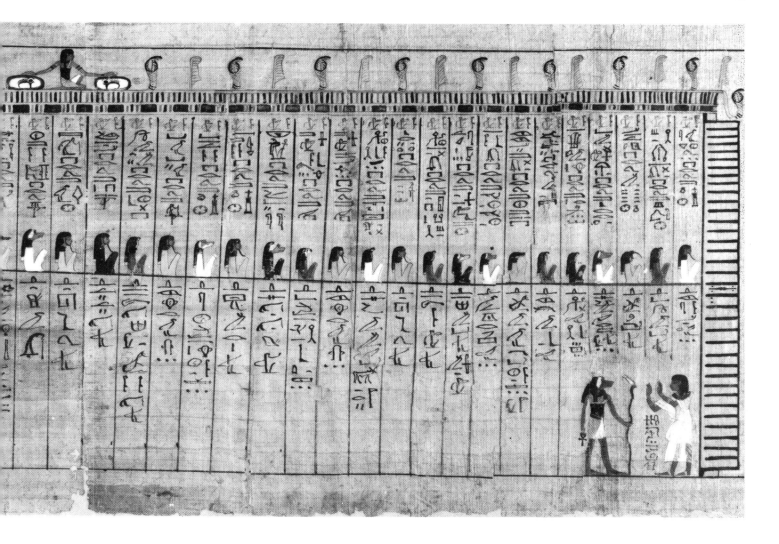

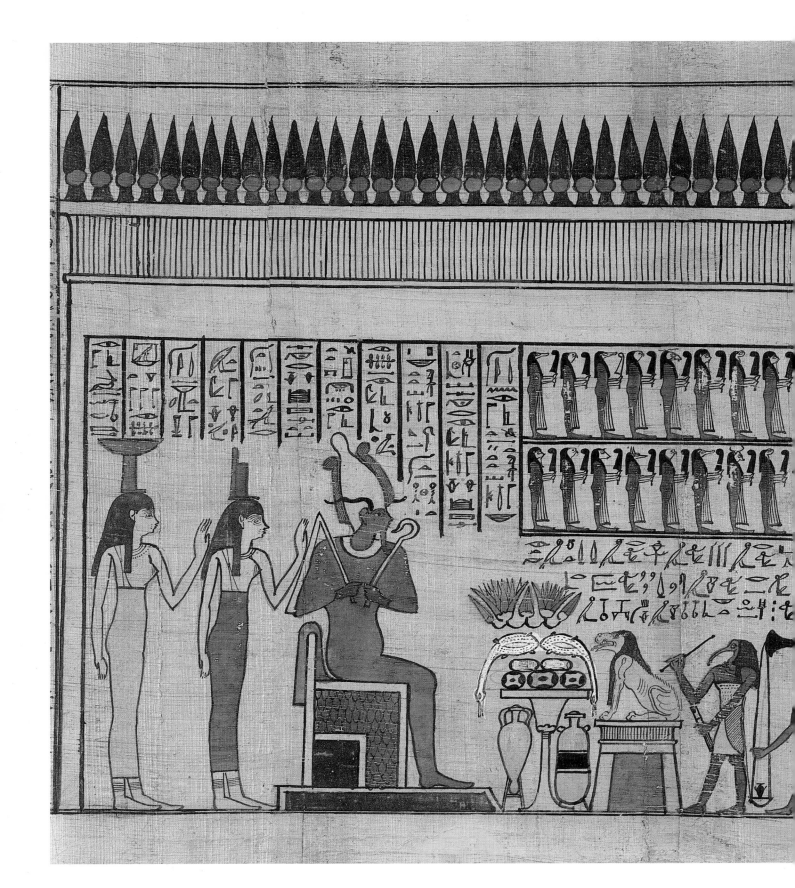

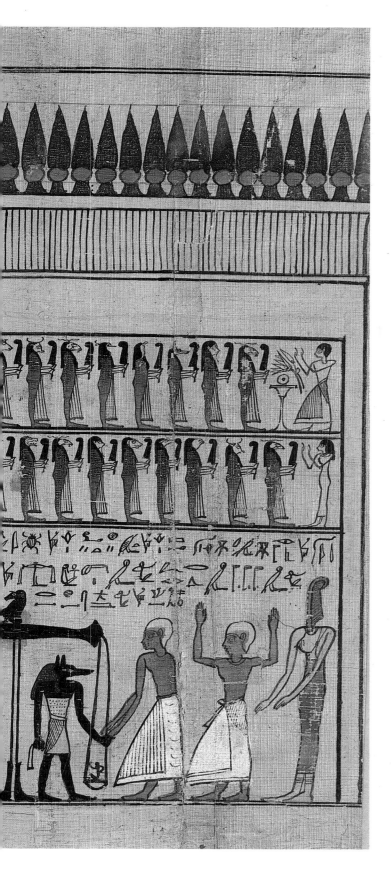

for anyone, I have not lessened the food-offerings in the temples, I have not destroyed the loaves of the gods, I have not taken away the food of the spirits, I have not copulated, I have not misbehaved, I have not lessened food-supplies, I have not diminished the aroura, I have not encroached upon fields, I have not laid anything upon the weights of the hand-balance, I have not taken anything from the plummet of the standing scales, I have not taken the milk from the mouths of children, I have not deprived the herds of their pastures, I have not trapped the birds from the preserves of the gods, I have not caught the fish of their marshlands, I have not diverted water at its season, I have not built a dam on flowing water, I have not quenched the fire when it is burning, I have not neglected the dates for offering choice meats, I have not withheld cattle from the god's-offerings, I have not opposed a god in his procession.

I am pure, pure, pure, pure! My purity is the purity of that great phoenix which is in Heracleopolis, because I am indeed the nose of the Lord of Wind who made all men live on that day of completing the Sacred Eye in Heliopolis *in the 2nd month of winter last day*, in the presence of the lord of this land. I am he who saw the completion of the Sacred Eye in Heliopolis, and nothing evil shall come into being against me in this land in this Hall of Justice, because I know the names of these gods who are in it.

### THE DECLARATION OF INNOCENCE BEFORE THE GODS OF THE TRIBUNAL

O Far-strider who came forth from Heliopolis, I have done no falsehood.

O Fire-embracer who came forth from Kheraha, I have not robbed.

O Nosey who came forth from Hermopolis, I have not been rapacious.

O Swallower of shades who came forth from the cavern, I have not stolen.

O Dangerous One who came forth from Rosetjau, I have not killed men.

O Double Lion who came forth from the sky, I have not destroyed food-supplies.

O Fiery Eyes who came forth from Letopolis, I have done no crookedness.

O Flame which came forth backwards, I have not stolen the god's-offerings.

*Spell 125: In a shrine surmounted by a kheker-frieze Osiris is enthroned, with Isis and Nephthys behind him, witnessing the Weighing of the Heart of Hor. Maat, with an ostrich feather for a head, introduces the deceased; Anubis and Horus help with the weighing; Thoth waits to write down the result and Ammit the monster perches on a shrine-shaped plinth before a heaped table of offerings ready to gobble down any heart weighed down by sin. At one corner Hor and his wife adore Thirty-five of the Forty-two Assessors of the Dead, each of whom holds the feather of Maat. 10479/6*

O Bone-breaker who came forth from Heracleopolis, I have not told lies.

O Green of flame who came forth from Memphis, I have not taken food.

O You of the cavern who came forth from the West, I have not been sullen.

O White of teeth who came forth from the Faiyum, I have not transgressed.

O Blood-eater who came forth from the shambles, I have not killed a sacred bull.

O Eater of entrails who came forth from the House of Thirty, I have not committed perjury.

O Lord of Truth who came forth from Maaty, I have not stolen bread.

O Wanderer who came forth from Bubastis, I have not eavesdropped.

O Pale One who came forth from Heliopolis, I have not babbled.

O Doubly evil who came forth from Andjet, I have not disputed except as concerned my own property.

O Wememty-snake who came forth from the place of execution, I have not committed homosexuality.

O You who see whom you bring who came forth from the House of Min, I have not misbehaved.

O You who are over the Old One who came forth from Imau, I have not made terror.

O Demolisher who came forth from Xois, I have not transgressed.

O Disturber who came forth from Weryt, I have not been hot-tempered.

O Youth who came forth from the Heliopolitan nome, I have not been deaf to words of truth.

O Foreteller who came forth from Wenes, I have not made disturbance.

O You of the altar who came forth from the secret place, I have not hoodwinked.

O You whose face is behind him who came forth from the Cavern of Wrong, I have neither misconducted myself nor copulated with a boy.

O Hot-foot who came forth from the dusk, I have not been neglectful.

O You of the darkness who came forth from the darkness, I have not been quarrelsome.

O Bringer of your offering who came forth from Sais, I have not been unduly active.

O Owner of faces who came forth from Nedjefet, I have not been impatient.

O Accuser who came forth from Wetjenet, I have not transgressed my nature, I have not washed out (the picture of) a god.

O Owner of horns who came forth from Asyut, I have not been voluble in speech.

O Nefertum who came forth from Memphis, I have done no wrong, I have seen no evil.

O Temsep who came forth from Busiris, I have not made conjuration against the king.

O You who acted according to your will, who came forth from Tjebu, I have not waded in water.

O Water-smiter who came forth from the Abyss, I have not been loud voiced.

O Commander of mankind who came forth from your house, I have not reviled God.

O Bestower of good who came forth from the Harpoon nome, I have not done...

O Bestower of powers who came forth from the City, I have not made distinctions for myself.

O Serpent with raised head who came forth from the cavern, I am not wealthy except with my own property.

O Serpent who brings and gives, who came forth from the Silent Land, I have not blasphemed God in my city.

## ADDRESS TO THE GOD OF THE HALL OF JUSTICE

*Thus says* N: Hail to you, you gods who are in this Hall of Justice! I know you and I know your names, I will not fall to your knives; you shall not bring the evil in me to this god in whose suite you are, no fault of mine concerning you shall come out, you shall tell the truth about me in the presence of the Lord of All, because I have done what was right in Egypt, I have not reviled God, and no fault of mine has come out regarding the reigning king.

Hail to you, O you who are in the Hall of Justice, who have no lies in your bodies, who live on truth and gulp down truth in the presence of Horus who is in his disc. Save me from Babai, who lives on the entrails of the old ones on that day of the great reckoning. Behold, I have come to you without falsehood of mine, without crime of mine, without evil of mine, and there is no one who testifies against me, for I have done nothing against him. I live on truth, I gulp down truth, I have done what men say and with which the gods are pleased. I have propitiated God with what he desires; I have given bread to the hungry, water to the thirsty, clothes to the naked and a boat to him who was boatless, I have given god's-offerings to the gods and invocation-offerings to the spirits. Save me, protect me, without your making report against me in the Presence, for I am pure of mouth and pure of hands, one to whom is said 'Twice welcome!' by those who see him, because I have heard that great word which the noble dead spoke with the Cat in the House of Him whose mouth gapes. He who testifies of me is He whose face is behind him, and he gives the cry. I have seen the dividing of the ished-tree in Rosetjau, I am he who succours the gods, who knows the affairs of their bodies. I have come here to bear witness to truth and to set the balance in its proper place within the Silent Land.

O You who are uplifted on your standard, Lord of the Atef-crown, who made your name as Lord of the Wind, save me from your messengers who shoot forth harm and create punishments and who show no indulgence, because I have done what is right for the Lord of Right. I am pure, my brow is clean, my hinder-parts are cleansed, and my middle is in the Pool of Truth, there is no member in me devoid of truth. I have bathed in the Southern Pool, I have rested in the Northern City, in the pure Field of Grasshoppers, in which is the crew of Re, in this second hour of the night and the third hour of the day, and the gods are calmed when they pass by it by night or by day.

## THE DEAD MAN IS QUESTIONED

'You have caused him to come,' say they about me. 'Who are you?' they say to me. 'What is your name?' they say to me.

'I am the lower part of the papyrus-plant; "He who is on his moringa-tree" is my name.'

'What have you passed by?' they say to me.

'I have passed by the city north of the moringa-tree.'

'What did you see there?'

'They were the calf and the thigh.'

'What did you say to them?'

'I have seen the rejoicings in these lands of the Fenkhu.'

'What did they give you?'

'A fire-brand and a pillar of faience.'

'What did you do with them?'

'I buried them on the river-bank of Maat with the night-ritual.'

'What did you find on it, the river-bank of Maat?'

'It was a staff of flint called "Giver of Breath".'

'What did you do with the fire-brand and the pillar of faience after you had buried them?'

'I called out over them, I dug them up, I quenched the fire, I broke the pillar and threw it into a canal.'

'Come and enter by this door of the Hall of Justice, for you know us.'

'We will not let you enter by us,' say the door-posts of this door, 'unless you tell our name.'

'"Plummet of Truth" is your name.'

'I will not let you enter by me,' says the right-hand leaf of this door, 'unless you tell my name.'

'"Scale-pan which weighs Truth" is your name.'

'I will not let you enter by me,' says the left-hand leaf of this door, 'unless you tell my name.'

'"Scale-pan of wine" is your name.'

'I will not let you pass by me,' says the floor of this door, 'unless you tell my name.'

'"Ox of Geb" is your name.'

'I will not open to you,' says the door-bolt of this door, 'unless you tell my name.'

'"Toe of his mother" is your name.'

'I will not let you enter by me,' says the hasp of this door, 'unless you tell my name.'

'"Living Eye of Sobk, Lord of Bakhu" is your name.'

'I will not open to you,' says this door, 'unless you tell my name.'

'"Breast of Shu which he placed as a protection for Osiris" is your name.'

'We will not let you enter by us,' say the cross-timbers, 'unless you tell our names.'

'"Children of uraei" are your names.'

'I will not open to you nor let you enter by me,' says the door-keeper of this door, 'unless you tell my name.'

'"Ox of Geb" is your name.'

'You know us; pass by us.'

'I will not let you tread on me,' says the floor of this Hall of Justice.

'Why not? I am pure.'

'Because I do not know the names of your feet with which you would tread on me. Tell them to me.'

'"Secret image of Ha" is the name of my right foot; "Flower of Hathor" is the name of my left foot.'

'You know us; enter by us.'

'I will not announce you,' says the door-keeper of this Hall of Justice, 'unless you tell my name.'

'"Knower of hearts, searcher-out of bodies" is your name.'

'To which god shall I announce you?'

'To him who is now present. Tell it to the Dragoman of the Two Lands.'

'Who is the Dragoman of the Two Lands?'

'He is Thoth.'

'Come!' says Thoth. 'What have you come for?'

'I have come here to report.'

'What is your condition?'

'I am pure from evil, I have excluded myself from the quarrels of those who are now living, I am not among them.'

'To whom shall I announce you?'

'You shall announce me to Him whose roof is fire, whose walls are living uraei, the floor of whose house is the waters.'

'Who is he?'

'He is Osiris.'

'Proceed; behold, you are announced. Your bread is the Sacred Eye, your beer is the Sacred Eye; what goes forth at the voice for you upon earth is the Sacred Eye.'

## RUBRIC TO THE PRECEDING SPELL

*The correct procedure in this Hall of Justice. One shall utter this spell pure and clean and clad in white garments*

*Spell 125 Anubis introduces Hunefer to the Weighing of his Heart against the feather of Maat. Anubis, depicted a second time, checks the accuracy of the balance; Thoth stands ready to write down the result, watched by the monster Ammit, who gobbles down hearts laden with sin. Vindicated, Hunefer is introduced by falcon-headed Horus-avenger-of-his-father to Osiris, who is enthroned in an elaborate booth with Isis and Nephthus behind him and the Four Sons of Horus standing on a lotus before. Above, behind an offering-table and adored by Hunefer, squat fourteen gods and goddesses who are witnesses to the judgement. 9901/3.*

and sandals, painted with black eye-paint and anointed with myrrh. There shall be offered to him meat and poultry, incense, bread, beer, and herbs when you have put this written procedure on a clean floor of ochre overlaid with earth upon which no swine or small cattle have trodden. As for him who makes this writing, he shall flourish and his children shall flourish, he shall not be in need, he shall be in the confidence of the king and his entourage, and there shall be given to him a shens-cake, a jug of beer, a persen-cake and a portion of meat from upon the altar of the Great God; he shall not be turned back from any gateway of the West, but shall be ushered in with the kings of Upper Egypt and the kings of Lower Egypt, and he shall be in the suite of Osiris. A matter a million times true.

## ——— SPELL 1 ———
[illustrated pp.24-5,38]

*Here begin the spells of going out into the day, the praises and recitations for going to and fro in the realm of the dead which are beneficial in the beautiful West, and which are to be spoken on the day of burial and of going in after coming out*

*Hail to you, Bull of the West* – so says Thoth, the King of Eternity, of me. I am the Great God, the protector. I have fought for you, for I am one of those gods of the tribunal which vindicated Osiris against his foes on that day of judgement. I belong to your company, O Osiris, for I am one of those gods who fashioned the Children of Nut, who slew the foes of Osiris and who imprisoned those who rebelled against him.

I belong to your company, O Horus, I have fought for you and have watched over your name; I am Thoth

day of placing the Bark of Sokar on its sledge; I am he who takes the hoe on the day of breaking up the earth in Heracleopolis.

*O you who cause the perfected souls to draw near to the House of* Osiris, may you cause the excellent soul of N to draw near with you to the House of Osiris. May he hear as you hear, may he see as you see, may he stand as you stand, may he sit as you sit.

*O you who give bread and beer to the perfected souls in the House of* Osiris, may you give bread and beer at all seasons to the soul of N, who is vindicated with all the gods of the Thinite nome, and who is vindicated with you.

*O you who open a path and open up roads for the perfected souls in the House of* Osiris, open a path for him, open up roads for the soul of N in company with you. May he come in freely, may he go out in peace from the House of Osiris, without being repelled or turned back. May he go in favoured, may he come out loved, may he be vindicated, may his commands be done in the House of Osiris, may he go and speak with you, may he be a spirit with you, may no fault be found in him, for the balance is voided of his misdoings.

## ——— SPELL 1B ———

*Spell for permitting the noble dead to descend to the Netherworld on the day of interment*

who vindicated Osiris against his foes on that day of judgement in the great Mansion of the Prince which is in Heliopolis. I am a Busirite, the son of a Busirite, I was conceived in Busiris, I was born in Busiris when I was with the men who lamented and the women who mourned Osiris on the Shores of Rekhty and who vindicated Osiris against his foes – so they say. O Re, Thoth has vindicated Osiris against his foes – so men say. Thoth has helped me so that I might be with Horus on the day of the clothing of the Dismembered One and of the opening of the caverns for the washing of the Inert One and the throwing open of the door of the secret things in Rosetjau; so that I might be with Horus as the protector of the left arm of Osiris who is in Letopolis. I go in and out among those who are there on the day of crushing the rebels in Letopolis so that I may be with Horus on the day of the Festival of Osiris; offerings are made on the days of the Sixth-day Festival and the Seventh-day Festival in Heliopolis.

I am the priest in Busiris for the Lion-god in the House of Osiris with those who raise up earth; I am he who sees the mysteries in Rosetjau; I am he who reads the ritual book for the Soul in Busiris; I am the Sem-priest at his duties; I am the Master Craftsman on the

Hail to you who are in the sacred desert of the West! N knows you and knows your name; may you save him from those snakes which are in Rosetjau, which live on the flesh of men and gulp down their blood, because N knows you and knows your names.

The First One, Osiris, Lord of All, mysterious of body, gives command, and he puts breath into those frightened ones who are in the midst of the West; what has been commanded for him is the governance of those who exist. May his place within the darkness be opened up for him, may a spirit-shape be given to him in Rosetjau, even to the Lord of gloom who goes down as the swallower of snakes in the West; his voice is heard but he is not seen. The Great God within Busiris, those who are among the languid ones fear him, they having gone forth under report to the shambles of the god.

I have come, even I the vindicated Osiris N, on business of the Lord of All, while Horus has taken possession of his throne and his father has given to him all those honours which are within his father's sacred bark. Horus has come with a report; he goes in that he may tell what he has seen in Heliopolis. Their great ones on earth wait on him, the scribes who are on their mats magnify him, and there has been given to him the mottled snake in Heliopolis. He has taken possession of the sky, he has inherited the earth, and who shall take this sky and earth from him? He is Re, the eldest of the gods; his mother has suckled him, she has given to him a nurse who is in the horizon.

This spell is to be recited after going to rest in the West, the Tjenenet-shrine being made content with its lord Osiris when going to and fro to the Sacred Bark of Re; his body on his bier shall be reckoned up, and shall be enduring in the Netherworld, namely that of N.

## SPELL 2

*Spell for going out into the day and living after death*

O you Sole One who shine in the moon, O you Sole One who glow in the sun, may N go forth from among those multitudes of yours who are outside, may those who are in the sunshine release him, may the Netherworld be opened to him when N goes out into the day in order to do what he wishes on earth among the living.

## SPELL 3

*Another like it*

O Atum who went forth as the Great One of the waters, having power as the Double Lion, announce in your own words to those who are in the Presence that N comes as one who is in their midst, and give command on his behalf to the crew of Re in the evening. May N live after death like Re every day. Was Re born yesterday? Then will N be born. May every god be joyful when N lives just as they were joyful when Ptah lived, when he came forth from the great Mansion of the Prince which is in Heliopolis.

## SPELL 4

*Spell for passing on the upper road of Rosetjau*

I am he who fixed the limits of the flood and who judged between the Rivals, I have come and I have removed the evil which was on Osiris.

## SPELL 5

*Spell for not doing work in the realm of the dead*

It is I who lift up the arm of Him who is inert; I have gone out of Hermopolis, I am a living soul, I have been initiated into the hearts of the baboons.

## SPELL 6

*Spell for causing a shabti to do work for a man in the realm of the dead*

O shabti, allotted to me, if I be summoned or if I be detailed to do any work which has to be done in the realm of the dead; if indeed obstacles are implanted for you therewith as a man at his duties, you shall detail yourself for me on every occasion of making arable the fields, of flooding the banks or of conveying sand from east to west; 'Here am I,' you shall say.

## SPELL 7

*Spell for passing by the dangerous coil of Apep*

O you waxen one who take by robbery and who live on the inert ones, I will not be inert for you, I will not be weak for you, your poison shall not enter into my members, for my members are the members of Atum. If I am not weak for you, suffering from you shall not enter into these members of mine. I am Atum at the head of the Abyss, my protection is from the gods, the lords of eternity, I am He whose name is secret, more holy of throne than the Chaos-gods; I am among them, I have gone forth with Atum, I am one who is not examined, I am hale, I am hale!

## SPELL 8
[illustrated p.39]

*Spell for opening up the West by day*

Hermopolis is opened and my head is sealed. O Thoth, the Eye of Horus is unblemished, the Eye of Horus saves me, and splendid are my ornaments from the brow of Re, father of the gods; I am this Osiris here in the West. Osiris knows his day, and if he does not exist in it, then I will not exist in it. I am Re who is with the gods and I will not perish; stand up, Horus, that I may number you among the gods.

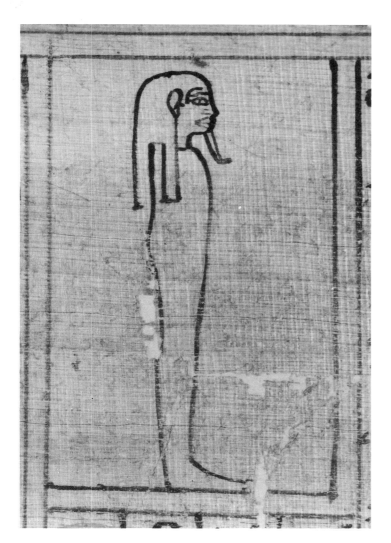

*Spell 6 Nebseny's shabti-figure which will carry out agricultural work on his behalf in the Other World. 9900/10.*

## SPELL 9
[illustrated p.39]

*Spell for going out into the day after opening the tomb*

O you Soul, greatly majestic, behold, I have come that I may see you; I open the Netherworld that I may see my father Osiris and drive away darkness, for I am beloved of him.

I have come that I may see my father Osiris and that I may cut out the heart of Seth who has harmed my father Osiris. I have opened up every path which is in the sky and on earth, for I am the well-beloved son of my father Osiris. I am noble, I am a spirit, I am equipped; O all you gods and all you spirits, prepare a path for me.

## SPELL 10
[illustrated p.40]

*Another spell for a man's going out into the day against his foes in the realm of the dead*

I have dug up the sky, I have hacked up the horizon, I have traversed the earth to its furthest extent, I have taken possession of the spirits of the great ones, because I am one who equips a myriad with my magic. I eat with my mouth, I defecate with my hinder-parts, for I am a god, lord of the Netherworld. I have given those things which were established in the past, I have planned appearance in glory.

## SPELL 11

*Spell for going out against a foe in the realm of the dead*

O you who consume your arm, prepare a path for me, for I am Re, I have come forth from the horizon against my foe. He has been given to me and he shall not be taken from me. I have extended my arm as Lord of the Wereret-crown, I have stridden out with the speed of the uraeus when my foe has not been put into my hand for me. Such is my foe; he has been given to me, he shall not be taken from me. I have arisen as Horus, I have sat down as Ptah, I am strong as Thoth, I am mighty as Atum, I walk with my legs, I speak with my mouth in order to seek out my foe; he has been given to me and he shall not be taken from me.

## SPELL 12

*Spell for going in and out*

Hail to you, O Re, guardian of the secrets of the gates which are on this neck of Geb, because of this balance of Re with which he weighs out justice daily. Behold, I have hacked up the earth, and I have been permitted to come, having grown old.

## SPELL 13
[illustrated p.41]

*Spell for going in and out of the West*

To me belong all men, I have given everything to myself. I have gone in as a falcon, I have come out as a phoenix, the god who worships Re. Prepare a path for me, that I may enter in peace into the beautiful West, for I belong to the Lake of Horus, I leash the hounds of Horus.

Above: **Spells 8 and 9** *In the left-hand detail (Spell 8), Ani is shown walking with staff and kerchief towards the falcon and feather on a stand which symbolise the West. The sand mound from which it protrudes is flanked by a beer jug and a loaf. On the right (Spell 9), Ani adores the divine soul represented as a ram wearing the Atef-crown and standing on a shrine-shaped plinth before a ewer on a stand which is topped by a lotus. 10470/18.*

Left: **Spell 1** *In the top illustration, above Ani's Canopic chest, which is topped by a jackal, servants carry grave-goods. Mourners walk behind his mummy, which is drawn on a boat-shaped bier under a canopy attended by his grieving widow, while a priest censes and libates before it. In the lower illustration, another priest lustrates more grave-goods, which are carried by servants behind a group of professional mourners. An attendant carries the foreleg cut from a still-bleating calf to the priests, clad in panther-skins, who are carrying out the Opening of the Mouth ceremony. The mummy is held up before a heaped offering-table and the pyramid-capped tomb chapel by a priest wearing a jackal's mask, while Ani's widow grieves on her knees. The Lector priest reads from a papyrus beside ritual objects depicted above a chest. 10470/5 and 6.*

Prepare a way for me, that I may go in and worship Osiris, the Lord of Life.

## ——— SPELL 14 ———

*Spell for removing anger from the heart of the god*

Hail to you, you who descend in power, chief of all secret matters! Behold, my word is spoken: so says the god who was angry with me. Wrong is washed away, and it falls immediately. O Lords of Justice, put an end to the evil harm which is in me. O you companions of the God of Justice, may this god be gracious to me, may my evil be removed for you. O Lord of Offerings, as mighty ruler, behold I have brought to you a propitiation-offering so that you may live on it and that I may live on it; be gracious to me and remove all anger which is in your heart against me.

*Spell 10 Ani spears a serpent symbolic of any force hostile to the dead.* 10470/18

## ——— SPELL 15 ———

*Worship of Re when he rises in the horizon until the occurrence of his setting in life*

Hail to you, O Re, at your rising, O Atum-Horakhty! Your beauty is worshipped in my eyes when the sunshine comes into being over my breast. You proceed at your pleasure in the Night-bark, your heart is joyful with a fair wind in the Day-bark, being happy at crossing the sky with the blessed ones. All your foes are overthrown, the Unwearying Stars acclaim you, the Imperishable Stars worship you when you set in the horizon of Manu, being happy at all times, and living and enduring as my lord.

Hail to you, O Re when you rise and Atum when you set. How beautiful are your rising and your shining on the back of your mother Nut, you having appeared as

King of the Gods. The Lower Sky has greeted you, Justice embraces you at all times. You traverse the sky happily, and the Lake of the Two Knives is in contentment. The rebel has fallen, his arms are bound, a knife has severed his spine, but Re will have a fair wind, for the Night-bark has destroyed those who would attack him. The southerners, northerners, westerners and easterners tow you because of the praise of you, O primeval god, whose images have come into being. The voice goes forth, and the earth is inundated with silence, for the Sole One came into existence in the sky before the plains and the mountains existed. The Herdsman, the Sole Lord, who made whatever exists, he has fashioned the tongue of the Ennead. O you who took what is in the waters, you issue thence on to the bank of the Lake of Horus. I breathe the air which comes out of your nose, the north wind which comes forth from your mother. You glorify my spirit, you make the Osiris my soul divine. I worship you; be content, O Lord of the Gods, for you are exalted in your firmament, and your rays over my breast are like the day.

### A HYMN TO OSIRIS

*Worship* of Osiris, Lord of Eternity, Wennefer.

Horakhty multiple of forms and great of shapes, Ptah-Sokar, Atum in Heliopolis, Lord of the Shetyt-shrine, who enriches Memphis; these are the gods who govern the Netherworld; they protect you when you go to rest in the Lower Sky. Isis embraces you in peace and drives away the adversary from your path. Turn your face to the West that you may illumine the Two Lands with fine gold. Those who were asleep stand up to look at you; they breathe the air, they see your face like the shining of the sun-disc in its horizon, their hearts are at peace because of what you have done, for to you belong eternity and everlasting.

### AN ADDRESS TO OSIRIS IN VARIOUS ASPECTS

*Hail to you,* Starry One in Heliopolis; Sun-folk in Kheraha; Wenti more powerful than the gods; Mysterious One in Heliopolis.

*Hail to you,* Heliopolitan in Iun-des; Great One; Horakhty the Far-Strider when he crosses the sky: he is Horakhty.

*Hail to you,* Ram of Eternity, Ram who is Mendes, Wennefer son of Nut: he is Lord of the Silent Land.

*Hail to you* in your rule of Busiris, the Wereret-crown is firm on your head: you are the Sole One who makes his own protection, and you rest in Busiris.

*Hail to you,* Lord of the naret-tree; Sokar is placed on his sledge, the rebel who did evil is driven off, and the Sacred Eye is set at rest in its place.

*Hail to you,* strong in your power, the great and

mighty one who presides over Naref, Lord of Eternity, maker of everlastingness: you are Lord of Heracleopolis.

*Hail to you* who are pleased with justice: you are Lord of Abydos, and your flesh has enriched the Sacred Land; you are he who detests falsehood.

*Hail to you*, occupant of the Sacred Bark, who brings the Nile from its cavern, over whose corpse the sun has shone; you are he who is in Nekhen.

*Hail to you* who made the gods, the vindicated King of Upper and Lower Egypt Osiris, who founded the Two Lands with his potent deeds: you are Lord of the Two Banks.

May you give me a path that I may pass in peace, for I am straightforward and true; I have not wittingly told lies, I have not committed a second fault.

### ANOTHER HYMN TO THE SUN

*Worship of Re when he rises* in the eastern horizon of the sky, when those who are in his following are joyful.

O Sun-disc, Lord of the sunbeams, who shines forth from the horizon every day: may you shine in the face of N, for *he worships you* in the morning, he propitiates you in the evening. May the soul of N go up with you to the sky, may he travel in the Day-bark, may he moor in the Night-bark, may he mix with the Unwearying Stars in the sky.

The Osiris N *says* when he honours his lord, the Lord of Eternity:

*Hail to you*, Horakhty, Khepri the self-created! How beautiful is your shining forth from the horizon when you illumine the Two Lands with your rays! All the gods are in joy when they see you as king of the sky, the royal serpent being firm on your head and the crowns of Upper and Lower Egypt on your vertex; she (the serpent) has made her seat on your brow. Thoth is established in the bow of your Sacred Bark, destroying all your foes, while those who are in the Netherworld have come out to meet you and to see this beautiful image.

*I have come* to you and I am with you in order to see your disc every day; I will not be restrained or repulsed, but my flesh will be renewed at seeing your beauty, like all those whom you favour, for I was one of those who were well esteemed by you on earth. I have arrived at the land of eternity, I have joined myself to the land of everlasting, and it is you who commanded it for me, O my lord.

*Hail to you* when you rise in your horizon as Re who is pleased with justice; when you cross the sky, all men see you, after your movements have been hidden from their sight. You display yourself from morning till evening on the day when celestial navigation with Your Majesty is successful; your rays are in men's faces, and fine gold does not know them, pigment does not report

*Spell 13 Horemheb returns to his tomb chapel after going forth into the West.* 10257/13

them when you illumine the lands of the gods, and it has not been seen in writing; the mountains of Punt disclose Him who was hidden. You did it alone when N's mouth was opened, and your shape was upon the primeval waters. He will travel just as you travel, and there will be no ceasing for him as for Your Majesty, not even for a little day, for you have passed through seasons of millions and hundreds of thousands of moments; when you have spent them you have gone to rest, you have also completed the hours of the night, and you have regulated and completed them according to your regular custom. The land becomes bright when you reveal yourself in your place as Re when he arises in the horizon.

The Osiris N *says* when he worships you at your shining, and speaks to you when you rise early to set your shape on high: You appear in glory in magnifying your beauty, creating yourself; you mould your own flesh. One who fashions but is not fashioned, as Re who shines in the sky. May you permit me to reach the eternal sky, the country of the favoured; may I join with the august and noble spirits of the realm of the dead; may I ascend with them to see your beauty when you shine in the evening. Your mother traverses for you the Lower Sky when you are placed in the West, and my arms are upraised in adoration at your setting, for you are he who made eternity. I worship you when you set in the Abyss, and I set you in my heart which is not inert, O you who are more divine than the gods.

Praise to you who rise in gold and who illumine the Two Lands by day at your birth ! Your mother Nut has borne you on her hand, and what the sun-disc encircles is bright because of you. Great Illuminator who shines forth from the Abyss, who knits his family together in the waters, who makes festal all estates, towns and households, who protects with his goodness, may your spirit be sustained with food and provisions. Greatly feared, Power of Powers, whose throne is far from the evil-doers; greatly majestic in the Night-bark, mightily long-lasting in the Day-bark, may you glorify N in the realm of the dead, may you cause him to endure in the West, he being devoid of evil. May you ignore my wrong-doing and may you set me as one honoured with the spirits; may you protect my soul in the Sacred Land, may it navigate in the Field of Rushes, because I have passed on in joy.

Right: *Vignette incorrectly termed Spell 16* The sun-god is depicted as a falcon wearing a sun-disc. He stands on the emblem of the West, and is protected by winged udjat-eyes which carry ostrich-feather fans and adored by rows of deities. Beneath dancing baboons Isis and Nephthys kneel in adoration, and below them the human-head soul of Anhai, shown twice, stands with arms raised in praise on a plinth set in the slopes of the eastern mountain. 10472/1

Left: *Vignette in four registers incorrectly termed Spell 16* Hor kneels in a boat steered by Horus adoring the sun-god. In the second register the sun-disc, streaming rays, is held up by two goddesses between the symbols of East and West, and is guarded by the Four Sons of Horus with knives on their knees. Below this the sun-disc is raised up between four representations of Hor's human-headed soul to be adored by baboons and protected by animated ankhs carrying ostrich-feather fans. In the bottom register Hor and his wife, seated separately beside offering-tables, are lustrated and censed by a priest. 10479/11

Below: *Part of Spell 17* Hunefer sits in a booth playing senet, while his human-headed soul stands on a shrine-shaped plinth with arms raised in praise. On the right Hunefer kneels in adoration of the two lions of the horizon over whose backs the sun rises daily. 9901/5

43

THE GOD REPLIES: You shall ascend to the sky, you shall traverse the firmament, you shall associate with the stars, who shall make acclamation to you in the Sacred Bark. You shall be summoned into the Day-bark, you shall see Re within his shrine, you shall propitiate his disc daily, you shall see the bulti-fish in its shape in the stream of turquoise, you shall see the abdju-fish in being, the serpent of evil having fallen according as was foretold for him, the sharp knives having cut his spine apart for me. Re shall sail with a fair wind, and the Night-bark shall be wiped clean for me. The crew of Re shall reach him with joy, and the Lady of Life will be happy when the hostile serpent has fallen to her lord. You shall see Horus whose face is kindly, with the standards of Thoth and Maat on his hands; all the gods will be in joy when they see Re coming in peace to vivify the hearts of the spirits, and the vindicated Osiris N shall be with them.

SPELL 16 DOES NOT EXIST. THIS NUMBER WAS ORIGINALLY ALLOTTED TO A VIGNETTE OF THE RISING SUN WHICH WAS INTENDED TO BE AN ILLUSTRATION TO ACCOMPANY A SUN-HYMN.

# SPELL 17
[illustrated pp.43,45,46,47,48,50-1]

THIS LENGTHY SPELL IS ACCOMPANIED BY AN EQUALLY LENGTHY SERIES OF VIGNETTES. THE SPELL, WHICH HAS A LONG HISTORY BEHIND IT, CONSISTS IN EFFECT OF A STATEMENT OF DOCTRINE REGARDING THE SUN-GOD, LATER BECOMING A SPELL ON BEHALF OF THE DECEASED, BUT AT FREQUENT INTERVALS THE TEXT IS INTERRUPTED BY A SERIES OF EXPLANATORY GLOSSES WHICH ATTEMPT TO ELUCIDATE THE SIGNIFICANCE OF WHAT HAS JUST PRECEDED. TO THE MODERN READER, THE GLOSSES ARE OFTEN MORE OBSCURE THAN THE MAIN TEXT.

*Here begin praises and recitations, going in and out of the realm of the dead,* having benefit in the beautiful West, being in the suite of Osiris, resting at the food-table of Wennefer, going out into the day, taking any shape in which he desires to be, playing at draughts, sitting in a booth, and going forth as a living soul by the Osiris N after he has died. It is beneficial to him who does it on earth.

Now come into being all the words of the Lord of All: I was Atum when I was alone in the Abyss; I was Re in his glorious appearings when he began to rule what he had made.

*What does it mean?* It means Re when he began to rule what he had made, when he began to appear as king, before the Supports of Shu had come into being, when he was upon the hill which is in Hermopolis, when he destroyed the Children of Impotence on the hill which is in Hermopolis.

I am the Great God, the self-created.

*Who is it?* The Great God, the self-created, is water, he is Nun, father of the gods. *Otherwise said:* He is Re.

He who created his names, Lord of the Ennead.

*Who is he?* It is Re who created his names and his members, it means the coming into existence of those gods who are in his suite.

I am he who is not opposed among the gods.

*Who is he?* He is Atum who is in his sun-disc. *Otherwise said:* He is Re when he rises in the eastern horizon of the sky.

To me belongs yesterday, I know tomorrow.

*What does it mean?* As for yesterday, that is Osiris. As for tomorrow, that is Re on that day in which the foes of the Lord of All were destroyed and his son Horus was made to rule. *Otherwise said:* That is the day of the 'We-remain' festival, when the burial of Osiris was ordered by his father Re.

The battle-ground of the gods was made in accordance with my command.

*What does it mean?* It is the West. It was made for the souls of the gods in accordance with the command of Osiris, Lord of the Western Desert. *Otherwise said:* It means that this is the West, to which Re made every god descend, and he fought the Two for it.

I know that Great God who is in it.

*Who is he?* He is Osiris. *Otherwise said:* His name is Re, his name is Praise-of-Re, he is the soul of Re, with whom he himself copulated.

I am that great phoenix which is in Heliopolis, the supervisor of what exists.

*Who is he?* He is Osiris. As for what exists, that means his injury. *Otherwise said:* That means his corpse. *Otherwise said:* It means eternity and everlasting. As for eternity, it means daytime; as for everlasting, it means night.

I am Min in his going forth, I have set the plumes on my head.

*What does it mean?* As for Min, he is Horus who protected his father. As for his going forth, it means his birth. As for his plumes on his head, it means that Isis and Nephthys went and put themselves on his head when they were the Two Kites, and they were firm on his head. *Otherwise said:* They are the two great and mighty uraei which are on the brow of his father Atum. *Otherwise said:* The plumes on his head are his eyes.

When I was in my land, I came into my city.

*Part of Spell 17* Osiris squats on a mat holding a crook and flail. To the right Hunefer adores the Phoenix, soul of Re, which stands behind an offering-table. 9901/6

*What is it?* It is the horizon of my father Atum.

I destroy what was done wrongly against me, I dispel what was done evilly against me.

*What does it mean?* It means that the navel-string of N will be cut.

All the ill which was on me has been removed.

*What does it mean?* It means that I was cleansed on the day of my birth in the two great and noble marshes which are in Heracleopolis on the day of the oblation by the common folk to the Great God who is in them. *What are they?* 'Chaos-god' is the name of one; 'Sea' is the name of the other. They are the Lake of Natron and the Lake of Maat. *Otherwise said:* 'The Chaos-god governs' is the name of one; 'Sea' is the name of the other. *Otherwise said:* 'Seed of the Chaos-god' is the name of one; 'Sea' is the name of the other. As for that Great God who is in them, he is Re himself.

I go on the road which I know in front of the Island of the Just.

*What is it?* It is Rosetjau. The southern gate is in Naref, the northern gate is in the Mound of Osiris; as for the Island of the Just, it is Abydos. *Otherwise said:* It is the road on which my father Atum went when he proceeded to the Field of Rushes.

I arrive at the Island of the Horizon-dwellers, I go out from the holy gate.

*What is it?* It is the Field of Rushes, which produced the provisions for the gods who are round about the shrine. As for that holy gate, it is the gate of the Supports of Shu. *Otherwise said:* It is the gate of the Netherworld. *Otherwise said:* It is the door through which my father Atum passed when he proceeded to the eastern horizon of the sky.

O you who are in my presence, give me your hands, for indeed I am he who grew up among you.

*What does it mean?* It means the blood which fell from the phallus of Re when he took to cutting himself. Then there came into being the gods who are in the presence of Re, who are Authority and Intelligence, while I followed after my father Atum daily.

I restored the Sacred Eye after it had been injured on that day when the Rivals fought.

*What does it mean?* It means the day when Horus fought with Seth when he inflicted injury on Horus's face and when Horus took away Seth's testicles. It was Thoth who did this with his fingers.

I lifted up the hair from the Sacred Eye at its time of wrath.

*What does it mean?* It means the right Eye of Re when it raged against him after he had sent it out. It was Thoth who lifted up the hair from it when he fetched it in good condition without its having suffered any harm. *Otherwise said:* It means that his Eye was sick when it wept a second time, and then Thoth spat on it.

I have seen this sun-god who was born yesterday from the buttocks of the Celestial Cow; if he be well, then will I be well, and vice versa.

*What does it mean?* It means these waters of the sky. *Otherwise said:* It is the image of the Eye of Re on the morning of its daily birth. As for the Celestial Cow, she is the Sacred Eye of Re.

Because I am one of those gods who are in the suite of Horus, who spoke before him all that my lord desired.

*Who are they?* They are Imsety, Hapy, Duamutef and Qebehsenuef.

Hail to you, Lords of Justice, tribunal which is behind

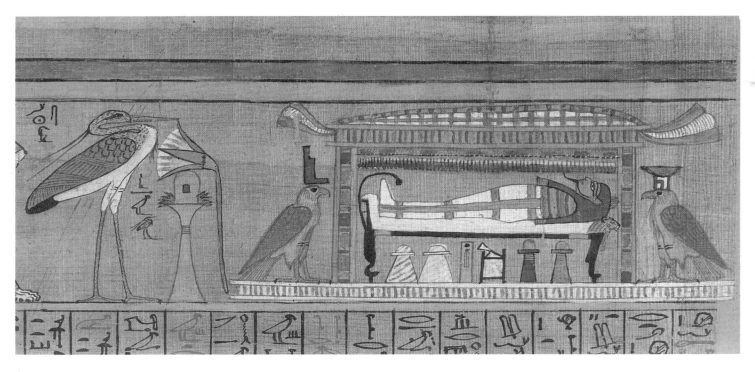

Above: *Part of Spell 17* The Phoenix, soul of Re, stands before a ewer on a stand, topped with a lotus. The mummy of Ani, wearing its mask, lies on a bed in the form of a lion, beneath which are a scribe's palette, a chest and two containers. The elaborate booth is flanked by Isis and Nephthys as kites. 10470/7

Below: *Part of Spell 17* The protective goddesses of Upper and Lower Egypt as cobras curl around the plant emblems of south and north. To the right, behind a heap of offerings and the Sacred Eye in a circle, two water-gods kneel on mats with representations of the Lake of Natron and the Lake of Maat between them. 9901/6

Osiris, who put terror into the doers of wrong, who are in the suite of Her who makes content and protects. Here am I; I have come to you that you may drive out all the evil which is on me just as you did for those seven spirits who are in the suite of the Lord of Sepa, whose places Anubis made ready on that day of 'Come thence'.

*Who are they?* As for those gods the Lords of Justice, they are Seth and Isdes, Lord of the West. As for the tribunal which is behind Osiris, Imsety, Hapy, Duamutef and Qebehsenuef, it is these who are behind the Great Bear in the northern sky. As for those who put terror into the doers of wrong, who are in the suite of Her who makes content and protects, they are Sobk and those who are in the waters. As for Her who makes content and protects, she is the Eye of Re. *Otherwise said:* She is a flame which follows after Osiris, burning up his enemies. As for all the evil which is on me, it is what I have done among the lords of eternity ever since I came down from my mother's womb. As for these seven spirits, Imsety, Hapy, Duamutef, Qebehsenuef, He who sees his father, He who is under his moringa-tree, and Horus the Eyeless, it is they who were set by Anubis as a protection for the burial of Osiris. *Otherwise said:* Behind the embalming place of Osiris. *Otherwise said:*

Above: *Part of Spell 17* A god squats in a shrine with open doors which represents the entrance to the Other World. 9901/7

Below: *Part of Spell 17* Thoth offers the udjat-eye to Mekhwert, the Celestial Cow, who reclines on a shrine-shaped plinth. In the centre Hunefer kneels in praise of a coffin-shaped chest from which a human head emerges and which is flanked by the mummiform Four Sons of Horus. 9901/8

As for these seven spirits, they are Nedjehdjeh, Aked-ked, Bull whose flame was set for him in front of his burning, He who entered into him who is in his hour, the Red-eyed who is in the Mansion of Red Linen, the Radiant One who comes out after having turned back, He who sees in the night what he shall bring by day. As for the head of this tribunal, his name is He who subdued the Great One. As for that day of 'Come to me', it means that Osiris said to Re, 'Come to me that I may see you' – so said he in the West.

I am his twin souls which are within the Two Fledglings.

*Who is he?* He is Osiris when he entered into Mendes. He found the soul of Re there and they embraced each other. Then his twin souls came into being. Now as for the Two Fledglings, they are Horus the Protector of his father and Horus the Eyeless. *Otherwise said:* As for his twin souls which are within the Two Fledglings, they are the soul of Re, the soul of Osiris, the soul which is in Shu, the soul which is in Nut, his twin souls which are in Mendes.

I am that great Cat who split the ished-tree on its side in Heliopolis on that night of making war on behalf of those who warded off the rebels and on that day in which were destroyed the enemies of the Lord of All.

*What does it mean?* As for that Cat, he is Re himself, who was called 'Cat' when Sia spoke about him; he was cat-like in what he did, and that is how his name of 'Cat' came into being. *Otherwise said:* He will be Shu making an inventory for Geb and for Osiris. As for the splitting of the ished-tree on its side in Heliopolis, it was when the Children of Impotence carried out what they did. As for that night of making war, it means that they entered into the east of the sky, and war broke out in the entire sky and earth.

O Re who are in your Egg, shining in your disc, rising in your horizon, swimming over your firmament, having no equal among the gods, sailing over the Sup-

ports of Shu, giving air with the breath of your mouth, illuminating the Two Lands with your sunshine, may you save me from that god whose shape is secret, whose eyebrows are the arms of the balance, on that night of reckoning up the robbers.

*Who is he?* It is he who uses his hand on that night of reckoning up the robbers, on that night of the flame against the fallen, when the lasso was put on the wrongdoers at the shambles for killing souls.

*Who is he?* He is Shesmu, he is the mutilator of Osiris. *Otherwise said:* He is Apep, he has only one head which bears righteousness. *Otherwise said:* He is Horus, he has two heads, one bearing right and one bearing wrong; he gives wrong to whoever does it and right to whoever comes with it. *Otherwise said:* He is Horus the Great, pre-eminent in Letopolis. *Otherwise said:* He is Thoth. *Otherwise said:* He is Nefertum, son of Bastet. These are the tribunal who take action against the enemies of the Lord of All.

Save me from those who deal wounds, the slayers whose fingers are sharp, who deal out pain, who decapitate those who follow after Osiris; they shall not have power over me, and I will not fall into their cauldrons.

*Who is he?* He is Anubis, he is Horus the Eyeless. *Otherwise said:* It is the tribunal who took action against the foes of the Lord of All. *Otherwise said:* He is the master-physician of the Court. Their knives shall not have power over me, I will not fall into their cauldrons, because I know them, I know their names, I know the name of that smiter among them who belongs to the House of Osiris, who shoots with his eye, yet is unseen. The sky is encircled with the fiery blast of his mouth and Hapi makes report, yet is unseen.

I was one who was hale on earth with Re and who

***Part of Spell 17*** *Five squatting ram-headed gods carrying ankhs are named as Re, Shu, Tefnut, Geb and the soul of Mendes. The cat of Re cuts up the evil serpent Apep before the sacred ished-tree of Heliopolis. 9901/8*

died happily with Osiris; your offerings will not come into being through me, O you who are in charge of your braziers, because I am in the suite of the Lord of All at the edict of Khepri. I fly up as a falcon, I cackle as a goose, I pass eternity like Nehebkau.

*What does it mean?* It means that as for those who are in charge of their braziers, they are the likeness of the Eye of Re and the likeness of the Eye of Horus.

O Re-Atum, Lord of the Great Mansion, Sovereign of all the gods, save me from that god whose face is that of a hound but whose skin is human, who lives by butchery, who is in charge of the windings of the Lake of Fire, who swallows corpses, who controls hearts, who inflicts injury unseen.

*Who is he?* 'Swallower of Myriads' is his name, and he dwells in the Lake of Wenet. Now as for that Lake of Fire, it is what is between Naref and the House of the Entourage. As for anyone who treads on it, beware lest he fall to the knives. *Otherwise said:* 'He of the Sharp Knife' is his name, and he is door-keeper of the West. *Otherwise said:* Babai is his name, and he is the guardian of this interior of the West. *Otherwise said:* 'He who is over his affairs' is his name.

O Lord of Terror who is at the head of the Two Lands, O Lord of Blood whose slaughter-blocks are flourishing, who lives on entrails.

*Who is he?* He is the heart of Osiris, and he devours all kinds of slaughtering.

To whom was given the Wereret-crown and joy in Heracleopolis.

*Who is he?* As for him to whom was given the Wereret-crown and joy in Heracleopolis, he is Osiris.

To whom was entrusted rulership among the gods on that day when the Two Lands were united in the presence of the Lord of All.

*Who is he?* As for him to whom was entrusted rulership among the gods, he is Horus son of Isis, who was made ruler in the place of his father Osiris on that day when the Two Lands were united. It means the union of the Two Lands at the burial of Osiris.

Potent Ram who is in Heracleopolis, who gives good fortune and drives off wrong-doers, to whom the way of eternity is shown.

*Who is he?* He is Re himself.

Save me from that god who steals souls, who laps up corruption, who lives on what is putrid, who is in charge of darkness, who is immersed in gloom, of whom those who are among the languid ones are afraid.

*Who is he?* He is Seth. *Otherwise said:* He is the great Wild Bull, he is the soul of Geb.

O Khepri in the midst of your Sacred Bark, primeval one whose body is eternity, save me from those who are in charge of those who are to be examined, to whom the Lord of All has given power to guard against his en-emies, who put knives into the slaughter-houses, who do not leave their guardianship; their knives shall not cut into me, I shall not enter into their slaughter-houses, I shall not fall victim to their slaughter-blocks, I shall not sit down in their fish-traps, no harm shall be done to me from those whom the gods detest, because I have passed on, having bathed in the Milky Way, one to whom has been given a meal of the faience which is in the Tjenenet-shrine.

*What does it mean?* As for Khepri in the midst of his bark, he is Re himself. As for those who are in charge of those who are to be examined, they are the two sun-apes, Isis and Nephthys. As for those things which the gods detest, they are faeces and falsehood. As for him who passed on, having bathed in the Milky Way, he is Anubis who is behind the chest which contains the entrails of Osiris. As for him to whom has been given a meal of the faience which is in the Tjenenet-shrine, he is Osiris. As for the meal of faience which is in the Tjenenet-shrine, it is sky and earth. *Otherwise said:* It means that Shu hammered out the Two Lands in Hera-cleopolis. As for faience, it is the Eye of Horus. As for the Tjenenet-shrine, it is the tomb of Osiris.

How well built is your house, O Atum! How well founded is your mansion, O Double Lion! Run, run to this! If Horus be respected, Seth will be divine, and vice versa. I have come into this land, I have made use of my feet, for I am Atum, I am in my city. Get back, O Lion, bright of mouth and shining of head; retreat because of my strength, take care, O you who are invisible, do not await me, for I am Isis. You found me when I had dis-arranged the hair of my face and my scalp was disor-dered. I have become pregnant as Isis, I have conceived as Nephthys. Isis drives out those who would await me, Nephthys drives off those who would disturb me. The dread of me follows after me, my dignity is before me, millions bend their arms to me, the common folk serve me, the associates of my enemies are destroyed for me, the Grey-haired ones uncover their arms for me, the well-disposed give sweet things to me, those who are in Kheraha and those who are in Heliopolis create things for me. Every god is afraid because so great and mighty is my protection of the god from him who would vilify him. Malachite glitters for me, I live according to my will, for I am Wadjet, Lady of the Devouring Flame, and few approach me.

*What does it mean?* 'Secret of shape, the arms of Hemen' is the name of the fish-trap. 'He who sees what he brings by hand' is the name of the storm-cloud. *Otherwise said:* The name of the slaughter-block. As for the Lion whose mouth is bright and whose head is shining, he is the phallus of Osiris. *Otherwise said:* He is the phallus of Re. As for my having disarranged the hair of my face and having disordered my scalp, it means that

Isis was in the shrine of Sokar and she rubbed her hair. As for Wadjet, Lady of the Devouring Flame, she is the Eye of Re. As for those few who approach her, it means that the confederacy of Seth are near her, because what is near her is burning.

If a man speaks this spell when he is in a state of purity, it means going forth after death into the day and assuming whatever shape he desires. As for anyone who shall read it daily for his own benefit, it means being hale on earth; he shall come forth from every fire and nothing evil shall reach him. It is a matter a million times true; I have seen and it has indeed come to pass through me.

# —— SPELL 20 ——

### THE DECEASED APPEALS TO THOTH TO VINDICATE HIM BEFORE THE TRIBUNALS OF THE GODS

O Thoth, you who vindicated Osiris against his enemies, may you entrap the enemies of N in the presence of the tribunals of every god and every goddess:

In the presence of the great tribunal which is in Heliopolis on that night of battle and of felling those who rebelled.

In the presence of the great tribunal which is in Busiris on that night of erecting the two djed-pillars.

In the presence of the great tribunal which is in Letopolis on that night of performing the night-ritual in Letopolis.

In the presence of the great tribunal which is in Pe and Dep on that night of confirming the heritage of Horus in respect of the property of his father Osiris.

In the presence of the great tribunal which is in the Two Banks on that night when Isis mourned for her brother Osiris.

In the presence of the great tribunal which is in Abydos on that night of the haker-festival and of the numbering of the dead and the spirits.

In the presence of the great tribunal which is on the Road of the Dead on that night of making inquiry into him who is nothing.

In the presence of the great tribunal which is in the Great Devastation.

In the presence of the great tribunal which is in Naref.

In the presence of the great tribunal which is in Rosetjau on that night when Horus was vindicated against his enemies.

Horus has become great happily, the Two Conclaves are pleased about it, and Osiris is glad. O Thoth, vindicate N against his enemies in the tribunal of every god and every goddess, and in those tribunals of Osiris which are behind the shrine.

*Part of Spell 17* Ani kneels in praise of the bark of the sun-god which sails on the sign for sky. In it squats Khepri, with a scarab for a head, protected by an udjat-eye and adored by two baboons. In the centre Atum, within his disc and accompanied by the hieroglyph for 'attendance', sails towards a lion which reclines on a shrine-shaped plinth. Wadjet, in cobra-form, is entwined in the overhanging papyrus plants which shade the lion. In front of the plinth is a ewer on a stand, topped by a lotus, and behind, a flame in a brazier. 10470/10

## —— SPELL 21 ——

*Spell for giving a mouth to N for him in the realm of the dead*

Hail to you, Lord of Light, pre-eminent in the Great Mansion, in charge of the twilight! I have come to you spiritualised and pure. Your arms are about you and your portion of food is before you; may you give me my mouth with which I may speak, and may my heart guide me at its hour of destroying the night.

## —— SPELL 22 ——

*Spell for giving a mouth to N for him in the realm of the dead*

I have arisen from the Egg which is in the secret land, my mouth has been given to me that I may speak with it in the presence of the Great God, Lord of the Netherworld; my hand shall not be thrust aside in the tribunal of all gods, for I am Osiris, Lord of Rosetjau. I will share with this one who is on the dais, for *I have come for what my heart desires into the Lake of Fire which is quenched for me.*

Right: **Spell 22** *The Keeper of the Scales touches the mouth of Nebseny to give him the power of speech.* 9900/5

## —— SPELL 23 ——
[illustrated p.53]

*Spell for opening the mouth of N*

*My mouth is opened by* Ptah and what was on my mouth has been loosened by my local god. Thoth comes indeed,

filled and equipped with magic, and the bonds of Seth which restricted my mouth have been loosened. Atum has warded them off and has cast away the restrictions of Seth.

*My mouth is opened, my mouth is split open by* Shu with that iron harpoon of his with which he split open the mouths of the gods. I am Sakhmet, and I sit beside Her who is in the great wind of the sky; I am Orion the Great who dwells with the Souls of Heliopolis.

*As for any magic spell or any words which may be uttered against me,* the gods *will rise up* against it, even the entire Ennead.

## —— SPELL 24 ——

### *Spell for bringing magic to N*

I am Atum-Khepri who came into being of himself upon the lap of his mother Nut, who gave jackals to those who are in the Abyss and hunting-dogs to those who are in the tribunal. *I have collected this magic in every place where it was, from the possession of anyone who possessed it, more speedily* than a hound, more swiftly than a shadow. *O you who bring the ferry-boat* of Re, strengthen your rope in the north wind. Ferry upstream to the Island of Fire beside the realm of the dead, *collect this magic* from wherever it may be, from the possession of anyone who may possess it, more speedily than a hound, more swiftly than a shadow. *Transform yourself* into a heron, the mother who created you; the gods are hushed, your mother has made you warm for the gods. *Now there is given to me* this magic, to whomsoever it may belong, more speedily than a hound, more swiftly than a shadow.

## —— SPELL 25 ——

### *Spell for causing that N be remembered in the realm of the dead*

A name has been given to me in the Per-wer, my name has been remembered in the Per-neser, on that night of reckoning the years and of counting the months. I am this builder, I sit on the eastern side of the sky. As for any god who shall not come following after me, I will declare his name to those who are yet to be.

## —— SPELL 26 ——

### *Spell for giving N's heart to him in the realm of the dead*

My heart is mine in the House of Hearts, my heart is mine in the House of Hearts, my heart is mine, and it is at rest there. I will not eat the cakes of Osiris on the eastern side of the Gay-water in the barge when you sail downstream or upstream, and I will not go aboard the boat in which you are. My mouth will be given to me that I may speak with it, my legs to walk, and my arms to fell my enemy. The doors of the sky are opened for me; Geb, chiefest of the gods, throws open his jaws for me, he opens my eyes which were closed up, he extends my legs which were contracted; Anubis strengthens for me my thighs which were joined together; the goddess Sakhmet stretches me out. I will be in the sky, a command shall be made for my benefit in Memphis, I shall

*Spells 25 and 26 In the right-hand detail (Spell 25) Ta-Amen-iw presents a papyrus scroll to a standing god and guarantees that her name will be remembered. On the left (Spell 26) she kneels clasping her heart before her human-headed soul, which wears a djed around its neck and stands on a plinth. 10086/5*

*Spells 27, 28 and 30 Ta-Amen-iw kneels, clasping her heart, before three gods who squat on a plinth (Spell 27). The central detail shows her standing with arms raised in praise before her heart on an offering-table, behind which squats a god on a plinth with a was-sceptre on his knee (Spell 28). On the left (Spell 30) Ta-Amen-iw adores the scarab in whose form is made the amulet which will guarantee her vindication at the Weighing of her Heart. 10086/5*

be aware in my heart, I shall have power in my heart, I shall have power in my arms, I shall have power in my legs, I shall have power to do whatever I desire; my soul and my corpse shall not be restrained at the portals of the West when I go in or out in peace.

## SPELL 27
[also illustrated p.55]

*Spell for not permitting a man's heart to be taken from him in the realm of the dead*

O you who take away hearts and accuse hearts, who recreate a man's heart (in respect of) what he has done, he is forgetful of himself through what you have done. Hail to you, lords of eternity, founders of everlasting! Do not take N's heart with your fingers wherever his heart may be. You shall not raise any matter harmful to him, because as for this heart of N, this heart belongs to one whose names are great, whose words are mighty, who possesses his members. He sends out his heart which controls his body, his heart is announced to the gods, for N's heart is his own, he has power over it, and he will not say what he has done. He himself has power over his members, his heart obeys him, for he is your lord and you are in his body, you shall not turn aside. I command you to obey me in the realm of the dead, even I, N, who am vindicated in peace and vindicated in the beautiful West in the domain of eternity.

## SPELL 28
[also illustrated p.56]

*Spell for not permitting N's heart to be taken from him in the realm of the dead*

O Lion, I am a weneb-flower; the shambles of the god is what I abhor, and my heart shall not be taken from me by those who fought in Heliopolis.

THE ORIGINAL SPELL ENDS HERE. WHAT FOLLOWS IS A VERY CORRUPT ADDITION WHICH IS VIRTUALLY UNTRANSLATABLE.

*Spell 23 Nakht, seated on a backless chair, has his mouth opened by a falcon-headed god using the ritual adze and so regains all his faculties for use in the Other World. 10471/8*

## ——— Spell 29 ———

*Spell for not permitting a man's heart to be taken away from him in the realm of the dead*

Get back, you messenger of any god! Have you come to take away this heart of mine which belongs to the living? I will not let you take away this heart of mine which belongs to the living who move about. The gods who rest for me have heard, falling headlong on their faces... in their own land.

Below: *Part of Spell 1 illustrating Spell 23* The Sem-priest, clad in a panther-skin, censes and lustrates behind a heap of offerings; other priests present containers and raise ritual implements to open the mouth of Hunefer's mummy, which is held upright by a priest wearing a jackal's mask and lamented by his widow, Nasha. Behind is a funerary stela standing before Hunefer's pyramid-capped tomb chapel. Below,

## ——— Spell 29a ———

*Spell for not taking away the heart of one whose conduct has been vindicated in the realm of the dead.*

My heart is with me and it shall not be taken away, for I am a possessor of hearts who unites hearts. I live by truth, in which I exist; I am Horus who is in hearts, he who is in the middle of what is in the body. I live by saying what is in my heart, and it shall not be taken away; my heart is mine, and none shall be aggressive

officiants carry a heart and foreleg cut from a still-bleating calf towards a table heaped with offerings, a chest and ritual implements laid out ready for the Opening of the Mouth ceremony. 9901/5

Right: *Spell 27* Ani stands in praise before his heart on a standard behind which squat four gods. 10470/16

against it, no terror shall subdue me. I take it that I may be in the body of my father Geb and of my mother Nut, for I have committed no sin against the gods, and nothing shall be deducted in that respect from my vindication.

## —— SPELL 29B ——
[illustrated p.158]

*Spell for a heart-amulet of sehret-stone*

I am the phoenix, the soul of Re, who guides the gods to the Netherworld when they go forth. The souls on earth will do what they desire, and the soul of N will go forth at his desire.

## —— SPELL 30A ——

*Spell for not letting N's heart create opposition against him in the realm of the dead*

O my heart which I had from my mother, O my heart which I had upon earth, do not rise up against me as a witness in the presence of the Lord of Things; do not speak against me concerning what I have done, do not bring up anything against me in the presence of the Great God, Lord of the West.

Hail to you, my heart! Hail to you, my heart! Hail to you, my entrails! Hail to you, you gods who are at the head of those who wear the sidelock, who lean on their staffs! May you say what is good to Re, may you make me to flourish, may powers be bestowed when I go forth, having been interred among the great ones who long endure upon earth.

Not dying in the West, but becoming a spirit in it.

## —— SPELL 30B ——

*See page 27*

# A Rubric for Spell 30a,b
[also illustrated p.53]

To be inscribed on a scarab made from nephrite, mounted in fine gold, with a ring of silver, and placed at the throat of the deceased. This spell was found in Hermopolis, under the feet of this god. It was written on a block of mineral of Upper Egypt in the writing of the god himself and was discovered in the time of the Majesty of the vindicated King of Upper and Lower Egypt Menkaure. It was the king's son Hordedef who found it while he was going around making an inspection of the temples.

## —— Spell 31 ——
[also illustrated p.58]

*Spell for driving off a crocodile which comes to take away N's magic from him in the realm of the dead*

Get back! Retreat! Get back, you dangerous one! Do not come against me, do not live by my magic; may I not have to tell this name of yours to the Great God who sent you; 'Messenger' is the name of one and Bedty is the name of the other.

THE CROCODILE SPEAKS: Your face belongs to righteousness. The sky encloses the stars, magic encloses its settlements, and my mouth encloses the magic which is in it. My teeth are a knife, my tusks are the Viper Mountain.

THE DECEASED REPLIES: O you with a spine who would work your mouth against this magic of mine, no crocodile which lives by magic shall take it away.

## —— Spell 32 ——

*Spell for repelling a crocodile which comes to take away a spirit's magic from him in the realm of the dead*

The Great One has fallen on his side, but the Ennead have pulled him together. I come, my soul speaks with my father, and I have this Great One from those eight crocodiles. I know them by their names and their lives, and I save my father from them.

Get back, you crocodile of the West, who lives on the Unwearying Stars! Detestation of you is in my belly, for I have absorbed the power of Osiris, and I am Seth.

Get back, you crocodile of the West! The nau-snake is in my belly, and I have not given myself to you; your flame will not be on me.

Get back, you crocodile of the East, who lives on those who are mutilated! Detestation of you is in my belly, and I have gone away, for I am Osiris.

Above: ***Spells 28, 30, 31 and 32*** *On the far right Mutirdais reveres her heart, which is on a stand before a falcon-headed god, who squats on a shrine-shaped plinth (Spell 28). Beside this she is shown adoring the scarab in whose form the amulet which guarantees her vindication at the Weighing of her Heart is made (Spell 30). The scarab is on a standard. On the left (Spells 31 and 32) the husband of Mutirdais repulses with a spear the crocodiles which would steal her magic. 9951/4*

Right: ***Spell 30*** *Ast-wert kneels clasping her heart before an offering table topped by a lotus. Behind is the scarab in whose form the amulet which will guarantee her vindication at the Weighing of her Heart is made. It holds a sun-disc in its back legs. 10039/3*

Get back, you crocodile in the East! The nau-snake is in my belly, and I have not given myself to you; your flame will not be on me.

Get back, you crocodile of the South, living on faeces, smoke and want! Detestation of you is in my belly, and my blood is not in your hand, for I am Sopd.

Get back, you crocodile in the South! I will erase you, for I become a bebet-herb, and I have not given myself to you.

Get back, you crocodile of the North, living on the ... which is in the midst of the stars! Detestation of you is in my belly, your poison is in my head; I am Atum.

Get back, you crocodile in the North! A scorpion is in my belly, but I will not give it birth.

I am one whose eyes are green, what exists is in my grasp, what does not exist is in my belly, I am clad and equipped with your magic, O Re, even this which is above me and below me. I am ..., I am exalted, my throat is wide open in the house of my father the Great One; he has given to me yon beautiful West which destroys the living; strong is its lord, who daily is weary in it. My vision is cleared, my heart is in its proper place, my uraeus is with me every day. I am Re, who himself protects himself, and nothing can harm me.

## —— SPELL 33 ——

*Spell for driving off a snake*

O Rerek-snake, take yourself off, for Geb protects me; get up, for you have eaten a mouse, which Re detests, and you have chewed the bones of a putrid cat.

## —— SPELL 34 ——

*Spell for not being bitten by a snake in the realm of the dead*

O cobra, I am the flame which shines on the brows of the Chaos-gods of the Standard of Years. *Otherwise said:* the Standard of Vegetation. Begone from me, for I am Mafdet!

## —— SPELL 35 ——

*Spell for not being eaten by a snake in the realm of the dead*

'O Shu,' says He of Busiris, and vice versa. Neith is wearing the head-cloth, Hathor makes Osiris glad, and who is he who will eat me? Depart, leave me, pass me by, you snake; it is the sam-plant which wards you off, this is the leek of Osiris which he asked for when he was buried. The clouded eyes of the Great One have fallen on you, and Maat will examine you for judgement.

## —— SPELL 36 ——

*Spell for repelling a beetle*

Begone from me, O Crooked-lips! I am Khnum, Lord of Peshnu, who despatches the words of the gods to Re, and I report affairs to their master.

**Spell 31** *Nakht wards off with a knife the crocodiles who seek to steal his magic.* 10417/16

**Spell 36** *Nakht repulses with a knife the apshai-insect, represented as a beetle.* 10471/16

## —— SPELL 37 ——
[also illustrated p.60]

*Spell for repelling two Songstress-snakes*

Hail to you, you two companions, sisters, Songstresses! I have divided you with my magic, for I am he who shines in the Night-bark, I am Horus, son of Isis, and I have come to see my father Osiris.

## —— SPELL 38A ——

*Spell for living by air in the realm of the dead*

I am Atum who ascended from the Abyss to the Celestial

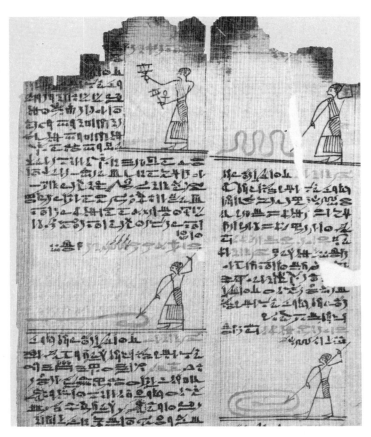 

Above: **Spells 33, 35, 38B and 39** *In each of the two right-hand details Horemheb repulses a snake with a spear (top: Spell 33, bottom: Spell 35). In the detail at the top left (Spell 38B) Horemheb raises two sails and an ankh which will enable him to breathe and live in the realm of the dead. Below this he repels with a spear the rerek-snake (Spell 39). 10257/4*

Above: **Spell 38A** *Nakht sits on a lion-footed chair holding a sail which will enable him to live by air in the Other World. 10471/8*

Below: **Spells 36 and 37** *On the left (Spell 36) Nakht spears a pig and a snake which would harm him. On the right (Spell 37) he wards off with a knife the two Songstress-snakes. 10471/14*

*Spells 37 and 38B The detail at the top shows Ta-amen-iw repulsing with two spears an undulating serpent which represents the two Songstress-snakes (Spell 37). In the bottom detail (Spell 38B) she holds a lotus and raises a sail before Osiris, who is enthroned behind an offering-table topped by a lotus, guaranteeing that she will live by air in the Other World. 10086/6*

attend on Re in his presence in the horizon, I daily live after death, I am strong through the Double Lion and I live after death, even I, N, who fills full the earth, who comes forth as the bloom of the lotus-plant, who makes the Two Lands content.

## ——— SPELL 38B ———
[also illustrated p.59]

*Spell for living by air in the realm of the dead*

I am the Double Lion, the first-born of Re, Atum of Chemmis; those who are in their booths (serve me), those who are in their holes guide me, there are made for me ways which encircle the Celestial Waters on the path of the bark of Atum. I stand on the deck of the Bark of Re, I proclaim his words to the common folk and I repeat his words to these whose throats are constricted; I have judged my forefathers at eventide, I open my mouth, I eat life, I live in Busiris, and I live again after death like Re every day.

## ——— SPELL 39 ———
[illustrated p.59]

*Spell for repelling a rerek-snake in the realm of the dead*

Get back! Crawl away! Get away from me, you snake! Go, be drowned in the Lake of the Abyss, at the place where your father commanded that the slaying of you should be carried out. Be far removed from that abode of Re wherein you trembled, for I am Re at whom men tremble; get back, you rebel, at the knives of his light. Your words have fallen because of Re, your face is turned back by the gods, your heart is cut out by Mafdet, you are put into bonds by the Scorpion-goddess, your sentence is carried out by Maat, those who are on the ways fell you.

Fall! Crawl away, Apep, you enemy of Re! O you who escape massacre in the east of the sky at the sound of the roaring storm, open the doors of the horizon before Re, that he may go forth, wearied with wounds. I do what you desire, O Re, I do what is good, I act as one who pleases, O Re, I cause your bonds to fall, O Re. Apep has fallen to your destruction, the southern, northern, western and eastern gods have bound their bonds on him, Rekes has felled him, he who is over the partisans has bound him, and Re is content, Re proceeds in peace. Apep the enemy of Re has fallen down, and what you have experienced is greater than that experience which is in the heart of the Scorpion-goddess; great is what she has done against you with the everlasting pains which are hers. You shall not become erect, you

Waters, I have taken my seat in the West and I give orders to the spirits whose seats are hidden, for I am the Double Lion, and acclamation is made to me in the Bark of Khepri. I eat in it and have become strong thereby, I live in it on air, and I drink in the Bark of Re. He opens a road for me, he throws open the gates of Geb. I have carried off those who are in the net of the Great One, I have governed those who are in their shrines, I have associated with Horus and Seth, the Two Lords. I despatch the Elders on my own account, I come and go without having my throat cut, I go aboard the Bark of the just, I join those who are in the Day-bark when I shall not copulate, O Apep, you enemy of Re. Opposition is made against you, O you whom Re hates when he looks on you.

Get back! You shall be decapitated with a knife, your face shall be cut away all round, your head shall be removed by him who is in his land, your bones shall be broken, your limbs shall be cut off; the earth-god has condemned you, O Apep, you enemy of Re.

O Re, your crew ... may you rest there, for your possessions are there. Bring to the house, bring your Eye to the house, bring what is good; may no evil opposition come forth from your mouth against me, being what you might do against me, for I am Seth, who can raise a tumult of storm in the horizon of the sky like one whose will is destruction – so says Atum.

Lift up your faces, you soldiers of Re, and keep Nendja away from the tribunal for me – so says Geb. Make yourselves firm, O you who are on your seats aboard the bark of Khepri. Take your ways and your weapons which are put into your hands for you – so says Hathor. Take your javelins – so says Nut. Come, drive away that enemy of his, namely Nendja, that those who are in his shrine may come and that he may ferry himself in solitude, even he the Lord of All, who shall not be opposed – so say those primeval gods who circumambulate the Lakes of Turquoise. Come, O Great One whom we worship; save us, O you whose shrines are great, from whom the Ennead came forth, to whom what is beneficial is done, to whom praise is given; may someone report it to you and me – so says Nut – for yonder Happy One – so say those who are among the gods. May he go forth, may he find the way, may he plunder the gods, may he rise early in front of Nut, and may Geb stand up – so says the Terrible One. The Ennead is on the move, the door of Hathor has been infringed, and Re is triumphant over Apep.

## —— Spell 40 ——
[illustrated p.62]

*Spell for repelling him who swallowed an ass*

Get back, you Male whom Osiris detests, whose head Thoth has cut off! I have done everything in respect of you which was said about you in the Ennead in order to carry out your destruction.

Get back, you whom Osiris in the Neshmet-bark detests when he sails southward with a fair wind! Purify yourselves, all you gods, and fell with shouting the enemies of Osiris, Lord of the Thinite nome.

Get back, you swallower of an ass, whom Ha who is in the Netherworld detests! I know, I know, I know, I know! Where are you? I am ...

## —— Spell 41 ——

*Spell for preventing the slaughter which is carried out in the realm of the dead*

O Atum, spiritualise me in the presence of the Double Lion, the Great God; may he open for me the portal of Geb, that I may do homage to the Great God who is in the realm of the dead; may you induct me into the presence of the Ennead who preside over the Westerners.

O you door-keeper of the City of the Bee which is in the West, may I eat and live by air, may he who is safe and great guide me to the Great Bark of Khepri, and may I speak to the evening crew; may I come and go, may I see who is there; I will raise him up, I will speak my words to him, when my throat is constricted. May I live, may I be saved after sleeping.

O Bringer of offerings who open your mouth, confirm the writings for offerings, establish Maat on her throne for me; confirm the tablets, establish the goddesses in the presence of Osiris the Great God, the ruler of eternity, who reckons up his seasons, who listens to them of the islands, who raises his right arm when he commissions the great ones whom he sends into the great tribunal which is in the realm of the dead.

*Spell 41* Ankhwahibre repulses with a spear the symbolic representation of slaughter, depicted as conventionally drawn vertebrae topped by a serpent. 10558/7

*Spell 40 Nakht spears the snake which is swallowing an ass.* 10471/16

## ——— Spell 42 ———

*Spell for preventing the slaughter which is carried out in Heracleopolis*

O Land of the Staff! O Crown of the Statue! O Standard which is rowed! I am the Child! O Great Kid, I speak to you today! The shambles is equipped with what you know, and you have come to it ... I am Re, continually praised; I am the knot of the god within the tamarisk. How beautiful is the ... with him!

I am Re, continually praised; I am the knot of the god within the tamarisk; if I am hale, then will Re be hale today.

My hair is Nun; my face is Re; my eyes are Hathor; my ears are Wepwawet; my nose is She who presides over her lotus-leaf; my lips are Anubis; my molars are Selket; my incisors are Isis the goddess; my arms are the Ram, the Lord of Mendes; my breast is Neith, Lady of Sais; my back is Seth; my phallus is Osiris; my muscles are the Lords of Kheraha; my chest is He who is greatly majestic; my belly and my spine are Sakhmet; my buttocks are the Eye of Horus; my thighs and my calves are Nut; my feet are Ptah; my toes are living falcons; there is no member of mine devoid of a god, and Thoth is the protection of all my flesh.

I am the daily sun, I am not grasped by my arms, I am not gripped by my hands, and there are no men, gods, spirits, dead men, patricians, common folk, sun-folk or robbers who shall harm me. I go forth hale, one whose name is unknown, I am Yesterday; one who views a million years; my name is one who passes on the paths of those who are in charge of destinies. I am the Lord of Eternity; may I be recognised as Khepri, for I am the Lord of the Wereret-crown.

I am he in whom is the Sacred Eye, and who is in the Egg, and it is granted to me to live by them.

I am he in whom is the Sacred Eye, namely the Closed Eye, I am under its protection. I have gone out, I have risen up, I have gone in, I am alive.

I am he in whom is the Sacred Eye, my seat is on my throne, I dwell in my abode with it, for I am Horus who treads down millions, my throne has been ordered for me, and I will rule from it. Behold, my mouth is what speaks and what keeps silence, and I am precise. Behold, my shape is turned upside down. I am Wennefer, season by season, whose attributes (come) into him one by one when he travels around.

I am he in whom is the Sacred Eye, and nothing shall come into being against me, no evil cutting off and no uproar, and there shall be no danger to me.

I am he who opened a door in the sky, who rules from his throne, who adjudges those who are born this day; there is no child who treads yesterday's road, and today is mine. O people on people, I am he who protects you for aeons. Are you in being, you sky-folk, earthlings, southerners, northerners, easterners and westerners, is the fear of me in your bellies? I am he who fashioned with his Eye, and I will not die again. My striking power is in your bellies, my shape is before me; I am ... and I ignore the wrath in your faces against me; I am joyful, and there can be found no season when he could harm me. Where is the sky? Where is the earth? Their offspring are rebuffed and they are disunited. My name overpasses it, namely everything evil, for great are the spoken words which I speak to you.

I am one who rises and shines, wall of walls, most unique of the unique ones, and there is no day devoid of its duties. Pass by! Behold, I have spoken to you, for I am the flower which came out of the Abyss, my mother is Nut. O you who created me, I am one who cannot tread, the great knot within yesterday; my arm is knotted into my hand, I will not know him who would know me, I will not grasp him who would grasp me. O Egg, O Egg, I am Horus who presides over myriads, my fiery breath is in the faces of those whose hearts would move against me. I rule from my throne, I pass time on the road which I have opened up. I am released from all evil, I am the golden baboon, three palms and two fingers high, which has neither arms nor legs, in front of Memphis. If I am hale, then will the baboon which is in front of Memphis be hale.

# Spell 43
[illustrated p.64]

*Spell for preventing a man's decapitation in the realm of the dead*

I am a Great One, the son of a Great One, I am a flame, the son of a flame, to whom was given his head after it had been cut off. The head of Osiris shall not be taken from him, and my head shall not be taken from me. I am knit together, just and young, for I indeed am Osiris, the Lord of Eternity.

# Spell 44
[illustrated p.66]

*Spell for not dying again in the realm of the dead*

My cavern is opened, the spirits fall within the darkness. The Eye of Horus makes me holy, Wepwawet has caressed me; O Imperishable Stars, hide me among you.

*Spell 42 Nakht wards off slaughter by adoring twenty major deities squatting in a shrine with open doors. Each of the deities is associated by name with a component part of Nakht's anatomy. 10471/17*

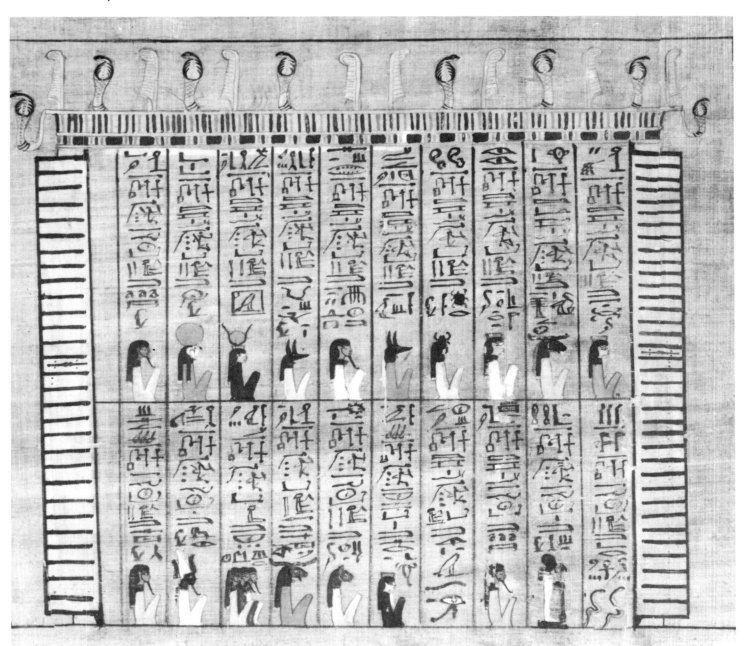

*Spell 43 Ani reveres three standing deities, who hold ankhs and was-sceptres, in the hope of avoiding decapitation. 10470/17*

My neck is Re, my vision is cleared, my heart is in its proper place, my speech is known.

THE GOD RE SPEAKS: I am Re who himself protects himself; I do not know you, I do not look after you, your father the son of Nut lives for you.

THE DECEASED REPLIES: I am your eldest son who sees your secrets, I have appeared as King of the Gods, and I will not die again in the realm of the dead.

## ——— SPELL 45 ———
[illustrated p.66]

*Spell for not putrefying in the realm of the dead*

Weary, weary are the members of Osiris! They shall not be weary, they shall not putrefy, they shall not decay, they shall not swell up! May it be done to me in like manner, for I am Osiris.

*As for him who knows this spell, he shall not putrefy in Osiris's realm of the dead*

## ——— SPELL 46 ———
[illustrated p.66]

*Spell for not perishing and for being alive in the realm of the dead*

O you young men of Shu of the morning, who have power over those who flash among the sun-folk, whose arms move about and whose heads sway to and fro; may I move about every day.

## ——— SPELL 47 ———

*Spell for preventing the taking of N's place and throne from him in the realm of the dead*

O Place of mine, O Throne of mine, come and serve me, for I am your lord. O you gods, come in my company, for I am the son of your lord, you are mine, for it was my father who made you.

*Spells 53 and 55 On the right Ta-Amen-iw is seated before a table of offerings behind which stands a mummiform god holding a crook and flail (Spell 55). On the left (Spell 55) she stands holding a lotus* *and a sail before an offering-table topped by a lotus; behind this stands Osiris holding a was-sceptre. 10086/6*

## ——— SPELL 50 ———
[illustrated p.66]

*Spell for not entering into the shambles of the god*

The four knots are tied about me by the guardian of the sky. He has made the knot firm for the Inert One on his thighs on that day of cutting off the lock of hair.

The knot was tied about me by Seth, in whose power the Ennead were at first, before uproar had come into being, when he caused me to be hale.

The knot was tied about me by Nut, when I first saw Maat, when the gods and the sacred images had not yet been born. I am a heavenborn, I am in the presence of the Great Gods.

## ——— SPELL 53 ———

*Spell for not eating faeces or drinking urine in the realm of the dead*

I am the horned bull who rules the sky, Lord of Celestial Appearings, the Great Illuminator who came forth from the heat, who harnesses the years; the Double Lion is glad, and the movement of the sunshine has been granted to me. I detest what is detestable, I will not eat faeces, I will not drink urine, I will not walk head downward.

I am the owner of bread in Heliopolis, bread of mine is in the sky with Re, bread of mine is on earth with Geb, and it is the Night-bark and the Day-bark which will bring it to me from the house of the Great God who is in Heliopolis. I am loosed from my windings, I make ready the ferry-boat of the sky, I eat of what they eat, I live on what they live on, I have eaten bread in every pleasant room.

## ——— SPELL 54 ———

*Spell for giving breath to N in the realm of the dead*

O Atum, give me the sweet breath which is in your nostril, for I am this Egg which is in the Great Cackler, I am the guardian of this great being who separates the earth from the sky. If I live, she will live; I grow young, I live, I breathe the air. I am he who splits iron, I go round about the Egg, tomorrow is mine through the striking-power of Horus and the strength of Seth. O you who sweeten the state of the Two Lands, you with whom are provisions, you with whom is lapis-lazuli, beware of Him who is in his nest; the Youth goes forth against you.

*Below:* ***Spell 50*** *Ani walks away from the shambles represented symbolically by a knife dripping blood on two supports which protrude from a sand mound.* 10470/16

*Above:* ***Spells 44, 45 and 46*** *On the left Ani sits on a chair with lions' feet, holding a staff and kherep-sceptre, before a table stacked with flat loaves (Spell 44). The central detail (Spell 45) shows Ani's mummy wearing a mummy mask and tended by Anubis, god of embalming. On the right a doorway is flanked by the phoenix and Ani's human-headed soul (Spell 46).* 10470/16

## —— SPELL 55 ——
[illustrated p.65]

*Spell for giving breath in the realm of the dead*

I am the jackal of jackals, I am Shu who draws the air into the presence of the sunshine to the limits of the sky, to the limits of the earth, to the limits of the plume of the nebeh-bird, and air is given to those youths who open my mouth so that I may see with my eyes.

## —— SPELL 56 ——

*Spell for breathing air among the waters in the realm of the dead*

O Atum, give me the sweet breath which is in your nostril, for I seek out that great place which is in Wenu, I have guarded that Egg of the Great Cackler. If I be strong, it will be strong; if I live, it will live; if I breathe the air, it will breathe the air.

# SPELL 57

[illustrated p.91]

*Spell for breathing air and having power over water in the realm of the dead*

O Hapi, Great One of the sky in this your name of 'The sky is safe', may you grant that I have power over water like Sakhmet who saved Osiris on that night of storm. Behold, the Elders who are before the throne of 'Abundance' have sent to me just as that august god whose name they do not know sent them, and they send me likewise. My nostrils are opened in Busiris, I rest in Heliopolis, my house is what Seshat built for me, Khnum stands up for me on his battlements.

If the sky comes with the north wind, I will dwell in the south; if the sky comes with the south wind, I will dwell in the north; if the sky comes with the west wind, I will dwell in the east; if the sky comes with the east wind, I will dwell in the west. I will pull the skin of my nostrils, I will open up at the place where I desire to be.

Above: **Spell 56** *Padiamennebnesutawy kneels in adoration of Atum, who squats wearing the Double Crown and holding a sail on his knee, thus guaranteeing breath in the Other World.* 10253/1

Below: **Spells 58 and 59** *On the left Ani and his wife Tutu stand in a pool with trees in the background, holding sails and raising water to their lips, thus guaranteeing themselves breath and power over water (Spell 58). On the right Ani kneels beside a pool and receives water and food from a tree goddess (Spell 59).* 10470/16

## SPELL 58
[illustrated p.67]

*Spell for breathing air and having power over water in the realm of the dead*

Open to me!
Who are you? What are you? Where did you grow up?
I am one of you.
Who is with you?
It is the two Songstress-serpents.
You shall separate head from head when approaching the Milky Way.
I shall cross to the Mansion of Him who finds faces; 'Collector of souls' is the name of the ferryman, 'Tresses of hair' is the name of the oars, 'Thorn' is the name of the bailer; 'Precise and accurate' is the name of the steering-oar, like him who smoothed things over when you buried yourself in the waters; you shall give me a jug of milk, a shens-loaf, a persen-loaf, a jug of beer and a portion of meat in the Mansion of Anubis.
*As for him who knows this spell, he will go in after coming out in the cemetery of the beautiful West.*

*Spell 61 Ani clasps his human-headed soul to his chest to prevent it being taken away in the Other world. 10470/15*

## SPELL 59
[illustrated p.67]

*Spell for breathing air and having power over water in the realm of the dead*

O you sycamore of the sky, may there be given to me the air which is in it, for I am he who sought out that throne in the middle of Wenu and I have guarded this Egg of the Great Cackler. If it grows, I will grow; if it lives, I will live; if it breathes the air, I will breathe the air.

## SPELL 61

*Spell for not letting a man's soul be taken away from him in the realm of the dead*

I am he, I am he who came forth from the flood, to whom abundance was given, that I might have power thereby over the River.

## SPELL 62

*Spell for drinking water in the realm of the dead*

May the great water be opened for Osiris, may the cool water of Thoth and the water of Hapi be thrown open for the Lord of the Horizon in this my name of Pedsu. May I be granted power over the waters like the limbs of Seth, for I am he who crosses the sky, I am the Lion of Re, I am the Slayer who eats the foreleg, the leg of beef is extended to me, the pools of the Field of Rushes serve me, limitless eternity is given to me, for I am he who inherited eternity, to whom everlasting was given.

## SPELL 63A
[illustrated p.70]

*Spell for drinking water and not being burnt by fire*

O Bull of the West, I am brought to you, for I am that oar of Re with which the Old Ones are rowed. I will be neither burnt up nor scorched, for I am Babai, the eldest son of Osiris, for whom all the gods have assembled within his Eye in Heliopolis; I am the trusted heir when the Great One is inert, my name will be strong for me, and assuredly you will live daily through me.

## —— SPELL 63B ——

*Spell for not being scalded with water*

I am that equipped oar with which Re is rowed when the Old Ones are rowed and the efflux of Osiris is upraised at the Lake of Flames which does not burn, I have climbed in the sunshine. O Khnum who is in charge of whips, come, cut away the bonds from him who travels on this road on which I have ascended.

## —— SPELL 65 ——

*Spell for going out into the day and having power over one's enemy*

Re sits in his Abode of Millions of Years, and there assemble for him the Nine Gods with hidden faces who dwell in the Mansion of Khepri, who eat abundance and who drink the drinks which the sky brings at dawn. Do not permit me to be carried off as booty to Osiris, for I have never been in the confederacy of Seth, O you who sit on your coils before Him whose soul is strong, let me sit on the throne of Re and take possession of my body before Geb; may you grant that Osiris may go forth vindicated against Seth; may the dreams of Seth be the dreams of a crocodile. O you whose faces are hidden, who preside over the Mansions of the King of Lower Egypt, who clothe the gods in the Sixth-day Festival, who weave for ever and who knot eternally, I have seen the Pig put into fetters, but indeed he who was put under ward has been released, the Pig has been loosed. I have been reborn, I have gone forth in the shape of a living spirit whom the common folk worship on earth. O you sick one who would harm me, be driven off from the wall of Re. Let me see Re, let me go forth against my enemies, let me be vindicated against them in the tribunal of the Great God in the presence of the Great God. If you do not let me go forth against that enemy of mine that I may be vindicated against him in the tribunal, then Hapi shall not ascend to the sky that he may live on truth, nor shall Re descend to the waters that he may live on fish. Then shall Re ascend to the sky that he may live on truth, and Hapi descend to the waters that he may live on fish, and the great day on earth shall end its condition. I have come against that enemy of mine, and he is given over to me, he is finished and silent in the tribunal.

## —— SPELL 66 ——

*Going out into the day*

I know that I was conceived by Sakhmet and borne by Satis. I am Horus who came forth from the Eye of Horus, I am Wadjet who came forth from Horus, I am Horus who flew up, I have lighted on the vertex of Re in the prow of his bark which is in the Abyss.

## —— SPELL 67 ——

*Spell for opening the tomb*

The cavern is opened for those who are in the Abyss, and those who are in the sunshine are released; the cavern is opened for Shu, and if he comes out, I will come out. I will go down into the earth-opening, I will receive ..., for I have grasped the lashings in the house of Him who is in charge of the mooring-posts. I will go down to my seat which is in the Bark of Re; may I not suffer through being deprived of my seat which is in the Bark of Re the great who rises and shines in the waterway of the lake.

## —— SPELL 68 ——

*Spell for going out into the day*

The doors of the sky are opened for me, the doors of the earth are opened for me, the door-bolts of Geb are opened for me, the shutters of the sky-windows are thrown open for me. It is he who guarded me who releases me, who binds his hand on me and thrusts his hand on to me on earth, the mouth of the Pelican is opened for me, the mouth of the Pelican is thrown open for me, the mouth of the Pelican is given to me, and I go out into the day to the place where I desire to be.

May I have power in my heart, may I have power in my heart, may I have power in my arms, may I have power in my legs, may I have power in my mouth, may I have power in all my members, may I have power over invocation-offerings, may I have power over water, may I have power over air, may I have power over the waters, may I have power over the streams, may I have power over riparian lands, may I have power over the men who would harm me, may I have power over the women who would harm me in the realm of the dead, may I have power over those who would give orders to harm me upon earth.

A GOD REPLIES: Surely it will be according to what

*Spell 63A Nakht stands in a pool cupping water to his lips, while a tree-goddess offers food and pours a stream of water over him. 10471/8*

you say to me. You shall live on the bread of Geb, and you shall not eat what you detest. You shall live on bread of white emmer and beer of red barley of Hapi in the pure place; you shall sit under the branches of the tree of Hathor who is pre-eminent in the wide solar disc when she travels to Heliopolis bearing the script of the divine words, the book of Thoth. You shall have power in your heart, you shall have power in your heart, you shall have power in your mouth, you shall have power in your arms, you shall have power over water, you shall have power over the waters, you shall have power over the streams, you shall have power over the riparian lands, you shall have power over the men who would harm you, you shall have power over the women who would harm you in the realm of the dead, you shall have power over those who would give orders to harm you on earth or in the realm of the dead. Raise yourself upon your left side, put yourself upon your right side, sit down and stand up, throw off your dust, may your tongue and your mouth be wise.

*As for whoever knows this book, he shall go out into the day, he shall walk on earth among* the living and he shall never suffer destruction. A matter a million times true.

## ——— SPELL 69 ———

*Spell for being the successor of Osiris*

I am the Radiant One, brother of the Radiant Goddess, Osiris the brother of Isis; my son and his mother Isis have saved me from my enemies who would harm me. Bonds are on their arms, their hands and their feet, because of what they have done evilly against me. I am Osiris, the first-born of the company of the gods, eldest of the gods, heir of my father Geb; I am Osiris, Lord of persons, alive of breast, strong of hinder-parts, stiff of phallus, who is within the boundary of the common folk.

I am Orion who treads his land, who precedes the stars of the sky which are on the body of my mother Nut, who conceived me at her desire and bore me at her will. I am Anubis on the Day of the Centipede, I am the Bull who presides over the field. I am Osiris, for whom his father and mother sealed an agreement on that day of carrying out the great slaughter; Geb is my father and Nut is my mother, I am Horus the Elder on the Day of Accession, I am Anubis of Sepa, I am the Lord of All, I am Osiris.

O you Eldest One who have come in, say to the collector of writings and to the door-keeper of Osiris that I have come, being a spirit, fully reckoned and divine; I have come that I myself may protect my body, that I may sit on the birth-stool of Osiris and get rid of his sore suffering. I am mighty and divine upon the birth-stool of Osiris, for I was born with him when he was very young. I uncover those knees of Osiris, I open the mouths of the gods because of them, I sit beside him, and Thoth has gone forth happy with a thousand of bread (and a thousand of beer) upon my father's altar, with my dappled cattle, long-horns, red cattle, geese and poultry for offering which I gave to Horus and offered to Thoth; my place of slaughter belongs to Him who is over the place of sacrifice.

—— SPELL 70 ——

*Otherwise said:* My place of slaughter belongs to Him who is over the place of sacrifice, I am happy and pleased with the altar of my father Osiris. I rule in Busiris, I travel about on its river-banks, I breathe the east wind because of its tresses, I grasp the north wind by its braided lock, I grip the south wind by its plaits, I grasp the west wind by its nape. I travel around the sky on its four sides, I give breath to the blessed ones among those who eat bread.

As for him who knows this book on earth, he shall come out into the day, he shall walk on earth among the living, and his name shall not perish for ever.

—— SPELL 71 ——

*Spell for going out into the day*

O you falcon who rise from the Abyss, Lord of the Celestial Waters, make me hale just as you made yourself hale. Release him, loose him, put him on earth, cause him to be loved: so says the One-faced Lord concerning me.

O you falcon within the shrine, may I be revealed to Him on whom is a fringed garment: so says Horus son of Isis.

O Horus son of Isis, make me hale as you made your-self hale. Release him, loose him, put him on earth, cause him to be loved: so says the One-faced Lord concerning me.

O Horus in the southern sky, O Thoth in the northern sky, pacify for me the raging fiery serpent, raise up Maat for me to Him whom she loves: so says Thoth.

O Thoth, make me hale just as you made yourself hale. Release him, loose him, put him on earth, cause him to be loved: so says the One-faced Lord concerning me.

I am the weneb-flower of Naref, the nebheh-flower of the hidden horizon: so says Osiris.

O Osiris, make me hale just as you made yourself hale. Release him, loose him, put him on earth, let him be loved: so says the One-faced Lord concerning me.

O you who are terrible on your feet, who are in action, Lord of the Two Fledglings: as the Two Fledglings live, make me hale just as you made yourself hale. Release him, loose him, put him on earth, cause him to be loved: so says the One-faced Lord concerning me.

O you of Nekhen who are in your Egg, Lord of the Celestial Waters, make me hale just as you made yourself hale. Release him, loose him, put him on earth, cause him to be loved: so says the One-faced Lord concerning me.

Rise up, O Sobk, in the midst of your river-bank; rise up, O Neith, in the midst of your riparian land. Release

*Spell 71 The Celestial Cow Mekhwert with an ankh around her neck reclines on a low plinth facing a falcon with upraised wings. 10086/7*

*Spell 72 Nakht walks out into the day from his pyramid-capped tomb chapel before which grows a tree.* 10471/14

him, loose him, put him on earth, cause him to be loved: so says the One-faced Lord concerning me.

O you seven knots, the arms of the balance on that night of setting the Sacred Eye in order, who cut off heads, who sever necks, who take away hearts, who snatch hearts, who make a slaughter in the Island of Fire: I know you, I know your names; may you know me just as I know your names; if I reach you, may you reach me; if you live through me, may I live through you; may you make me to flourish with what is in your hands, the staff which is in your grasp. May you destine me to life annually; may you grant to me many years of life over and above my years of life; many months over and above my months of life; many days over and above my days of life; many nights over and above my nights of life, until I depart. May I rise to be a likeness of myself, may my breath be at my nose, may my eyes see in company with those who are in the horizon on that day of dooming the robber.

As for him who shall recite this spell, it means prosperity on earth with Re and a goodly burial with Osiris; it will go very well with a man in the realm of the dead, and there shall be given to him the loaves which are issued daily in the Presence. A matter a million times true.

—— SPELL 72 ——

*Spell for going out into the day and opening up the tomb*

Hail to you, you owners of souls, who are devoid of wrong, who exist for all eternity! Open to me, for I am a spirit in my own shape, I have power by means of this my magic, and I am recognised as a spirit. Save me from aggressors in this land of the just, give me my mouth that I may speak with it, let my arms be extended in your presence, because I know you, I know your names, I know the name of that Great God before whom you place your provisions, whose name is Tjekem. He opens up the eastern horizon of the sky, he alights in the western horizon of the sky, he removes me so that I may be hale. The Milky Way will not reject me, the rebels will not have power over me, I shall not be turned away from your portals, the doors shall not be closed against me, because my bread is in Pe, my beer is in Dep, my hands shall be ... there, there shall be given to me my father Atum, there shall be established for me my houses in the sky and on earth, with uncounted emmer therein; offering shall be made to me there of food by my son of my body, you shall give invocation-offerings of bread and beer, incense and unguent, and all things good and pure whereon a god lives, in very deed for ever, in any shape which I desire, and faring downstream and upstream in the Field of Rushes, for I am the Double Lion.

*As for him who knows this book on earth or it is put in writing on the coffin, it is my word that he shall go out into the day in any shape that he desires and shall go into his place without being turned back, and there shall be given to him bread and beer and a portion of meat from upon the altar of Osiris. He shall enter safely into the Field of Rushes in order to learn this command of Her who is in Busiris, there shall be given to him barley and emmer therein, he shall be hale like he was upon earth, and he shall do what he wishes like those nine gods who are in the Netherworld. A matter a million times true.*

*Spell 75 Ast-wert walks with a staff towards the hieroglyph which represents Heliopolis. Between them is an offering-table topped by a lotus. 1039/4*

## ——— SPELL 74 ———

[illustrated p.74]

*Spell for being swift-footed when going out from the earth*

May you do what you are wont to do, O Sokar who are in your Mansion, possessing a foot in the realm of the dead. I shine in the sky, I ascend to the sky; though I am inert, I climb on the sunshine; though I am inert, I walk on the river-banks ... in the realm of the dead.

## ——— SPELL 75 ———

*Spell for going to Heliopolis and receiving a throne there*

I have gone forth from the limits of the earth that I may receive my fringed cloak for the heart of the Baboon; I have razed the Pure Mansions which were in Edfu, I have destroyed the Mansions of Him who beats with a stick, I have attacked the Mansions of Ikhsesef, I have forced the sacred gates, I have passed by the House of Kemkem, the 'knot-of-Isis' amulet has laid her hands on me, and she has commended me to her sister the Accuser by her own mother the Destroyer, she has set me in the eastern sky in which Re appears and in which Re is daily exalted. I have appeared in glory, I have been initiated, I have been ennobled as a god, and they have put me on that sacred road on which Thoth travelled when he pacified the Combatants and proceeded to Pe so that he might come to Dep.

## ——— SPELL 76 ———

*Spell for being transformed into any shape one may wish to take*

I have passed by the Palace, and it was an abyt-bird which brought you to me. Hail to you, you who flew up to the sky, the white and shining bird which guards the White Crown. I shall be with you and I shall join the Great God; make a way for me that I may pass on it.

## ——— SPELL 77 ———
[illustrated pp.75,76]

*Spell for being transformed into a falcon of gold*

I have appeared as a great falcon, having come forth from the Egg; I have flown up and alighted as a falcon of four cubits along its back, whose wings are of greenstone of Upper Egypt; I have gone up from the coffer into the Night-bark, I have brought my heart from the eastern mountains, I have alighted in the Day-bark, there are brought to me those of ancient times bowing down, and they give me worship when I appear, having been reassembled as a fair falcon of gold upon the pointed stone. Re comes in daily to give judgement, and I sit among those elder gods of the Lower Sky; He of the Field of Offerings bows to me in the Presence, and I eat

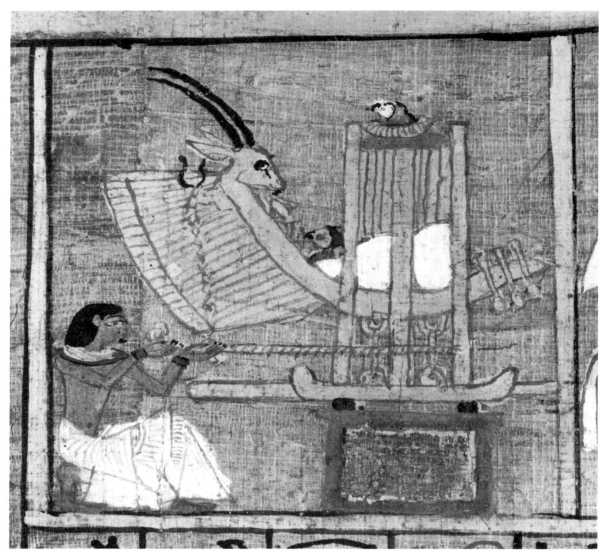

*Spell 74 Ani kneels before the sacred bark of the funerary god Sokar with the characteristic averted antelope's head at the prow. 10470/18*

of him and have power over him, I have abundance to my desire. The grain-god has given me smoked barley, and I have power over what appertains to my head.

# —— SPELL 78 ——
[illustrated p.78]

THIS SPELL IS IN DRAMATIC FORM, WITH VARIOUS CHARACTERS SPEAKING IN TURN, AND IT APPEARS TO BE PART OF THE TEXT OF A RELIGIOUS DRAMA RECITED AS A TEMPLE RITUAL. WHETHER ANY ACTION TOOK PLACE IS DOUBTFUL; MORE PROBABLY IT WAS A RECITATIVE PRONOUNCED BY VARIOUS PRIESTS IN TURN, POSSIBLY WITH APPROPRIATE GESTURES. HERE IT IS USED SIMPLY AS A MAGIC SPELL.

*Spell for being transformed into a divine falcon*

OSIRIS SPEAKS: O Horus, come to Busiris, clear my ways for me, and go all over my house, that you may see my form and extol my shape. May you inspire fear of me, may you create awe of me, that the gods of the Netherworld may fear me, that the gates may beware of me. Do not let him who has done me harm approach me, so that he sees me in the House of Darkness, and uncovers my weariness which is hidden from him.

THE GODS: 'Do thus', say the gods, who hear the voices of those who go in the suite of Osiris.

HORUS: Be silent, you gods; let a god speak with a god, let him hear the true message which I shall say to him. Speak to me, Osiris, and grant that what has come forth from your mouth concerning me be revoked. See your own form, form your shape, and cause him to go forth and to have power over his legs that he may stride and copulate among men, and you shall be there as the Lord of All. The gods of the Netherworld fear you, the gates beware of you. You move along with those who move along, while I remain on your mound like the Lord of Life. I ally myself with the divine Isis, I rejoice on account of him who has done you harm. May he not come so that he sees your weariness which is hidden from him. I shall go and come to the confines of the sky, that I may ask the word from Geb, that I may demand authority from the Lord of All. Then the gods shall fear you, even they who shall see that I send to you one of those who dwell in the sunshine. I have made his form as my form, his gait as my gait, that he may go and come to Busiris, being invested with my shape, that he may tell you my affairs. He shall inspire fear of you, he shall create awe of you in the gods of the Netherworld, and the gates shall beware of you.

THE MESSENGER: Indeed I am one who dwells in the sunshine, I am a spirit who came into being and was created out of the body of the god, I am one of those gods

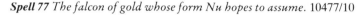

*Spell 77 The falcon of gold whose form Nu hopes to assume.* 10477/10

*Spell 77 The golden falcon with a flail at its shoulder stands on the hieroglyph for gold. 10470/25*

or spirits who dwell in the sunshine, whom Atum created from his flesh, who came into being from the root of his eye, whom Atum created and with whom he made spirits, whose faces he created, in order that they might be with him, while he was alone in the Abyss, who announced him when he came forth from the horizon, who inspired fear of him in the gods and spirits, the Powers and Shapes. I am one of those serpents which the Sole Lord made, before Isis came into being that she might give birth to Horus. I have been made strong, I have been made young and vigorous. I am distinguished above the other beings who dwell in the sunshine, the spirits who came into being along with me. I have made my appearance as a divine falcon, Horus has invested me with his shape in order that I might take his affairs to Osiris, to the Netherworld.

THE DOUBLE LION RAISES AN OBJECTION: The Double Lion who is in his cavern, warden of the House of the Royal Wig-cover, said to me: How can you reach the confines of the sky? Indeed you are equipped with the form of Horus, but you do not possess the Wig-cover. Do you speak on the confines of the sky?

THE MESSENGER: I am indeed he who takes the affairs of Horus to Osiris, to the Netherworld. Horus has repeated to me what his father Osiris said to him in the ... on the day of burial.

THE DOUBLE LION: Repeat to me what Horus has said as the word of his father Osiris in the ... on the day of burial. Then I shall give you the Wig-cover – so said the Double Lion to me – that you may come and go on the roads of the sky. Then those who dwell in the horizon shall see you, and the gods of the Netherworld shall fear you.

THE MESSENGER: You may jubilate concerning him, he has been initiated into the word of these gods, the Lords of All, who are at the side of the Sole Lord – so said he who is high on his dais, who dwells in holiness, concerning me.

THE DOUBLE LION IS SATISFIED: Take out the Wig-cover for him – so said the Double Lion concerning me.

THE MESSENGER, NOW POSSESSED OF HIS PASSPORT, THE ROYAL WIG-COVER, CONTINUES HIS JOURNEY: O Heret, clear my way for me. I am high in the form of Horus, and the Double Lion has taken out the Wig-cover for me, he has given me my wings, he has established my heart on his great standard. I do not fall on account of Shu, I am he who pacifies himself with his own beauty, the Lord of the two mighty royal serpents. I am he who knows the roads of Nut, the winds are my protection, and the raging bull shall not drive me back. I go to the place where dwells He who sleeps, being helpless, who is in the Field of Eternity, who was conducted to the painful western darkness, even Osiris. I come today from the House of the Double Lion, I have come forth from it to the House of Isis, to the secret mysteries, I have been conducted to her hidden secrets, for she caused me to see the birth of the Great God. Horus has invested me with his shape in order that I might say what is there, in order that I might say ... which shall drive back the fearful attack. I am the falcon who dwells in the sunshine, who has power through his light and his flashing. I go and come to the confines of the sky ... There is none who thwarts me ... Horus to the confines of the sky. Horus is upon his seats and his thrones, and I am he who is in his form. My arms are those of a divine falcon, I am one who has acquired (the position of) his lord, and Horus has invested me with his shape. I come forth to Busiris that I may see Osiris, I land at the Mansion of the Great Dead One; I inspire fear of him and create awe of him among the gods. I belong to the great shrine, even I the holy one of ... in front of whom one walks to and fro, and Nut shall walk to and fro when she sees me. The hostile gods have seen that she incites the Eyeless One against those who shall stretch forth their arms against me. The Powerful One stands up against the earth-gods, the holy roads are opened for me when they see my form and hear what I shall say. Down on your faces, you gods

of the Netherworld, whose faces are ... whose necks are outstretched, and who hide the face of the Great Demolisher! Clear the road of ... towards the majestic shape.

THE MESSENGER QUOTES THE COMMAND OF HORUS: Horus has commanded: Lift up your faces and look at him; he has made his appearance as a divine falcon, the Double Lion has taken out the Wig-cover for him, he has come with the word of Horus to Osiris. The Greyhaired Ones have ... he has united himself with the Powers. Get out of the way, you wardens of your gates, for him in front of me, clear the way for him. Let him pass by, O you who dwell in your caverns, wardens of the House of Osiris.

THE MESSENGER RESUMES HIS OWN SPEECH: I say: How mighty is Horus! I cause them to know that the terror of him is great, and that his horn is sharp against Seth; that Horus has taken authority and that he has acquired the might of Atum. I have followed Horus, Lord of All.

THE GODS GIVE THE MESSENGER PERMISSION TO PASS: Pass by in peace – so say the gods of the Netherworld to me. The wardens of their caverns, the wardens of the Mansion of Osiris rise up.

*Spell 79 Ani and his wife Tutu stand in adoration before three gods, who squat on a shrine-shaped plinth and represent the divine tribunal. 10470/24*

THE MESSENGER REPLIES: See, I come to you as an equipped spirit. The wardens of the gates walk for me, the Powers clear the roads for me, I have fetched the Grey-haired Ones whom Nenet has defied. The great ones who dwell in the horizon fear me, even the wardens of ... in the sky, who guard the roads. I make firm the gates for the Lord of All, I have cleared the roads towards him; I have done what was commanded, for Horus invested me with his shape. Let my wisdom be granted, for I desire triumph over my enemies. May the mysteries be uncovered for me, may the secret caverns be opened to me, may I enter into the Lord of the Soul, greatly majestic, may I come forth to Busiris and go all over his mansion, may I tell him the affairs of his son whom he loves, while the heart of Seth is cut out. May I see the Lord of Weariness, who is limitless, that he may know how Horus regulated the affairs of the gods without him.

THE MESSENGER ATTAINS HIS AIM AND ADDRESSES OSIRIS: O Lord of the Soul, greatly majestic, see, I have

*Spell 78 The divine falcon stands on a low plinth with a flail at its shoulder. 10470/25*

*Spell for becoming an elder of the tribunal*

I am Atum who made the sky and created what exists, who came forth from the earth, who created seed, Lord of All, who fashioned the gods, the Great God, the self-created, the Lord of Life, who made the Ennead to flourish.

Hail to you, you lords of pure offerings, whose thrones are secret! Hail to you, you lords of eternity, whose forms are hidden, whose shrines are secret, whose place is unknown! Hail to you, you gods who are in the Radiance! Hail to you, you gods who encircle the firmament! Hail to you, you gods who are in the West! Hail to you, Ennead which is in the Lower Sky! See, I have come to you pure, divine, possessing a spirit, mighty, besouled; I have brought to you a measure of incense and natron, that I may drive away slaver therewith from your mouths, I have come that I may remove the ill which is in your hearts, I have removed the evil which is on you. I have brought you what is good, I have raised up to you what is true, for I know you, I know your names, I know your forms which were unknown. I have come into being among you, I appear in glory as that god who eats men and lives on gods, I am mighty among you as that god who is uplifted on his standard, to whom the gods come in joy, at whom the goddesses exult when they see him. I have come to you, having appeared as son of you all; I sit in my seat which is in the horizon, I receive offerings upon my altar, I drink wine in the evening. Those who are in joy come to me, praise is given to me by those who are in the horizon in this my rank of the Lord of All. I am exalted as this noble god who is in the Great Mansion; the gods rejoice when they see him among those who go forth happily on the body of the Lower Sky when his mother Nut has borne him.

— SPELL 80 —

*Making transformation into a god and giving light and darkness*

I am he who donned the white and bright fringed cloak of Nun which is on his breast, which gives light in darkness, which unites the two companion-goddesses who are in my body by means of the great magic which is on my mouth. My fallen enemy who was with me in the valley of Abydos will not be raised up, and I am content. The remembrance of him is mine, I have taken authority in my city, for I found him in it, I have brought darkness by

come, the Netherworld has been opened for me, the roads in the sky and on earth have been opened for me, and there was none who thwarted me.

Be high upon your seat, O Osiris: may your breast live and may your buttocks be vigorous. Let your heart jubilate, for you triumph over Seth, and your son Horus has been placed upon your throne. Myriads have been assigned to him, the gods have brought him oblations, and the heart of Geb, who is older than the great ones, rejoices. The sky is strong and Nut jubilates when she sees what Atum has done, whilst he sat among the two Enneads and gave the authority which is on his mouth to Horus the son of Isis. He has become ruler over Egypt, the gods work for him, he has nurtured myriads and has brought up myriads by means of the Sole Eye, the Mistress of the Enneads, the Lady of All.

means of my power, I have rescued the Eye from its non-existence before the festival of the fifteenth day had come, I have separated Seth from the houses of the Above because of the Elder who was with him, I equipped Thoth in the Mansion of the Moon before the festival of the fifteenth day had come, I have taken possession of the Wereret-crown, and right is in my body, also the turquoise and faience of its monthly festival, and my field of lapis-lazuli is there on my river-bank. I am the Woman who lightens darkness, I have come to lighten the darkness, and it is bright. I have lightened the darkness, I have felled the evil spirits, those who were in darkness have given praise to me, I have made the mourners whose faces were hidden to stand up, even though they were languid when they saw me. As for you, I am the Woman of whom I do not permit you to hear.

## ——— SPELL 81A ———
[also illustrated p.80]

*Spell for being transformed into a lotus*

I am this pure lotus which went forth from the sunshine, which is at the nose of Re; I have descended that I may

*Spells 80 and 81A On the left a man's head emerges from a blue lotus flower flanked by buds and pads and floating in a pool: a symbolic representation of the sun-god's daily reappearance and a guarantee of resurrection for Ani (Spell 81A). On the right is a squatting god with sun-disc on his head whose form Ani hopes to assume (Spell 80). 10470/28*

seek it for Horus, for I am the pure one who issued from the fen.

## ——— SPELL 81B ———

*Spell for being transformed into a lotus*

O Lotus belonging to the semblance of Nefertum, I am the Man. I know your name, I know your names, you gods, you lords of the realm of the dead, for I am one of you. May you grant that I see the gods who lead the Netherworld, may there be given to me a seat in the realm of the dead in the presence of the lords of the West, may I take my place in the Sacred Land, may I receive offerings in the presence of the lords of eternity, may my soul go forth to every place that it desires, without being held back from the presence of the Great Ennead.

## SPELL 82
[illustrated p.82]

*Spell for becoming Ptah, eating bread, drinking beer,
purifying the hinder-parts, and being alive
in Heliopolis*

I have flown up as a falcon, I have cackled as a goose, I
have alighted on yonder road of the Mound of the Great
Festival. What I doubly detest, I will not eat; what I
detest is faeces, and I will not eat it; what I detest is excrement, and it shall not enter my body.

'What will you live on?' say the gods and spirits to me.

'I will live and have power through bread.'

'Where will you eat it?' say the gods and spirits to me.

'I will have power and I will eat it under the branches
of the tree of Hathor my mistress, who made offering of
bread, beer and corn in Heliopolis. I will don a loin-
cloth from the hand of Tayt, I will dwell in the place
where I wish to be.'

My head is that of Re who is united with Atum, the
four suns of the length of the land; I have gone forth, for
my tongue is that of Ptah, my throat is that of Hathor,
for I have recalled with my mouth the speech of Atum to
my father when he destroyed the majesty of the wife of
Geb, whose head was broken at his word. Be afraid
thereat and report it, the outcry at my strength. There
shall be assigned to me the heritage of the Lord of the
Earth, namely Geb, and I shall be cared for thereby; Geb
shall refresh me, for he has given to me his appearings in
glory. Those who are in Heliopolis bow their heads to
me, for I am their lord, I am their bull. I am mightier
than the Lord of Terror; I copulate and I have power
over myriads.

## SPELL 83
[also illustrated p.82]

*Spell for being transformed into a phoenix*

I have flown up like the primeval ones, I have become
Khepri, I have grown as a plant, I have clad myself as a
tortoise, I am the essence of every god, I am the seventh
of those seven uraei who came into being in the West,
Horus who makes brightness with his person, that god
who was against Seth, Thoth who was among you in that
judgement of Him who presides over Letopolis together
with the Souls of Heliopolis, the flood which was between them. I have come on the day when I appear in

*Spell 81A A long-stemmed blue lotus, symbolic of resurrection
for Nu. 10477/11*

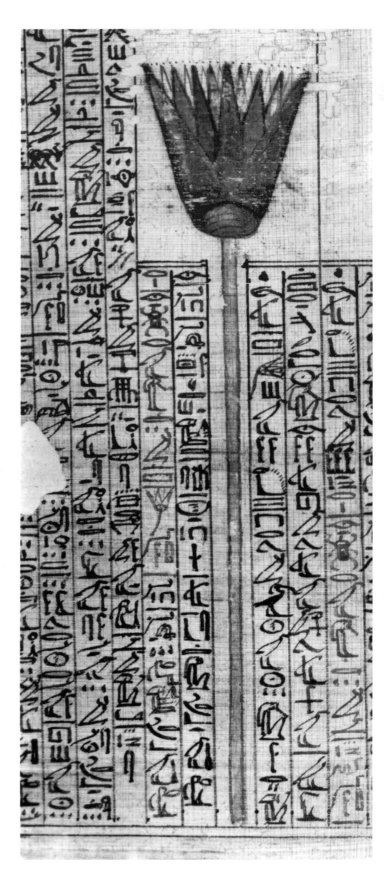

*Spells 83 and 86 On the left a swallow perches on a mound (Spell 86). On the right is the phoenix whose form Nu hopes to assume (Spell 83). 10477/10*

glory with the strides of the gods, for I am Khons who subdued the lords.

As for him who knows this pure spell, it means going out into the day after death and being transformed at will, being in the suite of Wennefer, being content with the food of Osiris, having invocation-offerings, seeing the sun; it means being hale on earth with Re and being vindicated with Osiris, and nothing evil shall have power over him. A matter a million times true.

## SPELL 84

[illustrated pp.82,83]

*Spell for being transformed into a heron*

I am the mightiest of the bulls, I am the forceful one among them, I am the twin braided locks which are on the head of the shorn priest, whom they of the sunshine worship, whose stroke is sharp. I am vindicated on earth, and the terror of me is in the sky – and vice versa; it is my strength which makes me victorious to the height of the sky, I am held in respect to the breadth of the sky, my strides are towards the towns of the Silent

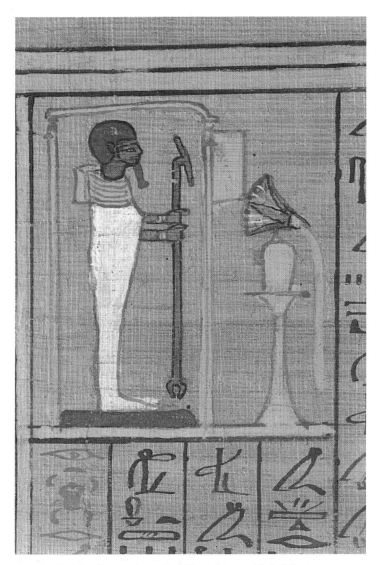

*Spell 82* Ptah, creator-god of Memphis, stands holding a was-sceptre in a shrine with an open door before a ewer on a stand, topped by a lotus. 10470/27

*Spells 83 and 84* Two phoenixes, two herons, or a phoenix and a heron: the artist has made no distinction except in size. 10471/13

## ——— SPELL 85 ———
[also illustrated p.84]

*Spell for being transformed into a living soul and not entering into the place of execution. He who knows it will never perish*

Land. I have gone and reached Wenu; I have ejected the gods from their paths, I have struck down those who are wakeful within their shrines. I do not know the Abyss, I do not know the emerging earth, I do not know the red ones who thrust with their horns, I do not know the magician, but I hear his words; I am this Wild Bull who is in the writings.

Thus said the gods when they lamented the past: 'On your faces! He has come to you while the dawn lacks you, and there is none who will protect you.' My faults are in my belly, and I will not declare them; O Authority, wrong-doing is of yesterday, but righteousness is of today. Righteousness runs on my eyebrows on the night of the festival 'The Old Woman lies down and her land is guarded'.

I am the soul of Re who issued from the Abyss, that soul of the god who created authority. Wrong-doing is my detestation, and I will not see it; I think about righteousness, and I live by it; I am Authority which will never perish in this my name of 'Soul'. I came into being of myself with the Abyss in this my name of Khepri, and I come into being in it daily.

I am the Lord of Light; death is my detestation, and I will not enter into the place of execution of the Netherworld. It is I who cause Osiris to be a spirit, and I have made content those who are in his suite. I desire that they grant fear of me and create respect of me among those who are in their midst, for I am lifted aloft on my standard, on my throne and on my allotted seat.

I am Nun, and the doers of wrong cannot harm me. I am the eldest of the primeval gods, the soul of the souls of the eternal gods; my body is everlasting, my shape is eternity, Lord of Years, Ruler of Everlasting. I am he who created darkness and who made his seat in the limits of the sky. I desire to reach their limits, and I walk afoot, I go ahead with my staff, I cross the firmament of those who ..., I drive away the hidden snakes which are upon my march to the Lord of the Two Regions.

I am the soul of the souls of the eternal gods, my body is everlasting, I am he who is on high, Lord of Tatjebu, I am young in my city, I am boyish in the field, and such is my name, for my name will not perish. I am the soul who created the Abyss, who made his seat in the realm of the dead. My nest will not be seen, my egg will not be broken, I have got rid of my ills, I have seen my father, the Lord of the Evening, and whose body it is which is in Heliopolis; I govern those who are in the dusk upon the western Mound of the Ibis.

*Spell 85 Horemheb's human-headed soul wearing a djed-pillar amulet around its neck. 10257/9*

*Spell 84 The heron whose form Ani hopes to assume. 10470/28*

---
# SPELL 86
[illustrated pp.81,86]

*Spell for being transformed into a swallow*

I am a swallow, I am a swallow, I am that Scorpion-goddess, the daughter of Re. O you gods, may your savour be sweet; a flame has gone up from the horizon. O you who are in the city, I have brought him who guards his coils; give me your hands, for I have spent the day in the Island of Fire, I have gone on an errand and I have returned with a report. Open to me; then I will tell what I have seen. Horus is in command of the Sacred Bark, and the throne of his father Osiris has been given to him, while that Seth the son of Nut is in bonds because of what he has done. What is in Letopolis has been allotted to me, and I have made obeisance to Osiris. I have gone to make inspection and I have returned to speak; let me pass, that I may report on my errand. I am one who goes in esteemed and who goes out distinguished at the portal of the Lord of All; I am pure on that great tomb-plateau, for I have got rid of my evil, I have discarded my wrong-doing, I have cast to the ground the ills which were on my flesh. O you keepers of the gate, make a way for me, for I am one like you. I go out into the day, I walk on my feet, I have power in my strides. O You of the sunshine, I know the secret ways of the portals of the Field of Rushes. See, I have come, having felled my enemies to the ground, and my corpse is buried.

*As for him who knows this spell, he shall go out into the day, and he shall not be turned away at any portal in*

*Spell 85 A ram, symbolic of the divine soul, stands on a low pedestal with the hieroglyph for the word 'soul' before it. 10470/27*

*the realm of the dead, and he shall assume the shape of a swallow. A matter a million times true.*

## SPELL 87
[illustrated p.86]

*Spell for being transformed into a snake*

I am a long-lived snake; I pass the night and am reborn every day. I am a snake which is in the limits of the earth; I pass the night and am reborn, renewed and rejuvenated every day.

## SPELL 88
[illustrated p.86]

*Spell for being transformed into a crocodile*

I am a crocodile immersed in dread, I am a crocodile who takes by robbery, I am the great and mighty fish-like being who is in the Bitter Lakes, I am the Lord of those who bow down in Letopolis.

## SPELL 89
[also illustrated pp.87,116]

*Spell for letting a soul rejoin its corpse in the realm of the dead*

O you who bring, you who run, you who are in the booth of the Great God, let my soul come to me from anywhere it is. If the bringing of my soul to me from anywhere it is be delayed, you will find the Eye of Horus standing up thus against you. O you Osirians, if you do not sleep, then will I not sleep in Heliopolis, the land of thousands of abodes. My soul shall be taken to me, and my spirit shall be vindicated with it wherever it may be.

Come for my soul, O you wardens of the sky! If you delay letting my soul see my corpse, you will find the Eye of Horus standing up thus against you. O you gods who are dragged in the Bark of the Lord of Millions of Years, who bring the Upper Sky to the Netherworld and who raise up the Lower Sky, who let souls draw near to the noble dead, may your hands be filled with your ropes, may your grip be on your harpoons, may you

*Spell 89 Nakht's human-headed soul stretches out its wings in protection above his mummy, which wears a mummy mask topped by an unguent cone and lies on a bed with lion-form feet. 10471/14*

drive off the enemy. The Sacred Bark will be joyful and the Great God will proceed in peace when you allow this soul of mine to ascend vindicated to the gods, while your buttocks are in the eastern horizon of the sky, so as to follow in peace to the place where it was yesterday, to the West. May it see my corpse, may it rest on my mummy, which will never be destroyed or perish.

*To be spoken over a human-headed bird of gold inlaid with semi-precious stones and laid on the breast of the deceased.*

—— SPELL 90 ——
[illustrated p.87]

*Spell for removing foolish speech from the mouth*

O you who cut off heads and sever necks and who put folly into the mouths of the spirits because of the magic which is in their bodies, you shall not see me with those eyes of yours with which you see, (you shall kneel) on your knees, you shall go about with your face behind you, you shall look on the tormentors belonging to Shu who follow after you to cut off your head and to sever your neck at the behest of Him who saved his lord, because of this which you have said you would do to me, namely the putting of folly into my mouth with intent to cut off my head, to sever my neck and to close my mouth because of the magic which is in my body, just as you did to the spirits because of the magic which was in their bodies. Turn away at the sentence which Isis spoke when you came to put folly into the mouth of Osiris at the desire of his enemy Seth, saying to you: 'May your face be downcast at seeing this face of mine!' May the flame of the Eye of Horus go forth against you within the Eye of Atum, which was injured on that night when it swallowed you. Get you back because of Osiris, for abhorrence of you is in him – and vice versa; get you back because of me, because abhorrence of you is in me – and vice versa. If you come against me, I will speak to you; if you do not come against me, I will not speak to you. Get back to the tormentors belonging to Shu ...

# SPELL 91
[illustrated pp.88,89]

*Spell for not restraining N's soul in the realm of the dead*

O you who are on high, who are worshipped, whose power is great, a Ram greatly majestic, the dread of whom is put into the gods when you appear on your great throne: you shall make a way for me and my soul, my spirit and my shade, for I am equipped. I am a worthy spirit; make a way for me to the place where Re and Hathor are.

As for him who knows this spell, he shall become an equipped spirit in the realm of the dead, he shall not be restrained at any gate of the West whether coming or going. A true matter.

Left: **Spell 86** *A swallow perches on a mound. 10470/25*

Below: **Spells 87 and 88** *On the left is the sa-ta snake walking on human legs (Spell 87), and on the right the crocodile-god Sobk reclines on a tall shrine-shaped plinth (Spell 88). 10470/27*

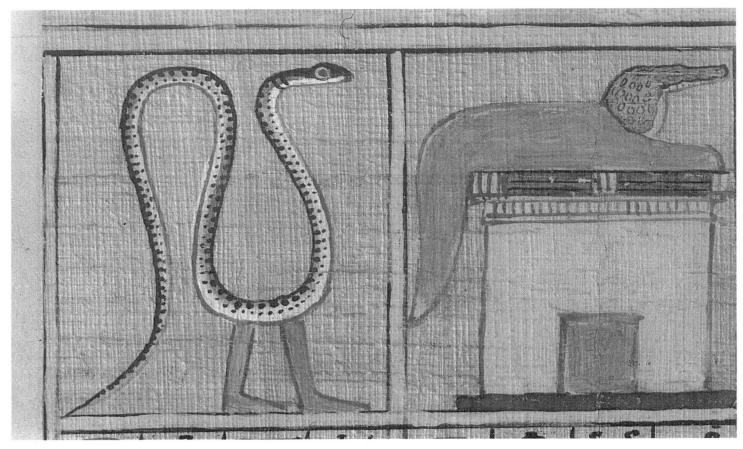

## SPELL 92

[illustrated pp.90,91]

*Spell for opening the tomb to N's soul and shade* so that he may go out into the day and have power in his legs.

Open and close! O you who sleep, open and close for my soul according to the command of Horus. O Eye of Horus, save me, establish my beauty on the vertex of Re. O Far-strider whose legs extend, make a way for me here, for my flesh is made ready.

I am Horus who protects his father, I am he who brought his father and who brought his mother with his staff; open a way for one who has power in his legs, who sees the Great God within the Bark of Re wherein souls are examined at the beginning of the reckoning of years. Save my soul for me, O Eye of Horus, who fixes ornaments on the vertex of Re. When the dusk is in your sight, you wardens of Osiris, do not restrain my soul or hold back my shade; open a way for my soul and my shade, that it may see the Great God within the shrine on the day of examining souls. May it speak again to Osiris. O you whose seats are hidden, wardens of the limbs of Osiris, who hold back spirits and who shut up

Above: *Spell 90* Horemheb extends a papyrus scroll to Thoth, who stands holding an ankh and was-sceptre. 10257/9

Below: *Spell 89* Ani's human-headed soul carrying a shen, symbolic of eternity, hovers protectively over his mummy, which wears a mummy mask and lies on a lion-form bed between two tall stands containing flames. 10470/17

thereby than the mighty ones. If I be ferried over and taken to the East with bound horns, or if any injury be done to me by rebels, I will swallow up the phallus of Re and the head of Osiris, I will be guided to the tomb of the decapitation of the gods in which they make answer; I will bind the horns of Khepri, I will become the stone in the Eye of Atum the Destroyer if I be seized and ferried over to the East, if the festival of the rebels be celebrated over me, or if anything terrible be evilly done to me.

## ——— SPELL 94 ———
[illustrated pp.92,93]

*Spell for requesting a water-pot and a palette*

O you great one who see your father, keeper of the book of Thoth, see, I have come spiritualised, besouled, mighty and equipped with the writings of Thoth. Bring me the messenger of the earth-god who is with Seth, bring me a water-pot and palette from the writing-kit of Thoth and the mysteries which are in them.

See, I am a scribe; bring me the corruption of Osiris that I may write with it and that I may do what the great and good god says every day, being the good which you have decreed for me, O Horakhty. I will do what is right and I will send to Re daily.

## ——— SPELL 95 ———
[illustrated p.95]

*Spell for being beside Thoth*

I am he who gave protection in the tumult, who guarded the Great Goddess in the war. I smote with my knife, I calmed Ash, I acted on behalf of the Great Goddess in the war. I made strong the sharp knife which was in the hand of Thoth in the tumult.

## ——— SPELLS 96 AND 97 ———

*Spell for being beside Thoth and for causing a man to be a spirit in the realm of the dead*

I am he who dwells in his Eye, I have come that I may give Maat to Re, I have propitiated Seth with the bodily fluids of Aker and the blood which is in the spinal cord of Geb.

O Night-bark, O Staff of Anubis, I have propitiated those four spirits who are in the suite of the Lord of Offerings, I am an owner of fields through their com-

***Spell 91*** *Ani's human-headed soul stands before the door of his tomb. 10470/17*

the shades of the dead, and who would harm me, you shall not harm me. 'Go far away, because your ka is with you as a soul,' say the wardens of the limbs of Osiris who hold back the shades of the dead, 'lest you be grasped by the sky and restrained by the earth; may the slayers not be with you, for you have power in your legs. Be far away from your corpse which is on earth.'

Get back, you who guard the tomb of Osiris!

## ——— SPELL 93 ———
[illustrated p.94]

*Spell for not letting N be ferried over to the East in the realm of the dead*

O you phallus of Re, this which is injured by uproar, whose inertness came into being through Babai, I am stronger thereby than the strong ones, I am mightier

*Spell 91 Nakht, with his human-headed soul flying before him,
walks towards his pyramid-capped tomb chapel, in front of which a
tree grows.* 10471/7

mand. I am the father of Bah who drives away thirst and who guards the waterways. See me, you great, elder and mighty gods who are at the head of the Souls of Heliopolis; I am high above your heads and I am one potent among you. See, I am one whose mighty, elder and great soul is respected; I will not be given over to this ill-will which has issued from your mouths, and harm will not turn round over me, for I am pure in the Island of Propitiation ... in the divine Eye under the tree of the goddess of the sky, which refreshes the vindicated ones, the lords who were aforetime.

Draw near quickly, you righteous ones! I was the most truly precise person on earth, I was an interpreter of speech, the sceptre of the Sole Lord, Re the Great God who lives by truth; do not injure me ...

## ——— Spell 98 ———

*Spell for fetching a ferry-boat in the sky*

Hail to you, you plateau which is in the sky north of the Great Waterway, for whoever sees it will not die. I stand upon you, I appear as a god, I have seen you and I will not die. I stand upon you, I appear as a god, I cackle as a goose, I fly up thence as the falcon upon the branches.

O Dew of the Great One, I cross the earth towards the sky, I stand up as Shu, I make the sunshine to flourish on the sides of the ladder which is made to mount up to the Unwearying Stars, far from decapitation. Bring me those who repel evil when I have passed you by at the polar region of Tepen.

'Where have you come from?'

'O Tepen, I have come from the Lake of Burning in the Field of Fire.'

'What did you live on in the Lake of Burning in the Field of Fire?'

'I lived on that noble tree of Ikaa who brought these boats from the Dried-up Lake for me. The water-jar was on ... that I might stand in the Sacred Bark and guide the waters; that I might stand in the Sacred Bark and conduct the god; that I might stand up, my staff being a rod.'

'Go aboard and sail.' The gates are opened for me in Letopolis, the earth is split open for me in Wenu, and the staffs have been given to me in respect of my inheritance.

89

*Spell 92 Ani opens up his tomb and is then depicted walking from it, while his human-headed soul carrying a shen, symbolic of eternity, flies protectively above him.* 10470/18

## ———— SPELL 99 ————
[illustrated pp.96,98]

THIS SPELL IS CONCERNED WITH THE PROVISION OF A BOAT FOR THE DECEASED TO CROSS THE CELESTIAL RIVER, EQUATED BY THE EGYPTIANS WITH THE MILKY WAY. IT FALLS INTO THREE PARTS. IN PART I THE DECEASED CALLS ON THE CELESTIAL FERRYMAN, WHOSE NAME IS MAHAF, TO AROUSE AQEN, WHO APPARENTLY HAS CHARGE OF THE BOAT AND WHO IS SOUND ASLEEP. THE FERRYMAN PROCEEDS TO QUESTION THE DECEASED AS TO HIS INTENTIONS AND TO MAKE ALL SORTS OF EXCUSES TO THE EFFECT THAT THE BOAT IS NOT IN A FIT STATE TO BE USED, AND SO ON, IN A KIND OF GAME OF CROSS QUESTIONS AND CROOKED ANSWERS.

THE NAME OF THE FERRYMAN MAHAF ORIGINALLY MEANT 'THE STERN IS BEHIND HIM', I.E. THE HELMSMAN, BUT OWING TO SIMILARITY OF SOUND THE MEANING OF THE NAME WAS EARLY MISUNDERSTOOD AS 'HE WHO SEES BEHIND HIM'; HENCE THE FERRYMAN IS DEPICTED IN THE MANUSCRIPTS OF THE *BOOK OF THE DEAD* AS SITTING IN A BOAT WITH HIS HEAD TURNED BACKWARDS.

IN PART II AQEN, HAVING BEEN AROUSED FROM SLEEP, IS CALLED UPON TO BRING THE BOAT, AND HE IN TURN PROCEEDS TO MAKE ALL KINDS OF DIFFICULTIES. IN PART III THE BOAT IS BROUGHT, BUT THE DECEASED HAS TO DECLARE THE NAMES OF THE VARIOUS PARTS AND FITTINGS. AT THE END OF PART II IS AN INTERESTING KIND OF SPELL OR GAME CONCERNED WITH COUNTING THE FINGERS, IN WHICH TEN SENTENCES OBSCURELY CORRESPOND TO EACH OF THE FINGERS AND THUMBS.

*Spell for bringing a ferry-boat in the realm of the dead*

O Ferryman, bring me this which was brought to Horus

**Spell 57 and 92** *Khary stands in a pool holding a sail and enveloped by streams of water (left), thus guaranteeing he will breathe air and have power over water (Spell 57). On the right Khary opens up the door of his tomb to enable his human-headed soul to fly out (Spell 92). 9949/3*

on account of his Eye and which was brought to Seth on account of his testicles; there leaps up the Eye of Horus which fell in the eastern side of the sky so that it may protect itself from Seth.

O Mahaf, as you are provided with life, awaken Aqen for me, for see, I have come.

*Who are you who comes?*

I am the beloved of my father, one who greatly loves his father, and I am he who awakens his sleeping father.

O Mahaf, as you are endowed with life, awaken Aqen for me, for see, I have come.

*Do you say that you would cross to the eastern side of the sky? If you cross, what will you do?*

I will raise up his head, I will lift up his brow, and he shall make a decree in your favour, and the decree which he shall make for you shall not perish nor become void

in this land for ever.

O Mahaf, as you are endowed with life, awaken Aqen for me, for see, I have come.

*Why should I awaken Aqen for you?*

That he may bring me the built-up boat of Khnum from the Lake of Feet.

*But she is in pieces and stored in the dockyard.*

Take her larboard side and fix it to the stern; take her starboard side and fix it to the bow.

*But she has no planks, she has no end-pieces, she has no rubbing-pieces, she has no oar-loops.*

Her planks are the drops of moisture which are on the lips of Babai; her end-pieces are the hair which is under the tail of Seth; her rubbing-pieces are the sweat which is on the ribs of Babai; her oar-loops are the hands of the female counterpart of Horus. She is built by the Eye of

**Spell 94** *Horemheb receives a scribe's palette and water-pot from Thoth, who holds an ankh.* 10257/10

Horus, who shall steer her to me.

O Mahaf, as you are endowed with life, awaken Aqen for me, for see, I have come.

*Who will guard this boat?*

Bring the tail of the senemty-animal and put it in her stern; that will guard her.

O Mahaf, as you are endowed with life, awaken Aqen for me, for see, I have come.

*Who will bring her to you and to me?*

Bring her to me with the best of the gods and his offspring, namely Imsety, Hapy, Duamutef and Qebehsenuef; he will command her, the tetwy-animal being placed at her bow, and he will steer her to the place where you are.

*What is she?*

She is the wings of the tetwy-animal.

*The weather is windy and she has no mast.*

Bring this phallus of Babai which creates children and begets calves.

*To what shall I make it fast?*

To the thighs which open out the shanks.

*What about her cable?*

Bring this snake which is in the hand of Hemen.

*Where shall I stow it?*

You shall stow it in her bilge.

*What about her sail?*

It is the cloth which came out of Sutyu when Horus and the Ombite kissed on New Year's Day.

*What about the gunwales?*

They are the sinews of Him whom all these fear.

*Who is he whom all these fear?*

It is he who lives in the night which precedes the New Year.

O Mahaf, as you are endowed with life, awaken Aqen for me, for see, I have come.

*Who are you who comes?*

I am a magician.

*How have you come and how have you gone up?*

I have gone up on this ...

*What have you done to her?*

I have trodden on her back, I have guided her ... aright.

*What else have you done to her?*

My right side was at her starboard, my front was towards her bow, my left side was at her larboard, my back was towards her stern.

*What else have you done to her?*

At night her bulls were slaughtered and her geese cut up.

*Who stands on her?*

Horus of the Rulers.

*Who takes her cordage?*

The Foremost One, the Ruler, the Oldest One.

*Who controls her bowls?*

The Foremost One, the Ruler, Baty.

*What else have you done to her?*

I went to Min of Coptos and Anubis the Commander of the Two Lands, and I found them celebrating their festivals and reaping their emmer in bundles of ears with their sickles between their thighs, from which you have made cakes. The god who ascends led me to the goddess who ascends, and the Lady of Pe led me to the Lady of Netjeru. Now as for the gods of Pe who are in front of their houses, I found them washing their head-cloths. They will come bearing the cakes of the gods, and they will make cakes for you when going downstream and bread when going upstream.

O Mahaf, as you are endowed with life, awaken Aqen for me, for see, I have come.

*Who are you who comes?*

I am a magician.

*Are you complete?*

I am complete.

*Are you equipped?*

I am equipped.

*Have you healed the limbs?*

I have healed the limbs.

*What are those limbs, magician?*

They are the arm and the leg.

*Take care! Do you say that you would cross to the east side of the sky? If you cross, what will you do?*

*Spell 94* Nebamun sits on a lion-footed chair sniffing a lotus before a
low table on which stands a scribe's palette and a water-pot. 9964/20

I will govern the towns, I will rule the villages, I will
know the rich and give to the poor, I will prepare cakes
for you when going downstream and bread when going
upstream.

O Mahaf, as you are endowed with life, awaken Aqen
for me, for see, I have come.

*Do you know the road on which you must go,
magician?*

I know the road on which I must go.

*Which is the road on which you must go?*

It is 'Power of Earth', and I shall go to the Field of
Rushes.

*Who will guide you?*

The Royal Twins will guide me.

*Who will tell your name to this august god?*

He who is content, the elder brother of Sokar.

O Mahaf, as you are endowed with life, awaken Aqen
for me, for see, I have come.

*He does not wake for me.*

You shall say: O Vulture-god who rebuilds a court-
yard, I will break your box, I will smash your pens, I
will tear up your books because of Him who is in the
Abyss. If I see, Shu will see; if I hear, Shu will hear; I

will give orders to the Imperishable Stars, and it will be
well with me on earth.

II

*'What is it?' says Aqen; 'I was asleep.'*

O Aqen, as you are endowed with life, bring me this,
for see, I have come.

*Who are you who comes?*

I am a magician.

*Are you complete?*

I am complete.

*Are you equipped?*

I am equipped.

*Have you taken care of the two limbs?*

I have taken care of the two limbs.

*What are the two limbs, magician?*

They are the arm and the leg.

O Aqen, as you are endowed with life, bring me this,
for see, I have come.

*Have you power over what I have not brought to you,
magician, that is to say this boat? She has no bailer.*

Bring that ... of Khnum through which I am made

*Spell 93* Ani stands holding a scribe's palette, his other arm raised
to send away the ferry-boat in which the ferryman squats, his head
turned back and a flail on his knee. 10470/17

alive, and put it in her.

O Aqen, as you are endowed with life, bring me this, for see, I have come.

*Have you power over what I have not brought to you, magician, that is to say this boat? She has no spars.*

What is missing from her?

*She has no beams, she has no rigging, she has no mooring-post, she has no warps.*

Go to that god who knows you and all that you would mention to him in respect of her spars; what he has given to you will come.

*Who is that god who knows me and all that I would mention to him in respect of her spars, so that what he has given to me will come?*

He is Horus with whom is a seal-ring.

O Aqen, as you are endowed with life, bring me this, for see, I have come.

*Have you power over what I have not brought to you, magician, that is to say this boat? She has no cable.*

Bring that snake which is in the hands of Hemen and of Anubis the Controller of the Two Lands, and put it in her, with its head in your hands and its tail in my hands, and we must pull it tight between us (in) its name of 'Pain' ... the waterways which are between those two cities; the river is in good order and the Lake of Offerings which connects with that river is in good order.

O Aqen, as you are endowed with life, bring me this, for see, I have come.

*What are those two cities, magician?*

They are the horizon and the malachite-region, or so I believe.

*Do you know those two cities, magician?*

94

*Spell 95 Nakht kneels in adoration of Thoth, who squats with an ankh on his knee. 10471/16*

I know them.
*What are those two cities, magician?*
They are the Netherworld and the Field of Rushes.
O Aqen, as you are endowed with life, bring me this, for see, I have come.
*Have you power over what I have not brought to you, magician? That august god will say: 'Have you ferried over to me a man who does not know the number of his fingers?'*
I know how to count my fingers; take one, take the second, quench it, remove it, give it to me, be friendly towards me; do not let go of it; have no pity on it; make the Eye bright; give the Eye to me.

### III

O you who bring the ferry-boat of the Abyss to this difficult bank, bring me the ferry-boat, make fast the warp for me in peace, in peace! Come, come; hurry, hurry, for I have come in order to see my father Osiris. O Lord of Red Cloth, who is mighty through joy; O Lord of Storm, the Male who navigates; O You who navigate over this sandbank of *Apep*; O You who bind on heads and make necks firm when escaping from wounds; O You who are in charge of the mysterious ferry-boat, who ward off *Apep*, bring me the ferry-boat, knot the warp for me, in order to escape from that evil land in which the stars fall upside down upon their faces and are unable to raise themselves up.

O Henswa who is the tongue of Re; O Indebu who governs the Two Lands; O Mengeb their helmsman; O Power who reveals the solar disc, who is in charge of redness, fetch me, do not let me be boatless, for there comes a spirit, my brother, who will ferry me over to the place I know of.
*'Tell me my name,' says the mooring-post.*

*Spell 95 A goose illustrating the spell 'to be in the presence of Thoth', which uniquely in the Book of the Dead of Userhat is entitled 'spell to become a goose'. 10009/3*

'Lady of the Two Lands in the shrine' is your name.
*'Tell me my name,' says the mallet.*
'Shank of Apis' is your name.
*'Tell me my name,' says the bow-warp.*
'Lock of hair of the mooring-post of Anubis in the craft of embalming' is your name.
*'Tell me my name,' says the steering-post.*
'Pillars of the realm of the dead' is your name.
*'Tell me my name,' says the mast-step.*
'Earth-god' is your name.
*'Tell me my name,' says the mast.*
'He who brought back the Great Goddess after she had been far away' is your name.
*'Tell me my name,' say the halyards.*
'Standard of Wepwawet' is your name.
*'Tell me my name,' says the mast-head.*
'Throat of Imsety' is your name.
*'Tell me my name,' says the sail.*
'Nut' is your name.
*'Tell me my name,' say the oar-loops.*
'You have been made with the hide of the Mnevis-bull and the tendons of Seth' is your name.

*Spell 99 Nu stands at the bow of a boat which has two steering-oars, a swelling sail and an udjat-eye painted on the prow, and which will ferry him across the celestial river. 10477/22*

*'Tell me my name,'* say the oars.
'The fingers of Horus the Elder' are your names.
*'Tell me my name,'* says the bailer.
'The hand of Isis which swabs up the blood from the Eye of Horus' is your name.
*'Tell me my name,'* say the ribs which are in her timbers.
'Imsety, Hapy, Duamutef and Qebehsenuef, Plunderer, He who takes by robbery, He who sees what he has brought, He who helps himself' are your names.
*'Tell me my name,'* says the hogging-beam.
'She who presides over gardens' is your name.
*'Tell me my name,'* says the rowing bench.
'Songstress' is your name.
*'Tell me my name,'* says the steering-oar.
'Accurate' is your name. 'That which rises from the water, whose blade is limited (in movement)' is your name.

*'Tell me my name,'* says the boat.
'That leg of Isis which Re cut off with a knife in order to bring blood to the Night-bark' is your name.
*'Tell me my name,'* says the skipper.
'Rebuffer' is your name.
*'Tell me my name,'* says the wind, *'since you are carried thereby.'*
'North wind which went forth from Atum to the nose of the Foremost of the Westerners' is your name.
*'Tell me my name,'* says the river, *'since you ferry over on me.'*
'He who sees them' is your name.
*'Tell me my name,'* says the bank of the river.
'Destroyer of those who stretch out the arm in the pure place' is your name.
*'Tell me my name,'* says the ground, *'since you tread on me.'*
'Nose of the sky which goes out from the Embalmer

*Spell 100 Nu stands at the stern of the boat of Re before two steering-oars topped by falcons' heads. In front of him stand Isis, Thoth, Khepri and Shu.* 10477/28

who is in the Field of Rushes, from which one goes out in joy' is your name.

*What is to be said to them:* Hail to you, you whose natures are kind, possessors of offerings who live for ever and ever! I have penetrated to you so that you may give me a funeral meal for my mouth with which I speak, namely the cake which Isis baked in the presence of the Great God, for I know that Great God to whose nose you present provisions, whose name is Tjekem. He reveals himself in the eastern horizon of the sky, he travels in the western horizon of the sky. When he departs, I will depart; when he is hale, I will be hale. You shall not repel me from the Milky Way, and those who are rebellious will not have power over this flesh of mine. My bread is in Pe, my beer is in Dep, your gifts of today shall be given to me, and the gifts due to me are barley and emmer, the gifts due to me are myrrh and clothing, the gifts due to me are life, welfare and health, the gifts due to me are what are issued by day in any shape in which I desire to go out to the Field of Rushes.

*As for him who knows this spell, he will go out into the Field of Rushes, and there will be given to him a cake, a jug of beer and a loaf from upon the altar of* the Great God, an aroura of land with barley and emmer by the Followers of Horus, *who will reap them for him. He will consume this barley and emmer and will rub his body with them, his body will be like these gods, and he will go out into* the Field of Rushes in any shape in which he desires to go out. A matter a million times true.

*Spell 99 Nakht kneels in a light boat with a papyrus-shaped prow and stern, holding two ropes to control the swelling sail.* 10471/12

## ——— SPELL 100 ———
[illustrated pp.97,100,120-1]

*The book of making a soul worthy and of permitting it to go aboard the Bark of Re with those who are in his suite.*

I have ferried over the phoenix to the East, Osiris is in Busiris, I have thrown open the caverns of Hapi, I have cleared the paths of the solar disc, I have dragged Sokar on his sledge, I have made the Great Goddess powerful in her moment of action, I have hymned and worshipped the solar disc, I have joined with him who is with the worshipping baboons, and I am one of them. I have acted as second to Isis, I have strengthened her powers, I have knotted the rope, I have driven off *Apep*, I have put a stop to his movements, Re has given his hands to me and his crew will not drive me away. If I am strong, the Sacred Eye will be strong – and vice versa. As for him who shall hold me back from the Bark of Re, he shall be held back from the Egg and the abdju-fish.

*To be said over this written text, which should be written on a clean blank roll with powder of green glaze mixed with water of myrrh. To be placed on the breast of the blessed dead without letting it touch his flesh. As for any blessed dead for whom this is done, he will go aboard the Bark of Re every day, and Thoth will take count of him in daily going and coming. A matter a million times true.*

## Spell 101

[illustrated p.100]

*Spell 103 Nakht kneels in praise of Hathor who squats on a mat with an ankh on her knee. 10471/16*

### Spell for protecting the Bark of Re

O you who emerge from the waters, who escape from the flood and climb on to the stern of your bark, may you indeed climb on to the stern of your bark, may you be more hale than you were yesterday. You have included N, a worthy spirit, in your crew; if you are hale, he will be hale.

O Re in this your name of Re, if you pass by the Eye of seven cubits with a pupil of three cubits, you will make N hale, the worthy spirit in your crew; if you are hale, he will be hale.

O Re in this your name of Re, if you pass by the dead who are upside down, you shall cause N the worthy spirit to stand up on his feet; if you are hale, he will be hale.

O Re in this your name of Re, if the mysteries of the Netherworld are opened to you in order to guide the hearts of your Ennead, you shall give N's heart to him; if you are hale, he will be hale.

Your body, O Re, is everlasting by reason of the spell.

*To be recited over a strip of royal linen on which this spell has been written in dried myrrh; to be placed on the*

99

throat of the blessed dead on the day of burial. If this protective spell is placed on his throat for him, praises will be made for him as for the gods, he shall be united with the Followers of Horus; the starry sky shall be made firm for him in the presence of Him who is with Sothis, his corpse shall be a god, together with his relatives, for ever, and a bush shall be planted for him over the breast by Menqet. It was the Majesty of Thoth who did this for the Majesty of the vindicated King of Upper and Lower Egypt Osiris through desire that the sunlight should rest on his corpse.

## —— SPELL 102 ——

*Spell for going aboard the Bark of Re*

O you who are great in your bark, bring me to your bark, so that I may take charge of your navigating in the duty which is allotted to one who is among the Unwearying Stars. What I doubly detest, I will not eat; my detestation is faeces, and I will not eat it, I will not consume excrement, I will not approach it with my hands, I will not tread on it with my sandals, because my bread is of white emmer and my beer of red barley. It is the Night-bark and the Day-bark who bring them to me, and the gifts of the towns are emptied on to the altar of the Souls of Heliopolis. Greeting to you, O Great One who acts in the rowing over the sky; the shens-cake which is in Thinis is that of which the dogs partake. I am not weary; I myself have come that I might save this god from those who would do him evil, namely the pain allotted to thigh, arm and leg. I have come that I may spit on the thigh, tie up the arm and raise the leg. 'Go aboard and navigate', is the command of Re.

## —— SPELL 103 ——
[illustrated p.99]

*Spell for being in the presence of Hathor*

I am one who passes by, pure and bald; O Sistrum-player, I will be in the suite of Hathor.

**Spells 100 and 101** *In the top vignette Horemheb poles a boat, containing the phoenix and a squatting falcon-headed sun-god with an ankh on his knee, towards Osiris, who stands before a djed-pillar symbolising the town of Busiris (Spell 100). The lower illustration shows Horemheb poling a boat containing the phoenix and a squatting falcon-headed sun-god, who carries a was-sceptre on his knee (Spell 101).* 10257/11

*Spell 104 Nebseny kneels holding a scribe's palette between two enthroned mummiform gods. 9900/8*

## —— SPELL 104 ——

*Spell for sitting among the great gods*

I have sat among the great gods, I have passed by the House of the Night-bark; it is the wasp which fetches me to see the great gods who are in the realm of the dead, and I am vindicated in their presence, I am pure.

## —— SPELL 105 ——
[illustrated p.102]

*Spell for propitiating N's ka for him in the realm of the dead*

Hail to you, my ka of my lifetime; behold, I have come to you, I have appeared in glory, I am strong, besouled and mighty, and I have brought to you natron and incense that I may cleanse you with them, that I may cleanse your slaver with them, even this evil phrase which I have spoken, this evil impurity which I have done, and nothing has been imputed to me, because to me belongs that papyrus-amulet which is on the neck of Re,

which was given to those who are in the horizon; if they are white, I will be white, and my ka will be like them, my ka's provisions will be like theirs, having been weighed in the balance. May truth be uplifted to the nose of Re, my head being supported by it, for I am an eye which sees and an ear which hears, I am not a bull for butchery, and none shall have an invocation-offering of me.

## —— SPELL 106 ——

*Spell for giving gifts to N in Memphis and in the realm of the dead*

O Great One, Lord of provisions; O Great One who presides over houses; O You who are above, who give bread to Ptah, the Great One who is on the Great Throne; may you give me bread, may you give me beer, may I eat of the shin of beef together with the roasted bread. O Ferryman of the Field of Rushes, bring me these loaves from your polar waters like your father the Great One who travels in the Bark of the God.

## —— SPELL 108 ——
[illustrated p.103]

*Spell for knowing the Souls of the Westerners*

As for that mountain of Bakhu on which the sky rests, it is in the east of the sky; it is three hundred rods long and one hundred and fifty rods broad. Sobk, Lord of Bakhu, is in the east of that mountain; his temple is of cornelian. A serpent is on the top of that mountain; it is thirty cubits long, eight cubits of its forepart are of flint, and its teeth gleam. I know the name of this serpent which is on the mountain; its name is 'He who is in his burning'. Now after a while he will turn his eyes against Re, and a stoppage will occur in the Sacred Bark and a great vision among the crew, for he will swallow up seven cubits of the great waters; Seth will project a lance of iron against him and will make him vomit up all that he has swallowed. Seth will place him before him and will say to him with magic power: 'Get back at the sharp knife which is in my hand! I stand before you, navigating aright and seeing afar. Cover your face, for I ferry across; get back because of me, for I am the Male! Cover your head, cleanse the palm of your hand; I am hale and I remain hale, for I am the great magician, the son of Nut, and power against you has been granted to me. Who is that spirit who goes on his belly, his tail and his spine? See, I have gone against you, and your tail is in my hand, for I

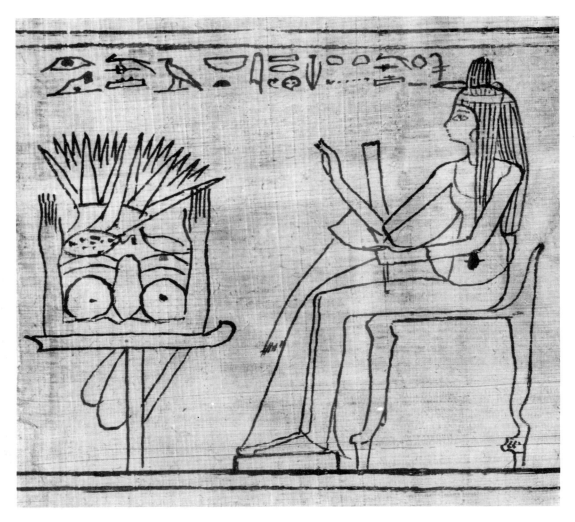

*Spell 105 Nesitanebtasheru, wearing a heart amulet and holding a kherep-sceptre, sits on a lion-footed chair before a standard on which upraised arms, symbolising the ka, embrace a heap of food offerings topped by lotus flowers. 10554/17*

am one who exhibits strength. I have come that I may rescue the earth-gods for Re so that he may go to rest for me in the evening. I go round about the sky, but you are in the fetters which were decreed for you in the Presence, and Re will go to rest alive in his horizon.'

I know those who govern the matter by reason of which *Apep* is repelled; I know the Souls of the Westerners, who are Atum, Sobk the Lord of Bakhu, and Hathor the Lady of the Evening.

## ——— SPELL 109 ———
[illustrated p.104]

*Spell for knowing the Souls of the Easterners*

I know the northern gate of the sky; its south is in the Lake of Waterfowl, its north is in the Waters of Geese, the place in which Re navigates by wind or by rowing. I am the whip-master in the Ship of the God, I am one who rows and does not tire in the Bark of Re.

I know those two trees of turquoise between which Re goes forth, which have grown up at the Supports of Shu at that gate of the Lord of the East from which Re goes forth.

I know that Field of Rushes which belongs to Re, the walls of which are of iron; the height of the barley is five cubits, its ear is two cubits and its stalk is three cubits; its emmer is seven cubits, its ear is of three cubits and its stalk of four cubits. They are spirits, each nine cubits tall, who reap it in the presence of the Souls of the Easterners.

I know the Souls of the Easterners; they are Horakhty, the sun-calf, and the Morning Star.

***Spell 108*** *Three squatting deities representing the Souls of the*
*Westerners and named as Atum, Sobk, Lord of Bakhu, and Hathor,*
*Mistress of the Evening.* 9900/7

## —— SPELL 110 ——
[illustrated pp.10,105,106-7,110-11]

N worships the Ennead which is in the Field of Offerings, and he says: Hail to you, you owners of kas! I have come in peace to your fields in order to receive the provisions which you give; I have come to the Great God in order that I may receive the provisions which his goodwill grants of bread and beer, oxen and fowl. Giving praise to the Ennead, doing homage to the Great God by N.

A boon which the King grants to Osiris and the Ennead which is in the Field of Offerings, that they may give invocation-offerings of bread and beer, oxen and fowl and all things good, and clothing and incense daily, which rest upon the altar every day; to receive senu-bread and khenef-bread, persen-bread, milk, wine and the provisions of one who follows the god in his pro-cession in his Festival of Rosetjau, bearing the water-jars of the Great God, for the benefit of N.

Here begin the spells of the Field of Offerings and spells of going forth into the day; of coming and going in the realm of the dead; of being provided for in the Field of Rushes which is in the Field of Offerings, the abode of the Great Goddess, the Mistress of Winds; having strength thereby, having power thereby, ploughing therein, reaping and eating therein, drinking therein, copulating therein, and doing everything that used to be done on earth by N.

He says: The Falcon has been taken by Seth, and I have seen the damage in the Field of Offerings; I have released the Falcon from Seth, I opened the paths of Re on the day when the sky was choked and stifled, when the Rejected One panted for breath in vivifying Him who was in the Egg and took Him who was in the womb from the Silent Ones.

*Spell 109* Nebseny stands in daily adoration of the spotted sun-calf and a squatting falcon-headed Re-Horakhty, who wears a sun-disc and cobra on his head. 9900/8

Now it befell that I rowed in the bark in the Lake of Offerings; I took it from the Limbs of Shu, and his northern stars, his Limbs, were set in due order; I rowed and arrived at its waterways and towns, I fared southward to the god who is in it, because I am he who would rest in his fields. I control the two Enneads whom he loves, I pacify the Combatants on behalf of those who are in the West; I create what is good, I bring peace, I pacify the Combatants on behalf of those who belong to them, I drive away mourning from their elders, I remove turmoil from their young; I wipe away harm of all kinds from Isis, I wipe away harm of all kinds from the gods, I remove turmoil from the Rivals, I separate the Authoritative One from his light, and I give abundance to souls and spirits; I have power over them.

I am one whom Hotep knows, I row on its waterways, I arrive at its towns. My utterance is mighty, I am more acute than the spirits, and they shall not have power over me. O Hotep, I acquire this field of yours which you love, the Lady of Air. I eat and carouse in it, I drink and plough in it, I reap in it, I copulate in it, I make love

in it, I do not perish in it, for my magic is powerful in it. I will not be aroused in it, my happy heart is not apprehensive in it, for I know the wooden post of Hotep, which is called Bequtet; it was made firm on the blood of Shu and it was lashed with the Bowstring of the Years on that day when the years were divided; my mouth is hidden and his mouth is silent. I say something mysterious, I bring eternity to an end and I take possession of everlasting.

ALL RUBRICS HEREAFTER REFER TO THE FIELD OF OFFERINGS (SEKHET-HOTEP) OR TO PARTS OF IT. HOTEP ALONE IS USED EITHER OF THE FIELD OR OF ITS PERSONIFICATION AS A DEITY.

*Being in Hotep,* Lord of the Field of Offerings. This is Horus; he is a falcon a thousand cubits long, life and dominion are in his hand, he comes and goes at will in its waterways and towns, he rises and sets in Qenqenet, the birth-place of the god. He does everything in it as it is done in the Island of Fire; there is no shouting in it, there is nothing evil in it.

This is Hotep who walks throughout this field of his;

*Spell 110* Kerquny carries out various activities in the Field of
Rushes, including offering incense, paddling across the Lake of
Offerings, ploughing, sowing seed, cutting corn and treading out the
grain. In the lowest register squats the Heron of Abundance and four
members of the Great Ennead, each holding and wearing an ostrich
feather. The boat with snake-headed prow and stern belongs to
Wennefer, the one which contains a throne is the sun-god's. 9911/2

he partakes of a meal in the birth-place of the god. If he
rests in Qenqenet, he will do everything in it as it is done
in the Island of Fire; there is no shouting in it, there is
nothing evil in it.

I live in Hotep, my bag and my bowl are on me,
which I have filled from baskets, being one whom the
spirits of the Lord of Plenty guide. I depart and ascend
to Him who brings it, and I have power through him, he
accepts on my behalf, for I am equipped and content.
This great magic of mine is powerful in this body of
mine, in these seats of mine; I am one who recalls to
himself that of which I have been forgetful. I plough and

I reap, and I am content in the City of God. I know the
names of the districts, towns and waterways which are in
the Field of Offerings and of those who are in them; I am
strong in them and I am a spirit in them; I eat in them and
travel about in them. I plough and reap in the Field; I rise
early in it and go to rest in it. I am a spirit in it as Hotep; I
shoot and travel about in it; at my word I row on its
waterways and I arrive at its towns as Hotep. My horns
are sharp, I give abundance to the souls and spirits, I
allot authoritative utterance to him who can use it. I
arrive at its towns, I row on its waterways, I traverse the
Field of Offerings as Re who is in the sky, and it is

Hotep who satisfies them. I have gone down to the earth, I have made Re content; I have gone up on high and I have caused joy to be made, I have taken power, I have promised peace.

*Being in Hotep.* O Field, I have come into you, my soul behind me and authority before me. O Lady of the Two Lands, establish my magic power for me, that by means of it I may recall what I had forgotten. I am alive without harm of any kind, and joy is given to me, peace is mine, I create seed, I have received air.

*Being in Hotep, Lord of Breezes.* I have come into you, having opened up my head and having aroused my body. I close my eye, yet I shine on the day of the Milk-goddess; I have slept by night, I have restored the milk to its proper level, and I am in my town.

*O Town of the Great Goddess,* I have come into you that I may allot abundance and cause vegetation to flourish; I am the bull of lapis-lazuli, unique and exalted, Lord of the Field, Bull of the Gods. Sothis speaks to me in her good time.

*O Swamp-land,* I have come into you, I have taken the Grey-haired One to the roof, for I am the moon, I have swallowed up the darkness.

*O Town of Fair Offerings,* I have come into you, I eat my meal, I have power over fowl and flesh, and the poultry of Shu which attend on my ka have been given to me.

*O Provision-town,* I have come into you, I have woven the eight-weave cloth, I have donned the fringed cloak as Re in the sky whom the gods who are in the sky serve.

*Being in Hotep, Lady of the Two Lands:* I have come into you, I have immersed the waterways as Osiris, Lord of Putridity, Lord of the Swamp-lands; as the Oldest One, Bull of vultures. I am a flamingo, which has eaten the like.

*O Qenqenet,* I have come into you, I have seen my father, I have recognised my mother, I have risen early, I have caught fish. I know the deep holes of the snakes, and I am saved. I know the name of this god; He whose mouth is put together, Lord of Holiness, whose hair is in good order, whose horns are sharp. If he reaps, I will plough and I will reap.

*O Town of the Milk-goddess,* I have come into you;

**Spell 110** *Hor pulls flax, treads grain, ploughs and sows seed, adores three of the Great Ennead and paddles across the Lake of Offerings, while his wife adores the Heron of Plenty. Beside a squatting god and staircase, representing the birthplace of the gods, are depicted the boats of Wennefer and the sun-god. In four registers Isis and Nephthys adore the scarab-headed sun-god squatting in a boat, Hor is introduced to Osiris and Isis by a god holding a was-sceptre and Hor kneels in adoration of six squatting gods each, with a crook and flail, who represent Authority, Intelligence, Sight and Hearing. 10479/7*

those who would oppose me and drive me off and who would follow after me are those who would follow after Horus; heads have been given to me, and I tie on the Head of Horus the blue-eyed, acting according to his desire.

O *Town of Union*, I have come into you; my head is whole and my heart is awake beneath the White Crown; I am guided above and I am hale below, I give joy to the bulls who are in charge of the Enneads, for I am a bull, Lord of the Gods, who proceeds into the place of turquoise.

O *Mighty Woman*, I have come into you, I have taken the Grey-haired One to the roof, I have fashioned Authority, I am in the middle of my Eye.

O *barley and emmer of the District of the God*, I have come into you, I fare upstream, I sail on the Waterway of Horns, Lady of Pure Things, I drive in the mooring-post in the upper waterways. I have borne aloft the storm of the Disturber and I have upheld the Supports of the Old One.

## —— SPELL 112 ——

*Spell for knowing the Souls of Pe*

O you female Souls of the Night, Marsh-dwellers, Women of Mendes, you of the Fish-nome and of the

*Spells 113 and 115 On the left Horemheb adores the Souls of Heliopolis named as falcon-headed Re, Shu and lioness-headed Tefnut (Spell 115). The right-hand vignette shows Horemheb adoring the Souls of Nekhen, named as falcon-headed Horus wearing a Double Crown, Duamutef and Qebehsenuef (Spell 113). 10257/12*

Mansion of Iapu, Sunshade-bearers of the Adoration, who prepare beer of Nubia, do you know why Pe was given to Horus? You do not know it, but I know it. It was Re who gave it to him in compensation for the mutilation in his Eye; I know it.

It so happened that Re said to Horus: 'Let me see your eye since this has happened to it.' He looked at it and said: 'Look at that black stroke with your hand covering up the sound eye which is there.' Horus looked at that stroke and said: 'Behold, I am seeing it as altogether white.' And that is how the oryx came into being. And Re said: 'Look again at yonder black pig.' And Horus looked at this black pig, and Horus cried out because of the condition of his injured eye, saying: 'Behold, my eye is like that first wound which Seth inflicted on my eye', and Horus fainted before him. Then Re said: 'Put him on his bed until he is well.' It so happened that Seth had transformed himself into a black pig and had projected a wound into his eye, and Re said: 'The pig is detestable to Horus.' 'We wish he were well,' said the gods. That is how the detestation of the pig came about for Horus's sake by the gods who are in the suite.

Now when Horus was a child, his sacrificial animal was a pig before his eye had suffered – Imsety, Hapy,

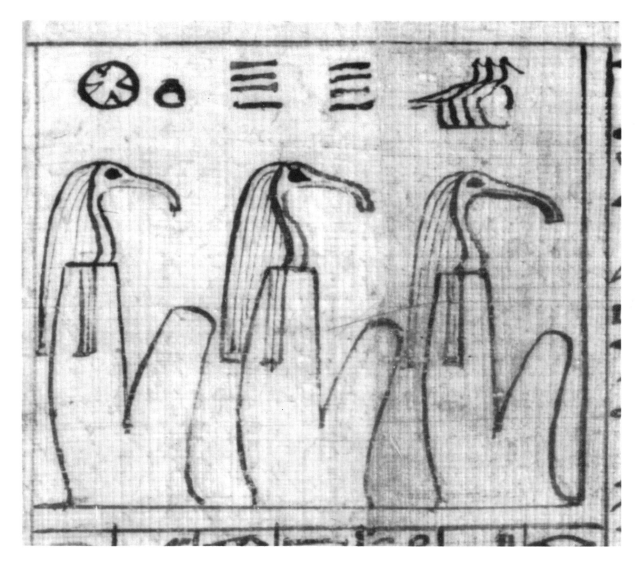

*Spell 114* *Three squatting ibis-headed gods represent the Souls of*
*Hermopolis.* 9900/7

Duamutef and Qebehsenuef, whose father was Horus the Elder and whose mother was Isis – and he said to Re: 'Give me two in Pe and two in Nekhen from this second company. May I be an allotter of eternity, an opener of everlasting and a queller of strife in this my name of "Horus who is on his papyrus-column".'

*I know the Souls of Pe; they are Horus, Imsety and Hapy.*

## ——— Spell 113 ———

*Spell for knowing the Souls of Nekhen*

I know the mystery of Nekhen; it is the hands of·Horus of his mother's making which were thrown into the water when she said: 'You shall be the two severed portions of Horus after you have been found.' And Re said, 'This son of Isis is injured by reason of what his own mother has done to him; let us fetch Sobk from the back of the waters, so that he may fish them out and that his mother Isis may cause them to grow again in their proper place.' And Sobk from the back of the waters said: 'I have fished and I have sought; they slipped from my hand on the bank of the waters, but in the end I fished them up with a fish-trap.' *That is how the fish-trap came into being.*

*Knowing the mystery of Nekhen.* Thus said Re: 'Has Sobk any fish as well as finding Horus's hands for him?' *That is how Fish-worship-town came into being.* Then Re said: 'Hidden are the mysteries concerning this fish-trap which brought Horus's hands to us; the sight is

*Spell 110* *Ani carries out agricultural activities in the Field of Rushes, including cutting corn, treading out the grain and ploughing. He worships three members of the Great Ennead, the Western Falcon and the Heron of Plenty and paddles across the Lake of Offerings. Among the islands and waterways are depicted the boats of Wennefer and the sun-god and heaps of grain.* 10470/35

*Spell 117 Anubis leads Nakht towards a False Door, entrance to the Other World, before which stands a tree. 10471/8*

cleared because of it in the monthly festival and the half-monthly festival in Fish-worship-town.' And Re said: 'Nekhen is set in his embrace and the sight is cleared on account of his hands in this Nekhen which I have given to him, and what is in them is shut up in the half-monthly festival.'

Then Horus said: 'Indeed I have placed Duamutef and Qebehsenuef with me so that I may watch over them, for they are a contentious company; further, they are to be there while Nekhen is mine, according to the word of Re, "Place them in the prison of Nekhen, for they have done what used to be done by Her who is in the Broad Hall" ; "They are with me", you shall say, and they will end up with you until Seth knows that they are with you and complains.'

O you who are in Nekhen, power is given to me, and I know the mystery of Nekhen; it is the hands of Horus and what is in them, for I have been introduced to the Souls of Nekhen. Open to me, that I may join with Horus.

*I know the Souls of Nekhen: they are Horus, Duamutef and Qebehsenuef. Not to be said when eating pig.*

## —— SPELL 114 ——
[illustrated p.109]

*Spell for knowing the Souls of Hermopolis*

The plume is stuck into the shoulder of Osiris, the Red Crown shines in the bowl, the Eye is eaten and he who sought it is fetched. I know it, for I have been initiated into it by the Sem-priest, and I have never spoken nor made repetition to the gods. I have come on an errand for Re in order to cause the plume to grow into the shoulder of Osiris, to make complete the Red Crown in the bowl and to pacify the Eye for him who numbered it. I have entered as a Power because of what I know, I have not spoken to men, I have not repeated what was said.

Hail to you, Souls of Hermopolis! Know that Re desires the plume which grows and the Red Crown which is complete at this temple, and rejoice at the allotting of what is to be allotted.

*I know the Souls of Hermopolis. What is great in the half-month and small in the full month, that is Thoth.*

## —— SPELL 115 ——
[illustrated p.108]

*Spell for ascending to the sky, opening up the tomb, and knowing the Souls of Heliopolis*

I have spent yesterday among the great ones, I have become Khepri, I have cleared the vision of the Sole Eye, I have opened up the circle of darkness. I am one of them, I know the Souls of Heliopolis, into which the High-priest of Heliopolis was not initiated through revelation; (I know) the hostile acts by Him who would destroy the heirs of Heliopolis; I know why a braided lock is made for a man.

Re disputed with the serpent, 'Him who is in his burning', and his mouth was injured, and that is how the reduction in the month came about. He said to the serpent: 'I will take my harpoon, which men will inherit', and that is how the harpoon came into being. The serpent said: 'The Two Sisters will come into being', and that is how Re's passing by came into being.

It so happened that He of the red cloth heard, and his arm was not stopped. He transformed himself into a woman with braided hair, and that is how the priest of Heliopolis with braided hair came into being. It so happened that the mighty one was stripped in the temple, and that is how the stripped one of Heliopolis came into being. It so happened that the heritage of the heir came into being, and great will be he who shall see it; he will become High-priest of Heliopolis.

I know the Souls of Heliopolis; they are Re, Shu and Tefnut.

## —— SPELL 117 ——
[also illustrated p.114]

*Spell for taking the road in Rosetjau*

The ways which are above the waters lead to Rosetjau; I am he who clothed my standard which came forth from the Wereret-crown. I have come that I may establish offerings in Abydos, I have opened the ways in Rosetjau, I have assuaged the pains of Osiris. It is I who created water, who discerned my throne, who prepared my way in the valley and on the waterway. O Great One, prepare a way for me, for it is yours. It was I who vindicated Osiris against his enemies, so may I be vindicated against my enemies. May I be like one of you, a friend of the Lord of Eternity, may I walk like you walk, may I stand like you stand, may I sit like you sit, may I speak like you speak before the Great God, Lord of the West.

## —— SPELL 118 ——

*Spell for arriving in Rosetjau*

I am one who was born in Rosetjau, and benefits have been given to me by those who are among the noble dead, with the pure things of Osiris; I received praise in Rosetjau when I conducted Osiris to the Mounds of Osiris. I am unique, having conducted them to the Mounds of Osiris.

## —— SPELL 119 ——
[illustrated p.114]

*Spell for going forth from Rosetjau*

I am the Great One who created his own light; I have come to you, Osiris, that I may worship you, for pure is the efflux which was drawn from you, the name of which was made in Rosetjau; may you be mighty thereby in Abydos. Raise yourself, Osiris, that you may go round about the sky with Re and see the people; O Unique One, travel around as Re. See, I have spoken to you, Osiris; I have the rank of a god, I say what comes to pass, and I will not be turned away from you, Osiris.

## —— SPELL 122 ——

*Spell for entering after coming out*

To me belongs everything, and the whole of it has been given to me. I have gone in as a falcon, I have come out as a phoenix; the Morning Star has made a path for me, and I enter in peace in to the beautiful West. I belong to

the Garden of Osiris, and a path is made for me so that I may go in and worship Osiris the Lord of Life.

## —— SPELL 123 ——
[illustrated p.116]

*Spell for entering into the Great Mansion*

Hail to you, Atum! I am Thoth who judged between the Rivals. I have stopped their fighting, I have wiped away their mourning, I have seized the buri-fish when it would flee away, I have done what you commanded in the matter, and afterwards I spent the night within my Eye (the moon). I am devoid of ill-will, and I have come that you may see me in the Mansion of Him of the double face in accordance with what was commanded; the old men are under my control and the little ones belong to me.

## —— SPELL 124 ——
[illustrated p.117]

*Spell for going down to the Tribunal of Osiris*

My soul has built an enclosed place in Busiris, and I am flourishing in Pe; I plough my fields in my own shape, and my dom-palm is that upon which Min is.

What I doubly detest, I will not eat; my detestation is faeces, and I will not eat it, I will not consume excrement, I will not approach it with my hands, I will not tread on it with my sandals, because my bread is of white emmer and my beer is of red barley. It is the Night-bark and the Day-bark which bring it to me, and I will eat beneath the branches, for I know the bearers of what is good. Then I will recite glorifications of the White Crown, and I will be raised aloft by the uraei. O you door-keepers of Him who pacified the Two Lands, bring me those who prepare offerings and let the branches be raised for me; may the sunshine open its arms to me, may the Ennead be silent when the sun-folk speak to me. May I guide the hearts of the gods, and may they protect me, may I be mighty among those who suspend themselves on high. As for any god or any goddess who shall oppose themselves to me, they shall be handed over to those who are in charge of the year, who live on hearts, while the preparation of senu-bread is before me; may Osiris eat it when going forth from the East, may it be allotted to those who are in the presence of Re, may it be allotted to those who are in the presence of the Sunshine-god who covers the sky among the great ones who belong to it.

Place bread in my mouth; I will go into the Moon-god, so that he may speak to me, that the followers of the gods may speak to me, that the sun may speak to me, and that the sun-folk may speak to me. The dread of me is in the twilight and in the Celestial Waters which are his on his forehead; I am there with Osiris, and my mat is his mat among the Elders. I have told him the words of men, and I have repeated to him the words of the gods. My spirit comes equipped, for I am an equipped spirit and I have equipped all the spirits.

## —— SPELL 125 ——

*See page 29*

## —— SPELL 126 ——
[illustrated pp.118-19]

O you four baboons who sit in the bow of the Bark of Re, who raise up truth to the Lord of All, who judge poor and rich, who propitiate the gods with the breath of your mouths, who give god's-offerings to the gods and invocation-offerings to the spirits, who live on truth and gulp down truth, whose hearts have no lies, who detest falsehood: expel my evil, grip hold of my falsehood, and I will have no guilt in respect of you. Grant that I may open up the tomb, that I may enter into Rosetjau, and that I may pass by the secret portals of the West. There shall be given to me a shens-cake, a jug of beer and a persen-loaf, just like those spirits who go in and out in Rosetjau.

THE BABOONS REPLY: Come, so that we may expel your evil and grip hold of your falsehood so that the dread of you may be on earth, and dispel the evil which was on you on earth. Enter into Rosetjau, pass by the secret portals of the West, and there shall be given to you a shens-cake, a jug of beer, and a persen-loaf, and you shall go in and out at your desire, just like those favoured spirits who are summoned daily into the horizon.

## —— SPELL 127 ——
[illustrated pp.120-1]

The book of worshipping the gods of the caverns; what a man should say there when he reaches them in order to go in to see this god in the Great Mansion of the Netherworld.

Hail to you, gods of the caverns which are in the West! Hail to you, door-keepers of the Netherworld who guard this god and who bring news to the presence of Osiris! May you be alert, may you have power, may you destroy the enemies of Re, may you make brightness, may you dispel your darkness, may you see the holiest of the Great Ones, may you live as he lives, may you give praise to Him who is in his sun-disc, may you guide N to your doors. May his soul pass by your hidden things, for he is one of you. May he strike evil into Apep, may his wrong-doing be smitten down in the West. You are triumphant over your enemies, O Great God who are in your sun-disc; you are triumphant over your enemies, O Osiris, Foremost of the Westerners; you are triumphant, O N, over your enemies in sky and earth and in the tribunals of every god and every goddess. Osiris, Foremost of the Westerners, speaks in front of the Valley and he is vindicated in the great tribunal.

O you door-keepers who guard your portals, who swallow souls and who gulp down the corpses of the dead who pass by you when they are allotted to the House of Destruction, who cause that the soul of every potent, great and holy spirit shall be led aright to the place of the Silent Land, even he who is a soul like Re who is praised and like Osiris who is praised. May you guide N, may you open the portals for him, may the earth open its caverns to him, may you make him triumphant over his enemies. So shall he give gifts to Him of the Netherworld; he shall make the head-cloth potent for its wearer within the hidden chamber as the image of Horakhty. 'May the soul of the potent spirit be led aright; how mighty is that which is in his hands!', say the two great and mighty gods concerning N. They rejoice over him, they acclaim him with what is in their hands, they give him their protection so that he may live. N has appeared as a living one who is in the sky, it has been commanded to him to assume his own shape, he is vindicated in the tribunal, and the gates of sky, earth and the Netherworld are opened for him as for Re.

N says: Open for me the gates of sky, earth and the Netherworld, for I am the soul of Osiris, and I am at peace thereby. I pass by their courts, and they give praise when they see me; I have gone in favoured and I have come out beloved; I have journeyed, and no fault of any kind has been found in me.

## ——— SPELL 128 ———
[illustrated p.122]

### Worshipping Osiris

Hail to you, Osiris Wennefer, the vindicated, the son of Nut! You are the first-born son of Geb, the Great One who came forth from Nut; King in the Thinite nome; Foremost of the Westerners; Lord of Abydos; Lord of Power, greatly majestic; Lord of the Atef-crown in Heracleopolis; Lord of Might in the Thinite nome; owner of a tomb; greatly powerful in Busiris; Lord of offerings and multiple of festivals in Mendes. Horus exalts his father Osiris in every place which Isis the goddess and her sister Nephthys protect; Thoth speaks with his great incantations which are in his body and which issue from his mouth; and Horus's heart is made more glad than those of all the gods. Raise yourself up, Horus son of Isis, so that you may protect your father Osiris.

Shout with joy, Osiris, for I have come to you; I am Horus, I have saved you alive today, and there are invocation-offerings of bread and beer, oxen and fowl and all good things for Osiris. Raise yourself up, Osiris; I will smite your enemies for you, for I have saved you from them. I am Horus in this happy day as one who appears happily in glory with your power.

He exalts you with himself today in your tribunal; shout for joy, Osiris, for your ka has come to you, accompanying you, that you may be content in this your name of 'Contented Ka'; he glorifies you in this your name of

*Spell 124: Horemheb stands before the Four Sons of Horus, who carry was-sceptres and ankhs.* 10257/13

'Divine Spirit'; he worships you in this your name of 'Magician'; he opens up paths for you in this your name of 'Opener of Paths'.

Shout with joy, Osiris, for I have come to you that I may put your enemies under you in every place where you are vindicated in the tribunals of the Ennead.

Shout with joy, Osiris; take your mace and your staff, with your stairway below you. Control the food of the gods; control the offerings of those who are in their tombs; give your greatness to the gods, O You whom the Great God created. May you be with them in your mummy-form, may you collect yourself because of all the gods, for you have heard the voice of Maat today.

*Recite an offering-formula to* this god in the Wag-festival.

## ——— SPELL 130 ———
[illustrated pp.120-1]

*Another spell for making a spirit worthy on the birthday of Osiris and for making a soul to live for ever*

May the sky be opened, may the earth be opened, may the West be opened, may the East be opened, may the chapel of Upper Egypt be opened, may the chapel of Lower Egypt be opened, may the doors be opened, may the eastern portals be thrown open for Re when he ascends from the horizon. May the doors of the Night-bark be opened for him, may the portals of the Day-bark be thrown open for him, may he breathe Shu, may he create Tefnut, may those who are in the suite serve him, may they serve me like Re daily.

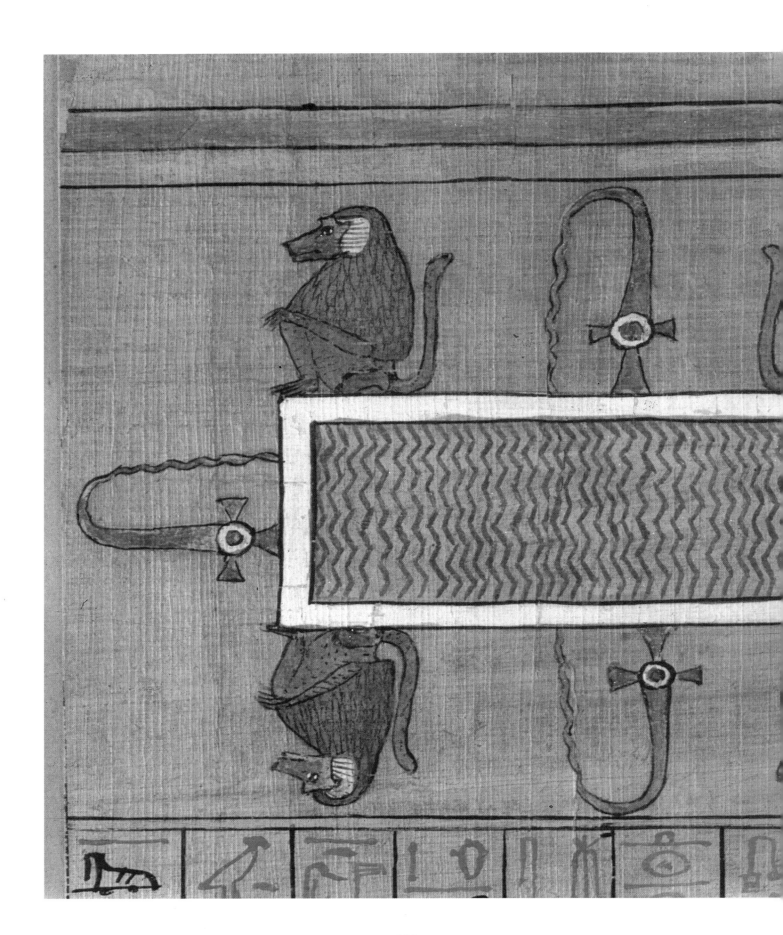

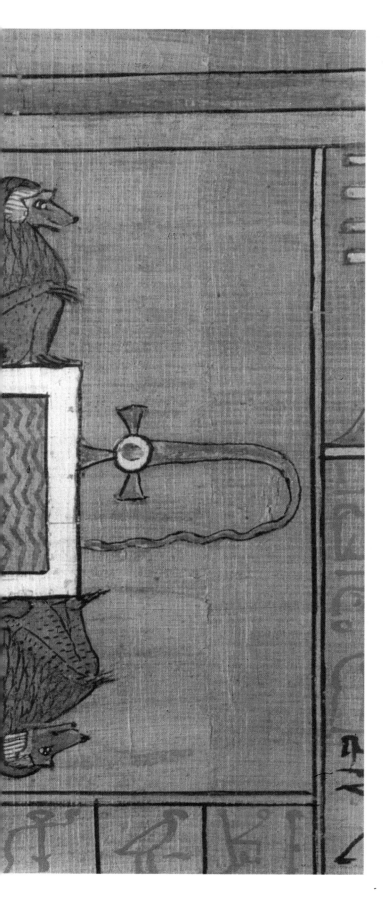

I am a follower of Re, who receives his firmament; the god occupies his shrine, Horus having approached his lord, whose seats are secret, whose shrine is pure, messenger of the god to him whom he loved. I am one who takes hold of Maat, having presented her before him; I am he who knots the cord and lashes his shrine together. What I detest is storm, and there will be no heaping up of waters in my presence, I will not be turned back because of Re, I will not be driven off by whoever acts with his hands, I will not go into the Valley of Darkness, I will not enter into the Lake of Criminals, I will not be in the weakening of striking-power, I will not fall as plunder, I will go in among those who are taken before him, behind the slaughter-block of the shambles of Sopd.

Hail to you, you squatting gods! The seclusion of the god is in the secrecy of the arms of Geb at dawn; who is he who will guide the Great One? He will number the children in his good time, while Thoth is in the secret places; he will make purity for Him who counts the myriads who are to be counted, who opens up the firmament and dispels all cloudiness. I have reached him in his place, I grasp the staff, I receive the head-cloth for Re, whose fair movements are great. Horus flames up around his eye, and his two Enneads are about his throne; if they remove the sore pain which he suffers, then will I remove the pain, that I may be made comfortable thereby. I will open up the horizon for Re, and I have built his ship 'She who proceeds happily'; the face of Thoth will be made bright for me, and I will worship Re, he will hearken to me, for he has implanted an obstacle on my behalf against my enemies. I will not be left boatless, I will not be turned back from the horizon, for I am Re. I will not be left boatless in the great crossing by Him whose face is on his knee and whose hand is bent down, because the name of Re is in my body, his dignity is in my mouth. So he has told me, and I hear his word.

Praise to you, Re, Lord of the Horizon; hail to you for whom the sun-folk are pure, for whom the sky is controlled in the great moment when the hostile oarsmen pass by. See, I have come among those who make truth known, because I am far away in the West; I have broken up the storm of *Apep*, O Double Lion, as I promised you. See, I have come; O you who are before the Great Throne, hearken to me. I go down into your tribunal, I rescue Re from *Apep* every day, and there is no-one who can attack him, for those who are about him are awake. I lay hold of the writings, I receive offerings, I equip Thoth with what was made for him, I cause truth to circulate over the Great Bark, I go down vindicated into the tribunal, I establish the Chaos-gods, I lead the

*Spell 126 The Four Baboons who sit in the bark of Re squat around a Lake of Fire with flaming braziers between them.* 10470/33

119

Entourage, I grant to them a voyage in utter joy, when the crew of Re goes round about following his beauty. Maat is exalted so that she may reach her lord, and praise is given to the Lord of All.

I take the staff, I sweep the sky with it, and the sun-folk give me praise as to Him who stands and does not tire. I extol Re in what he has made, I dispel cloudiness, I see his beauty, I display the terror of him, I make his oarsmen firm when his Bark travels over the sky at dawn. I am the Great One within his Eye, who kneels at the head of the Great Bark of Khepri. I come into being and what I have said comes into being, I am this one who traverses the sky towards the West, and those who heap up the air stand up in joy; they have taken the bow-warp of Re from his crew, and Re traverses the sky happily in peace by my command; I will not be driven away, the fiery breath of your power will not carry me off, the power of repulsion in your mouth will not go forth against me, I will not walk on the paths of pestilence, for to fall into it is the detestation of my soul; what I detest is the flood, and it shall not attack me. I go aboard your Bark, I occupy your seat, I receive my dignity, I control the paths of Re and the stars, I am he who drives off the Destructive One who comes at the flame of your Bark upon the great plateau. I know them by their names, and they will not attack your Bark, for I am in it, and I am he who prepares the offerings.

*To be said over a Bark of Re drawn in ochre on a clean place. When you have placed a likeness of this spirit in front of it, you shall draw a Night-bark on its right side and a Day-bark on its left side. There shall be offered to them in their presence bread and beer and all good things on the birthday of Osiris. If this is done for him, his soul will live for ever and he will not die again.*

## —— SPELL 131 ——
[illustrated p.123]

*Spell for being in the presence of Re*

I am that Re who shines in the night. As for anyone who

*Spells 127, 129 and 130 On the left Horemheb stands in a boat behind the falcon-headed sun-god and two other deities all carrying ankhs and was-sceptres (Spell 130). The central detail shows*

*Horemheb paddling the phoenix in a boat towards Osiris, who stands before his djed-pillar (Spell 129: the text, being identical to Spell 100, is translated under that number). On the right*

is in his suite or who lives in the suite of Thoth, he will give appearance in glory to this Horus in the night and joy to me, because I am one of these, and my enemies will be driven off from the Entourage; I am a follower of Re who has received his firmament. I have come to you, my father Re; I have travelled in the air, I have summoned this Great Goddess, I have adorned the god of Authority, I have passed by that Destructive One who is in the road to Re, and it is well with me. I have reached this Old One who is at the limits of the horizon, whom I have driven off. I take possession of the Great Goddess, I lift up your soul when you have become strong, and my soul is in the dread of you and the awe of you; I am he who enforces the commands of Re in the sky.

Hail to you, Great God in the east of the sky! I go aboard your Bark, O Re; I pass by as a divine falcon, I give orders, I smite with my sceptre and govern with my staff. I go aboard your Bark, O Re, in peace; I navigate in peace to the beautiful West, and Atum speaks to me.

THE REMAINDER OF THIS SPELL IS TOO CORRUPT TO YIELD AN INTELLIGIBLE TEXT.

*Horemheb adores the Gods of the Caverns, three of whom stand with was-sceptres, while the others squat with feathers on their heads (Spell 127).* 10257/14

## —— SPELL 132 ——
[illustrated p.124]

*Spell for causing a man to turn about in order to see his house upon earth*

I am the Lion who went out with a bow, I have shot and I have ... The Eye of Horus belongs to me, I have opened the Eye of Horus at this time, I have reached the riverbank.

Come in peace, O N.

## —— SPELL 133 ——
[illustrated p.125]

*Writing for making a spirit worthy; to be recited on the first of the month*

Re appears in his horizon, his Ennead following after him; the god issues from the secret place, and trembling falls on the eastern horizon of the sky at the voice of Nut; she clears the ways for Re before the Oldest One, who turns about. Raise yourself, O Re who are in your shrine, that you may lap up the breezes. May you swallow the north wind, may you swallow the spine, may you entrap the day, may you kiss Maat, may you divide your suite, may you sail the Sacred Bark to the Lower Sky, may the Elders run to and fro at your voice; may

*Spell 128 Hor stands pulling on a djed-pillar before Osiris, Isis, Nephthys and the falcon-headed Horus, who wears the Double Crown. Isis, Nephthys and Horus carry a was-sceptre and a kerchief. 10479/9*

you reckon up your bones, may you gather your members together, may you turn your face to the beautiful West, may you return anew every day, for you are that golden image which bears the likeness of the sun-disc, the sky being possessed with trembling at your recurrence every day. The horizon is joyful, and there is acclamation within your bounds.

As for the gods who are in the sky who behold N, they have offered up praise as though to Re, for N is a great one who seeks out the Wereret-crown of Re and reckons up his needs; N is one alone whose affairs flourish in that first company of those who are in the presence of Re; N is hale on earth and in the realm of the dead, N is hale like Re every day, N will run and will not tire in this land for ever. How happy are those who see with their eyes and who hear truth with their ears as Re and who ply the oar in the suite of Nun! N will not tell what he has seen nor will he repeat what he has heard of the secret matters, and there is acclamation for N. The god's body of Re crosses the Abyss among those who propitiate the will of the god with what he has desired, and N is a falcon whose shape is great.

*To be spoken over a Sacred Bark of four cubits' length made of pieces of malachite, and having upon it the* tribunal of the nomes. There shall be made a sky with stars purified with natron and incense. Make an image of Re with ochre in a new bowl placed in front of this bark, and put an image of this spirit which you desire to be made worthy within this bark; it means that he will sail in the Bark of Re, and that Re himself will see him in it. This spirit will be deemed worthy in the heart of Re, he will be caused to have power over the Ennead, and they will be with him; the gods will see him as one of themselves, the dead will see him, and they will fall on their faces when he is seen in the realm of the dead by means of the rays of the sun.*

—— SPELL 134 ——
[illustrated p.125]

*Another spell for making a spirit worthy*

Hail to Him who dwells in his shrine, who rises and shines, who imprisons myriads at his will and who gives commands to the sun-folk, Khepri who dwells in his Bark, for he has felled *Apep*. It is the children of Geb who will fell you, you enemies of N, who would demolish the Bark of Re. Horus has cut off their heads in the sky like birds, and their goat-buttocks are in the Lake of Fish. As for any male or female adversary who would do harm to N, whether he is one who shall descend from the sky or ascend from the earth, who shall come by water or travel in company with the stars, Thoth the son of an eggshell who came out of the two eggshells shall decapitate them. Be dumb, be deaf before N! This is Re, this god mightily terrible and greatly majestic; he will bathe in your blood, he will drink of your gore, O you who would do much harm to N in the Bark of his father Re. N is Horus; his mother Isis bore him, Nephthys nursed him, just as they did for Horus, in order to drive away the confederacy of Seth, and they see the Wereret-crown firm-planted on his head. The spirits of men and gods and the spirits of the dead fall on their faces when they see N as Horus, with the Wereret-crown firm-planted on his head; they fall on their faces when N is triumphant over his enemies in the Upper Sky and the Lower Sky and in the tribunals of every god and every goddess.

*To be spoken over a falcon standing with the White Crown on his head; Atum, Shu and Tefnut, Geb and Nut, Osiris and Isis, Seth and Nephthys being drawn in ochre on a new bowl placed in the Sacred Bark, together with an image of this spirit whom you wish to be made worthy, it being anointed with oil. Offer to them incense on the fire and roasted ducks, and worship Re. It means that he for whom this is done will voyage and be with Re every day in every place he desires to travel, and it means that the enemies of Re will be driven off in very deed. A matter a million times true.*

—— SPELL 135 ——

*Another spell to be said* when the moon is new on the first day of the month.

Open, O cloudiness! The bleared Eye of Re is covered, and Horus proceeds happily every day, even he the great of shape and weighty of striking-power, who dispels bleariness of eye with his fiery breath. Behold, O Re, I have come voyaging, for I am one of these four gods who are at the side of the sky, and I show you Him who is present by day.

Make your cable fast, for there is no opposition to you.

*As for him who knows this spell,* he will be a worthy spirit in the realm of the dead, and he will not die again in the realm of the dead, and he will eat in the presence of Osiris. As for him who knows it on earth, he will be like Thoth, he will be worshipped by the living, he will not fall to the power of the king or the hot rage of Bastet, and he will proceed to a very happy old age.

**Spell 131** *Horemheb kneels in a boat adoring the falcon-headed Re, who wears a sun-disc and cobra on his head and squats within a large sun-disc holding a was-sceptre on his knee. 10257/15*

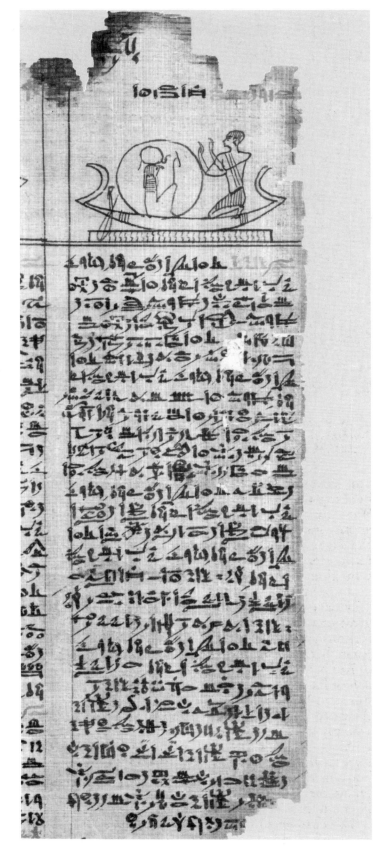

*Spell 132 Nebamun stands with a staff in hand before his earthly house, which is built of mud bricks. 9964/20*

*Spell 133 Nebseny stands in daily adoration before the falcon-headed Re, who is enthroned in his boat wearing a sun-disc, with a cobra on his head and carrying a was-sceptre. 9900/23*

*Spell 134 Nebseny prays with his daughter before a boat on whose prow perches a falcon with a flail and the White Crown. In the boat stand Shu, Tefnut, Geb, Nut, Osiris, Isis, Horus and Hathor. 9900/6*

## —— SPELL 136A ——
[illustrated pp.126-7]

*Another spell for making a spirit worthy on the Festival of the Sixth Day*

Behold the starry sky is in Heliopolis, and the sun-folk are in Kheraha. The god is born, his fillet is bound on, his oar is grasped, and N gives judgement with them in the lotus-bark at the dockyard of the gods; N takes over the bark in it which has lotus-flowers on its ends; N ascends to the sky, N sails in it to Nut, he sails in it with Re, he sails in it with apes, he repels the waves which are over yonder polar region of Nut at that stairway of Sebeg. Geb and Nut are happy, there is repeated the renewed and rejuvenated name of Wennefer, Re is his power, Wenti is what he is called: 'You are abundance, the greatest of the gods, widespread of sweet savour among all those who are not ignorant of you. Your war-shout is harsh, O swiftest of the Ennead, you being stronger, more besouled and more effective than the gods of Upper and Lower Egypt and their powers. May you grant that N be great and mighty in the sky just as you are greatest of the gods; may you save him from anything that those who hunt with yonder Adversary may do against him. May his heart be valiant, may you make N mightier than all the gods, the spirits and the dead.'

N is mighty, the Lord of Might; N is the master of righteousness, whom Wadjet made; N's protection is the protection of Re in the sky. May you permit N to pass into your Bark, O Re, in peace; prepare a path for N who navigates the Bark, for N's protection is its protection. N is he who daily drives off the aggressor against Re; N has come like Horus into the holy place of the horizon of the sky; N is he who makes Re known at

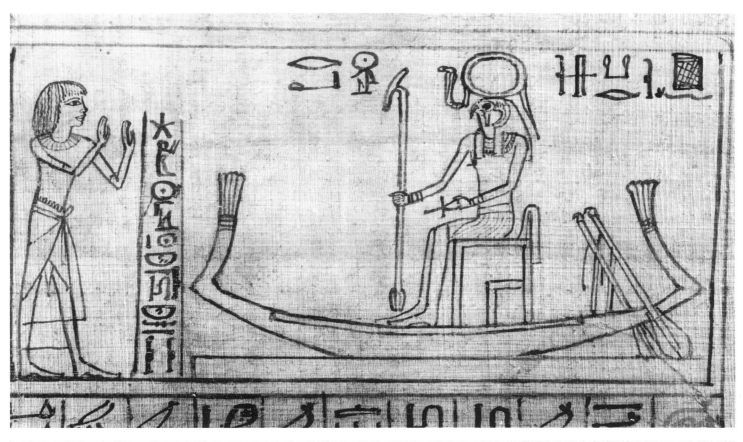

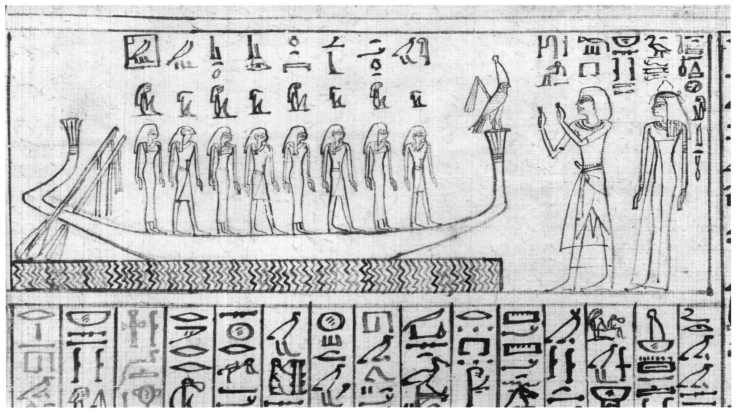

the gates, and the gods who meet N rejoice over him, for the greatness of a god is on N, the Destroyer will not attack him, the keepers of the gates will not ignore him. N is he whose face is hidden within the Great Mansion, even he the master of the god's shrine; N is he who despatches the words of the gods to Re; N has come that he may report business to its lord; N is stout of heart and weighty of action among those who prepare offerings.

*To be recited over an image of this spirit placed in this bark, you being cleansed, purified and censed in the presence of Re, with bread, beer, roast meat and ducks; it means that he will be conveyed in the Bark of Re. As for any spirit for whom this is done, he will be among the living, and he will never perish. He will be a holy god, and nothing evil shall ever harm him; he will be a potent spirit in the West, and he will not die again. He will eat and drink in the presence of Osiris every day; he will be admitted with the kings of Upper Egypt and the kings of Lower Egypt every day, he will drink water from the stream, he will go out into the day like Horus, he will live and be like a god, and he will be worshipped by the living like Re every day. A matter a million times true.*

*Spell 136A and B Atum, Hathor and three other enthroned deities, all holding was-sceptres, pull on ropes attached to a boat on whose prow squats Horus as a child. Nakht stands in the boat poling,*

## —— Spell 136b ——

*Spell for sailing in the Great Bark of Re and for passing over the circle of fire*

This is the fire which shines behind Re and which is concentrated behind him; the storm is afraid of the shining and splendid Bark of Re. I have come with Him whose face is wiped into his sacred lake, I have seen Him who attains to righteousness, who has fallen among those whose forms are holy, who are in sarcophagi; and the reed-dwellers are many. I have looked there, and we rejoice; their great ones are in joy and their little ones are in happiness. A path is made for me at the head of the Sacred Bark, and I am lifted up as the sun disc; I am bright in its sunshine ...

Down on your faces, you evil snakes! Let me pass, for I am a mighty one, Lord of the mighty ones; I am a noble of the Lord of Righteousness, whom Wadjet made. My protection is the protection of Re. See, I am he who went

*alongside a large falcon's head wearing a sun-disc. In the following boat, steered by Thoth, the falcon-headed sun-god sits enthroned behind the scarab-headed Khepri and Isis.* 10471/9

round about in the Field of Offerings of the Two Lands; a greater god than you, who reckons up his Enneads among those who give offerings.

## —— SPELL 137A ——
[illustrated p.128]

*Spell for four torches for the ceremonies which are carried out for a spirit. You shall make four basins of clay beaten up with incense and filled with milk of a white cow; the torches are to be quenched in them*

The torch comes to your ka, O Osiris, Foremost of the Westerners, and the torch comes to your ka, O N. There comes he who promises the night after the day; there come the two sisters of Re; there comes she who was manifested in Abydos, for I cause it to come, even that Eye of Horus which was foretold before you, O Osiris, Foremost of the Westerners. It is safe in your outer chamber, having appeared on your brow, for it was

foretold before you, O N, and it is safe on your brow.

The Eye of Horus is your protection, O Osiris, Foremost of the Westerners; it spreads its protection over you, it fells all your enemies for you, and your enemies have indeed fallen to you.

The Eye of Horus is your protection, O N, it spreads its protection over you, it fells all your enemies for you, and your enemies have indeed fallen to you.

To your ka, O Osiris, Foremost of the Westerners! The Eye of Horus is your protection; it spreads its protection over you, it fells all your enemies for you, and your enemies have indeed fallen to you.

To your ka, O N! The Eye of Horus is your protection; it spreads its protection over you, it fells all your enemies for you, and your enemies have indeed fallen to you.

The Eye of Horus comes intact and shining like Re in the horizon; it covers up the powers of Seth who would possess it, for it is he who would fetch it for himself, and it is hot against him when he is at the feet of the intact Eye of Horus. Eat the food of your body, possessing it, and worship it.

May the four torches go in to your ka, O Osiris, Foremost of the Westerners; may the four torches go in to your ka, O N. O you Children of Horus, Imsety,

*Spell 137A Four men carry torches towards a mummiform figure*
*before whom are set four prescribed basins.* 10477/26

Hapy, Duamutef, Qebehsenuef, as you spread your protection over your father Osiris, Foremost of the Westerners, so spread your protection over N as when you removed the impediment from Osiris, Foremost of the Westerners, so that he might live with the gods and drive Seth from him; as when at dawn Horus became strong that he himself might protect his father Osiris when wrong was done to your father when you drove Seth off.

To your ka, Osiris, Foremost of the Westerners! The Eye of Horus is your protector which spreads its protection over you; it fells all your enemies for you, and your enemies have indeed fallen to you. Remove the impediment from N that he may live with the gods; smite the enemies of N and protect N. At dawn may Horus become strong that he may protect N when wrong is done to N, and may you drive Seth off.

To your ka, N! The Eye of Horus is your protector, it fells all your enemies for you and your enemies have indeed fallen to you.

Osiris, Foremost of the Westerners, is he who causes a torch to be bright for the potent souls in Heracleopolis; may you make the living soul of N strong with his torch, so that he may not be repelled nor driven off from

*Spell 137в The hippopotamus-goddess Opet, Mistress of Protection,
sets fire to incense in a bowl on a tall stand. 9900/6*

the portals of the West. Then there will be brought in to him his bread, beer and clothing among the possessors of offerings; you will send up thanks for power, for N will be restored to his true shape, his true god-like form.

*To be spoken over four torches of red linen smeared with best quality Libyan oil in the hands of four men on whose arms are inscribed the names of the Children of Horus. They are to be lighted in broad daylight, in order to give this spirit power over the Imperishable Stars. As for him for whom this spell is recited, he will never perish, his soul shall live for ever, and this torch shall strengthen his spirit like Osiris, Foremost of the Westerners. A matter a million times true.*

*Beware greatly lest you do this before anyone except yourself, with your father or your son, because it is a great secret of the West, a secret image of the Netherworld, since the gods, spirits and dead see it as the shape of the Foremost of the Westerners. He will be mighty like this god, and you shall cause this spell of these four torches to be recited for him every day, so that his image shall be made to arrive at every gate of these seven gates of Osiris. It means being a god, having power in the company of the gods and spirits for ever and ever, and entering into the secret portals without his being turned away from*

*Osiris.* As for him for whom this is done, he shall go in and out without being turned away; he shall not be arrested or left out on the Day of Judgement when he who is detestable to Osiris will suffer. A true matter.

You shall recite this writing when this spirit is pure, made worthy and cleansed and when his mouth is opened with a wand of iron. This text was copied when it was found in writing by the king's son Hordedef, being what he found in a secret chest written in the god's own hand in the temple of Wenut, Mistress of Wenut, when he was travelling upstream inspecting the temples in the fields and mounds of the gods. What is done is a secret of the Netherworld belonging to the Mysteries of the Netherworld, a secret image in the realm of the dead.

Left: **Spell 138** *Ast-wert adores Anubis, who reclines on a plinth before the emblem of the Thinite nome: a head-shaped container with plumes and a cobra on a pole. 10039/3*

Below: **Spell 140** *Horemheb kneels in adoration before Anubis, who reclines on a shrine-shaped pedestal with a kherep-sceptre. Behind, a kneeling god with arms upraised carries an udjat-eye on his head. 10257/16*

*Vignette incorrectly termed Spell 143 which illustrates Spells 141 and 142.* The two barks of the sun-god, the upper protected by an udjat-eye, are shown above ten deities, most of them members of the Heliopolitan Ennead. 10479/4

## SPELL 137B

[illustrated p.129]

*Spell for kindling a torch for N*

The bright Eye of Horus comes, the glorious Eye of Horus comes; welcome, O you who shine like Re in the horizon. It drives off the powers of Seth from upon the feet of Him who brings it. It is Seth who would take possession of it, but its heat is against him; the torch comes. When will it arrive? It comes now, traversing the sky behind Re on the hands of your two sisters, O Re. Live, live, O Eye of Horus within the Great Hall! Live, live, O Eye of Horus, for he is the Pillar-of-his-Mother priest.

## SPELL 138

[illustrated p.130]

*Spell for entering into Abydos and being in the suite of Osiris*

O you gods who are in Abydos, the whole and complete company, come joyfully to meet me and see my father Osiris whom I have recognised and from whom I have come forth. I am this Horus, Lord of the Black Land and of the Red Land, I have taken possession entirely of Him who cannot be conquered, whose Eye is victorious over his enemies, who protects his father who is saved from the floodwaters and also his mother; who smites his enemies, who drives away the robber thereby, who counters the strength of the Destructive One; ruler of multitudes, monarch of the Two Lands, who smoothly takes possession of his father's house. I have been judged and I have been vindicated, I have power over my enemies, I get the better of those who would harm me, my strength is my protection. I am the son of Osiris, my father is in his own place, his body is in ...

## SPELL 140

[illustrated p.130]

*Book to be recited in the second month of winter, last day, when completing* the Sacred Eye in the second month of winter, last day

The Mighty One appears, the horizon shines, Atum appears on the smell of his censing, the Sunshine-god has risen in the sky, the Mansion of the Pyramidion is in joy and all its inmates are assembled, a voice calls out within the shrine, shouting reverberates around the Netherworld, obeisance is done at the utterance of Atum-Horakhty. His Majesty gives a command to the Ennead

attendant on His Majesty, for His Majesty is happy in contemplating the Sacred Eye: 'Behold my body to which protection has been given and all my members have been made to flourish.' His Majesty's utterance goes forth, his Eye rests in its place upon His Majesty in this fourth hour of the night, and the land is happy in the second month of winter, last day. The Majesty of the Sacred Eye is in front of the Ennead, His Majesty shines as on the First Occasion and the Sacred Eye is in his head; Re, Atum, the Sacred Eye, Shu, Geb, Osiris, Seth and Horus, Mont, Bah, Re the Everlasting, Thoth who travels eternity, Nut, Isis, Nephthys, Hathor the victorious, the two Songstress-goddesses, Maat, Anubis of the land, born of eternity, and the Soul of Mendes: when the Sacred Eye *has been reckoned* up in the presence of the Lord of this land, and it stands complete and content, these gods are joyful on this day; their hands support it and the festival of all the gods is celebrated. They say:

Hail to you and praise to Re! The crew navigate the Sacred Bark and *Apep* is felled.

Hail to you and praise to Re! The shape of Khepri has been brought into being.

Hail to you and praise to Re! Rejoice over him, for his enemies have been driven off.

Hail to you and praise to Re! The heads of the *Children of Impotence* have been removed.

Worship to you and praise to N!

*To be spoken over* a Sacred Eye of real lapis-lazuli or cornelian, decorated with gold; there shall be offered to it everything good and pure before it when Re shows himself in the second month, last day; and there shall be made another Sacred Eye of red jasper which is to be placed for a man on every member which he wishes. He who utters this spell will be in the Bark of Re when it is taken out with these gods, and he will be like one of them, he will be raised up in the realm of the dead.

As for him who utters this spell, *also the offerings* when the Sacred Eye is complete: *four braziers* for the Sacred Eye and *four* for Re-Atum; *four braziers* for the Sacred Eye and *four* for these gods, *each one of them* ; five good loaves of white bread, five cones of incense, five thin flat biscuits, one basket of incense, one basket of fruit and one of roast meat.

## SPELL 141

[illustrated p.131]

*Book which a man should recite for his father and son: it is an utterance for the festivals of the West. It means that he will be deemed worthy by Re and by the gods and that he will be with them. To be spoken on the day of the Festival of the New Moon.*

An offering of bread and beer, oxen and fowl, roast meat and incense on the fire to Osiris, Foremost of the Westerners; to Re-Horakhty; to Nun; to Maat; to the Bark of Re; to Atum; to the Great Ennead; to the Lesser Ennead; to Horus, Lord of the Wereret-crown; to Shu; to Tefnut; to Geb; to Nut; to Isis; to Nephthys; to the Mansion of Kas, the Mistress of All; to the Storm in the sky which bears the god aloft; to the Silent Land and Her who dwells in its place; to Her of Chemmis, the noble divine Lady; to Her who is greatly beloved, the red-haired; to Her who protects in life, the particoloured; to Her whose name has power in her craft; to the Bull, the male of the herd; to the Good Power, the good steering-oar of the northern sky; to the Wanderer who guides the Two Lands, the good steering-oar of the western sky; to the Sunshine-god who dwells in the Mansion of Images, the good steering-oar of the eastern sky; to Him who dwells in the Mansion of the Red Ones, the good steering-oar of the southern sky; to Imsety; to Hapy; to Duamutef; to Qebehsenuef; to the Southern Conclave; to the Northern Conclave; to the Night-bark; to the Day-bark; to Thoth; to the Southern Gods; to the Northern Gods; to the Western Gods; to the Eastern Gods; to the Squatting Gods; to the Gods of the Offerings; to the Per-wer; to the Per-neser; to the Gods of the Mounds; to the Gods of the Horizon; to the Gods of the Fields; to the Gods of the Houses; to the Gods of the Thrones; to the Southern Roads; to the Northern Roads; to the Eastern Roads; to the Western Roads; to the Gates of the Netherworld; to the Portals of the Netherworld; to the Secret Doors; to the Secret Gates; to the Keepers of the Doors of the Netherworld; to Those with hidden faces who guard the roads; to the Guardians of those who utter cries; to the Guardians of the Deserts who display kindly faces; to Those of the heat who give fire; to Those of the braziers; to Those who open up and quench the flame of fire in the West.

# —— SPELL 144 ——
[illustrated pp.134-5]

*The first gate.* 'He whose face is inverted, the many-shaped' is the name of the keeper of the first gate; 'Eavesdropper' is the name of him who guards it; 'The loud-voiced' is the name of him who makes report in it.

*The second gate.* 'He whose hinder-parts are extended' is the name of the keeper of the second gate; 'Shifting of face' is the name of him who guards it; 'Burner' is the name of him who makes report in it.

*The third gate.* 'He who eats the corruption of his hinder-parts' is the name of the keeper of the third gate; 'Vigilant' is the name of him who guards it; 'He who curses' is the name of him who makes report in it.

*The fourth gate.* 'He who defends from the noisy' is the name of the keeper of the fourth gate; 'Wakeful' is the name of him who guards it; 'Grim of visage who repels the aggressor' is the name of him who makes report in it.

*The fifth gate.* 'He who lives on snakes' is the name of the keeper of the fifth gate; 'Fiery' is the name of him who guards it; 'Hippopotamus-faced, raging of power' is the name of him who makes report in it.

*The sixth gate.* 'The bread-shaper, the harsh-voiced' is the name of the keeper of the sixth gate; 'He who looks to and fro' is the name of him who guards it; 'Sharp of glance, warden of the Lake' is the name of him who makes report in it.

*The seventh gate.* 'He who cuts them down' is the name of the keeper of the seventh gate; 'Loud-voiced' is the name of him who guards it; 'He who defends from those who would work harm' is the name of him who makes report in it.

O you gates, O you who keep the gates because of Osiris, O you who guard them and who report the affairs of the Two Lands to Osiris every day: I know you and I know your names; I was born in Rosetjau, and the power of the Lord of the horizon was given to me. I was ennobled in Pe like the priest of Osiris; I receive food in Rosetjau and lead the gods in the horizon in the entourage about Osiris; I am one of them as one who leads them. I am a spirit, a master of spirits, a spirit who acts. I am one who celebrates the monthly festival and announces the half-monthly festival, I go round about bearing the fiery Eye of Horus which the hand of Thoth bears on the night when he crosses the sky in vindication. I pass by in peace, I sail in the Bark of Re, and my protection is the protection of the Bark of Re. Mine is a name greater than yours, mightier than yours upon the road of righteousness; I detest any deduction, for my protection is the protection of Horus, the first-born of Re, whom his will created. I will not be arrested, I will not be driven off from the gates of Osiris, I am he who equips the Double Lion, one who is purified daily in the suite of Osiris, Foremost of the Westerners. My lands are in the Field of Offerings among the wise ones, among those who serve me in the presence of Thoth and among those who make offerings. Anubis has commanded those who are among the offerings that my offerings shall be in my possession, and they shall not be taken from me by those who are among the plunderers.

I have come like Horus into the holy place of the horizon of the sky; I announce Re at the gates of the horizon, the gods are joyful at meeting me, and the costly stones of the gods are on me. The Destructive One shall not attack me, and those who keep their gates shall not be ignorant of me. I am one whose face is hidden within the Great Mansion, the Upper Place, the shrine of

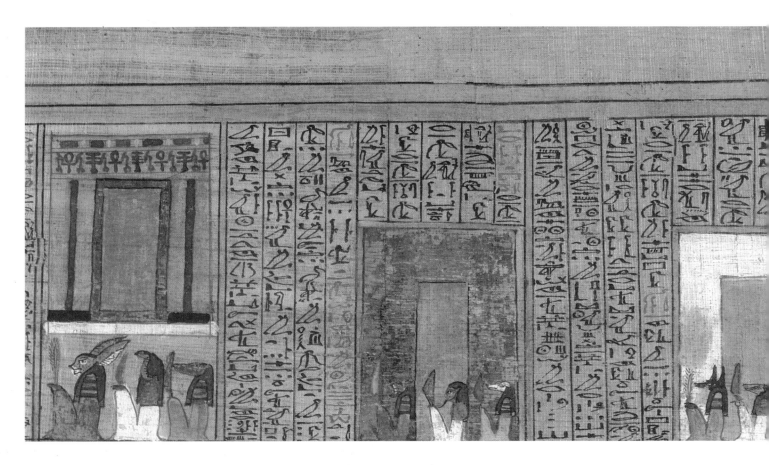

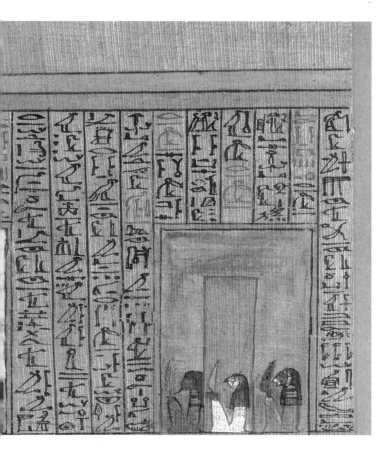

the god, and I have reached there after the purification of Hathor. I am one who creates a multitude, who raises up Truth to Re and who destroys the might of *Apep*; I am one who opens up the firmament, who drives off the storm, who makes the crew of Re alive, and who raises up offerings to the place where they are. I have caused the Sacred Bark to make its fair voyages; a way is prepared for me that I may pass on it. My face is that of a Great One, my hinder-parts are the Double Crown, I am a possessor of power, I am content in the horizon, and I am joyful at felling you. O you who are awake, prepare a path for your lord Osiris.

*To be recited over these directions which are in writing, and which are to be inscribed in ochre with the two companies of the Bark of Re. Offer to them foodstuffs, poultry and incense in their presence. It means that a spirit will be made to live and be given power over these gods; it means that he will not be driven off or turned away at the portals of the Netherworld. You shall make recitation over an image of this spirit in their presence, and he will be permitted to arrive at every gate according to what is written. Make recitation at every gate in accordance with what is written, and make offering to each of them with a foreleg, head, heart and side of a red bull and four bowls of blood, not leaving out a heart of costly stone; sixteen white loaves, eight persencakes, eighteen shens-cakes, eight khenef-loaves, eight hebnenet-loaves, eight measures of beer, eight bowls of grain, four clay basins filled with milk of a white cow, green herbs, fresh moringa-oil, green and black eye-paint, first quality unguent and incense on the fire. To be recited and erased, item by item, after reciting these directions, four hours of the day having passed, and taking great care as to the position (of the sun) in the sky. You shall recite this book without letting anyone see it; it means that the movements of a spirit will be extended in the sky, on earth and in the realm of the dead, because it will be more beneficial to a spirit than anything which is done for him, and what is needed will be at hand this day. A matter a million times true.*

## —— SPELL 146 ——
[illustrated pp.138-9]

*Here begin the spells for entering by the mysterious portals of the House of Osiris in the Field of Rushes*

*What is to be said by N when arriving at the first portal of Osiris.* Make a way for me, for I know you, I know

*Left above and left:* **Spell 144** *The Seven Gates of the Underworld, each addressed individually and accompanied by its keeper, guard and announcer, shown as squatting figures with knives on their knees.* 10470/11 and 12

your name, and I know the name of the god who guards you. 'Mistress of trembling; Lofty of battlements; Chieftainess; Mistress of destruction; One who foretells matters, who repels storms and who rescues the robbed among those who come from afar' is your name. 'Terrible' is the name of her Door-keeper.

*What is to be said by N when arriving at the second portal of Osiris.* Make a way for me, for I know you, I know your name, and I know the name of the god who guards you. 'Mistress of the sky; Lady of the Two Lands; She who licks (her calves); Mistress of the world who numbers all men' is your name. 'He who fashions the end' is the name of her door-keeper.

*What is to be said by N when arriving at the third portal of Osiris.* Make a way for me, for I know you, I know your name, and I know the name of the god who guards you. 'Mistress of altars, great of oblations, who pleases every god therewith on the day of faring upstream to Abydos' is your name. 'He who makes brightness' is the name of her door-keeper.

*What is to be said by N when arriving at the fourth portal of Osiris.* Make a way for me, for I know you, I know your name, and I know the name of the god who guards you. 'Mighty of knives; Lady of the Two Lands, who destroys the enemies of the Inert One, who does what is wise and who is devoid of wrong' is your name. 'Long-horned Bull' is the name of her door-keeper.

*What is to be said by N when arriving at the fifth portal of Osiris.* Make a way for me, for I know you, I know your name, and I know the name of the god who guards you. 'Fiery One, Mistress of heat; Joyful One who asks that something be given to her without the swift of glance entering into her' is your name. 'He who cuts up an opponent' is the name of her door-keeper.

*What is to be said by N when arriving at the sixth portal of Osiris.* Make a way for me, for I know you, I know your name, and I know the name of the god who guards you. 'Mistress of Darkness, loud of shouts; its height cannot be known from its breadth, and its extent in space cannot be discovered. Snakes are on it, of which the number is not known; it was fashioned before the Inert One' is your name. "He who was joined together' is the name of her door-keeper.

*What is to be said by N when arriving at the seventh portal of Osiris.* Make a way for me, for I know you, I know your name and I know the name of the god who guards you. 'Shroud which veils the Limp One; Mourner who wishes to hide the body' is your name. 'Ikenty' is the name of her door-keeper.

*What is to be said by N when arriving at the eighth portal of Osiris.* Make a way for me, for I know you, I know your name, and I know the name of the god who guards you. 'Hot of flames, destructive of heat, sharp of blaze, swift of hand, who kills without warning, whom

none pass by for fear of her pain' is your name. 'He who protects himself' is the name of her door-keeper.

*What is to be said by N when arriving at the ninth portal of Osiris.* Make a way for me, for I know you, I know your name, and I know the name of the god who guards you. 'She who is at the forefront; Mistress of power; Contented of heart, who bore her lord. Its circuit is 350 rods, strewn with green-stone of Upper Egypt. She who raises the secret image on high, who veils the Limp One, who pleases her lord daily' is your name. 'Himself' is the name of her door-keeper.

*What is to be said by N when arriving at the tenth portal of Osiris.* Make a way for me, for I know you, I know your name, and I know the name of the god who guards you. 'Loud-voiced whose cries arouse, who calls at the top of her voice, terrible and majestic, but who does not drive out whoever is in her' is your name. 'The Great User of reed rafts' is the name of her door-keeper.

*What is to be said by N when arriving at the eleventh portal of Osiris.* Make a way for me, for I know you, I know your name, and I know who is within you. 'She who always bears knives, who burns up the rebellious; Mistress of every portal, to whom acclamation is made on the day of darkness' is your name. She is under the supervision of Him who veils the Limp One.

*What is to be said by N when arriving at the twelfth portal of Osiris.* Make a way for me, for I know you, I know your name, and I know who is within you. 'She who summons her Two Lands, who destroys those who come at dawn; Bright One; Mistress of spirits, who hears the voice of her lord' is your name. She is under the supervision of Him who veils the Limp One.

*What is to be said by N when arriving at the thirteenth portal of Osiris.* Make a way for me, for I know you, I know your name, and I know who is within you. 'She on whom Osiris has extended his hands, who illumines Hapi in his abode' is your name. She is under the supervision of Him who veils the Limp One.

*What is to be said by N when arriving at the fourteenth portal of Osiris.* Make a way for me, for I know you, I know your name, and I know who is within you. 'Mistress of wrath, who dances in blood, for whom the haker-festival is celebrated on the day of Her who hears sins' is your name. She is under the supervision of Him who veils the Limp One.

The fifteenth portal. 'She who has a soul, red of plaited hair, dim-eyed when going out by night, who grasps the rebel by his belly, who gives her hand to the Inert One at his critical moment, who makes her comings and goings.' She is under the supervision of Him who veils the Limp One.

The sixteenth portal. What is to be said by N when arriving at this portal. 'The Terrible One, Lady of Pestilence, who casts away thousands of human souls, who

136

hacks up human dead, who decapitates him who would go out, who creates terror.' She is under the supervision of Him who veils the Limp One.

The seventeenth portal. 'She who dances in blood ... Mistress of Fire.' She is under the supervision of Him who veils the Limp One.

What is to be said by N when arriving at the eighteenth portal. 'Lover of heat, clean of brand-mark, who loves to cut off heads; the venerated Mistress of the Castle, who quells rebels in the evening.' She is under the supervision of Him who veils the Limp One.

What is to be said by N when arriving at the nineteenth portal. 'She who announces the dawn in her time, flaming hot, Mistress of the powers of the writings of Thoth himself.' She is under the supervision of the veiled ones of the treasury.

What is to be said by N when arriving at the twentieth portal. 'She who is within the cavern of her lord; She whose name is hidden; Mysterious of shape, who takes hearts for food.' She is under the supervision of the veiled ones of the treasury.

What is to be said by N when arriving at the twenty-first portal. 'Sharp of knife against the talker, who acts the slayer, who descends in her own flame.' She is under secret governance.

## —— SPELL 148 ——
[illustrated pp.142,143]

*Spell for making provision for a spirit in the realm of the dead*

Hail to you, You who shine in your disc, a living soul who goes up from the horizon! I know you and I know your name; I know the names of the seven cows and their bull who give bread and beer, who are beneficial to souls and who provide daily portions; may you give bread and beer and make provision for me, so that I may serve you, and may I come into being under your hinder-parts.

THE NAMES OF THE CATTLE ARE:

Mansion of Kas, Mistress of All.
Silent One who dwells in her place
She of Chemmis whom the god ennobled.
The Much Beloved, red of hair.
She who protects in life, the particoloured.
She whose name has power in her craft.
Storm in the sky which wafts the god aloft.
The Bull, husband of the cows.

May you grant bread and beer, offerings and provisions which shall provide for my spirit, for I am a worthy spirit who is in the realm of the dead.

THE NAMES OF THE FOUR STEARING-OARS OF THE SKY:

O Good Power, the good steering-oar of the northern sky;
O Wanderer who guides the Two Lands, good steering-oar of the western sky;
O Shining One who dwells in the Mansion of Images, good steering-oar of the eastern sky;
O Pre-eminent who dwells in the Mansion of the Red Ones, good steering-oar of the southern sky;

May you grant bread and beer, offerings and provisions which are beneficial to my spirit, may you grant me life, prosperity, health, joy and long duration on earth; may you grant to me sky and earth and what is beneficial in Heliopolis and the Netherworld, for I know them all; may you do the like for me.

O fathers of the gods and mothers of the gods who are over sky and earth and who are in the realm of the dead, save me from all kinds of harm and injury, from the trap with painful knives and from all things bad and harmful which may be said or done against me by men, gods, spirits or the dead, by day, by night, in the monthly festival, in the half-monthly festival, in the year or in what appertains to it.

*To be spoken by a man, when Re manifests himself, over these gods depicted in paint on a writing-board. There shall be given to them offerings and provisions before them, consisting of bread, beer, meat, poultry and incense. The invocation-offering for this spirit shall be made to them in the presence of Re; it means that this soul will have provision in the realm of the dead; it means that a man will be saved from anything evil. Do nothing on behalf of anyone except your own self, for it is the Book of Wennefer. As for him for whom this is done, Re will be his helmsman and his protection, and none of his enemies will know him in the realm of the dead, in the sky, on earth, or in any place where he may walk; it means that this spirit will be provisioned in very deed. A true matter.*

## —— SPELL 149 ——
[illustrated pp.140-1]

The first mound; green. *N says:* As for this Mound of the West in which men live on shens-loaves and jugs of beer, doff your head-cloths at meeting me as at the likeness of the greatest among you. May he knit my bones together, may he make my members firm. May the Sistrum-player, Lord of Hearts, be brought to me that he may shape my bones and establish the Wereret-crown of Atum. Make my head firm for me, O Bestower of Powers; complete and make firm my spine, that you may rule among the gods, O Min the Builder.

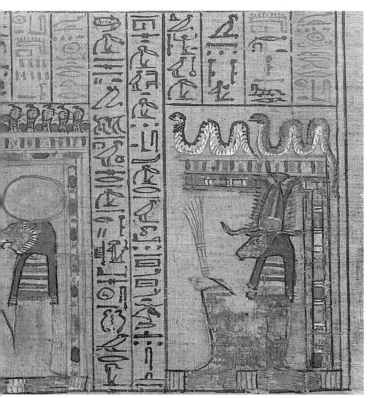

The second mound; green. The god who is in it is Re-Horakhty. *N says:* I am one rich in possessions in the Field of Rushes. As for this Field of Rushes, its walls are of iron, the height of its barley is five cubits, its ear is two cubits and its stalk is three cubits. Its emmer is seven cubits, its ear is three cubits and its stalk is four cubits. They are spirits, each nine cubits tall, who reap it in the presence of Re-Horakhty. I know the gate in the middle of the Field of Rushes from which Re goes out into the east of the sky, of which the south is the Lake of Water-fowl and the north is the Waters of Geese, the place where Re navigates by wind or by rowing. I am the whip-master in the God's Ship, I row and never tire in the Bark of Re. I know those two trees of turquoise between which Re goes forth, and which have grown up at the Supports of Shu at that door of the Lord of the East from which Re goes forth. I know that Field of Rushes which belongs to Re; the height of its barley is five cubits, its ear is two cubits and its stalk is three cubits. Its emmer is seven cubits, its ear is three cubits and its stalk is four cubits. They are spirits nine cubits tall who reap it in the presence of the Souls of the East.

The third mound; green. The Mound of Spirits. *N says:* As for the Mound of Spirits over which none travel, it contains spirits, and its flame is efficient for burning. As for the Mound of Spirits whose faces are downcast, cleanse your mounds, being what it was commanded that you should do for me by Osiris, Lord of Eternity, for I am a Great One. The Red Crown which is between the horns of the Sunshine-god makes the whole world to live with the flame of its mouth, and Re is saved from *Apep.*

The fourth mound; green. The very high twin mountains. *N says:* As for the Chief of the mysterious mound, as for the very high mountain which is in the realm of the dead, on which the sky rests, it is 300 rods long by 150 rods wide; a snake is on it called 'Caster of knives', and it is 70 cubits when it glides; it lives by decapitating the spirits of the dead in the realm of the dead. I rise up against you (the snake), so that navigation may be carried out aright; I have seen the way to you, and I will gather myself together against you, for I am the Male. Cover your head, for I am hale, hale, I am one mighty of magic and my eyes have caused me to benefit therefrom. Who is this spirit who goes on his belly and whose tail is on his mountain? See, I have gone against you, and your tail is in my hand. I am one who displays strength; I have come that I may care for the earth-snakes of Re, so that he will be pleased with me in the evening. I circumambulate the sky, while you are in

Left above and left: *Spell 146 Nine of the Twenty-one Portals of the House of Osiris, each addressed individually and shown as an elaborate entrance containing the squatting figure of its door-keeper.* 10470/11 *and* 12

139

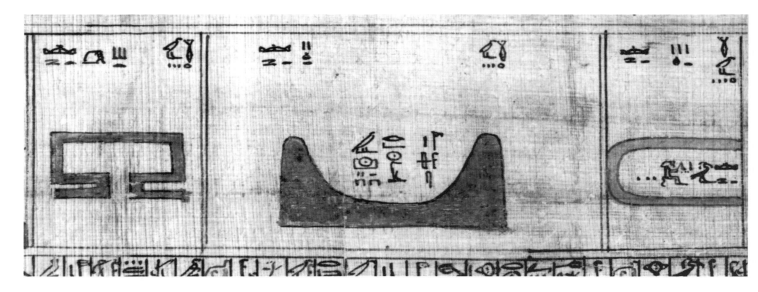

bonds; that is what was commanded for you upon earth.

The fifth mound; green. *N says:* As for this Mound of Spirits by which men do not pass, the spirits who are in it are seven cubits from their buttocks, and they live on the shades of the inert ones. As for the Mound of Spirits, open your roads for me until I pass by you when I travel to the beautiful West; that is what was commanded by Osiris, a spirit and master of spirits, so that I might live by my magic power. I am one who celebrates exactly every monthly festival and half-monthly festival; the Eye of Horus which my hand holds goes round about for me in the suite of Thoth. As for any god or any dead who shall lick his lips over me this day, he shall fall into the depths.

The sixth mound; green. *N says:* As for this cavern sacred to the gods, secret from spirits and inaccessible to the dead, the god who is in it is called 'Feller of the adju-fish'. Hail to you, you cavern! I have come to see the gods who are in you. Clear your vision, doff your head-cloths when meeting me as at the likeness of the greatest among you. I have come to prepare your flat cakes, and the Feller of the adju-fish shall not have power over me, the slayers shall not pursue me, the adversaries shall not pursue me, and I shall live on the offerings which are with you.

*Spell 149 The three details show the fourteen mounds of the Field of Rushes represented pictorially and named. Eleven of them are termed 'green', the remainder 'yellow'. The sixth (below) contains an eel-like fish, the ninth a crocodile nuzzling a jar-shaped area, the tenth a cobra over a man brandishing knives and the eleventh a jackal-headed demon with knives inside a stepped area. 10477/28, 29 and 30*

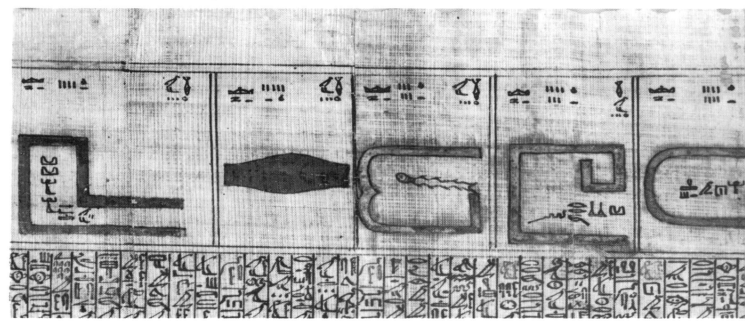

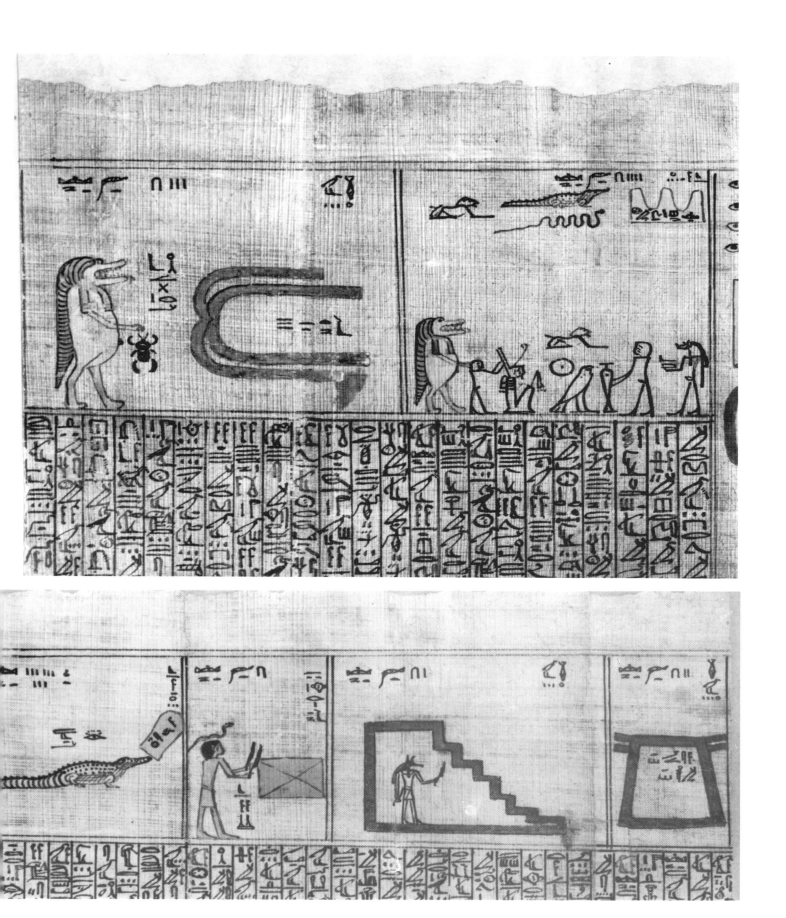

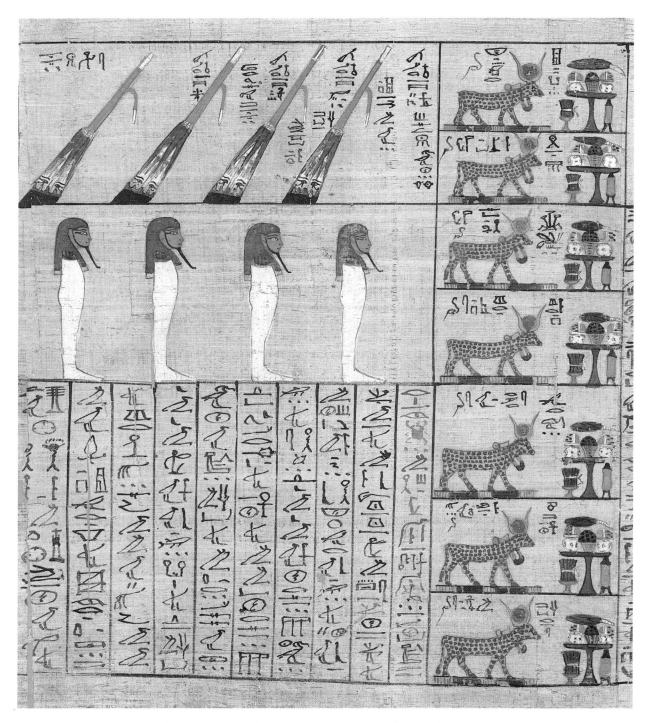

Above: **Spell 148:** *The Seven Celestial Cows, who, together with the Bull of Heaven (not illustrated), provide sustenance for the deceased, stand behind heaped offering-tables. Behind them are the Four Rudders of Heaven, which represent the four cardinal points, and four mummiform figures. 10471/9*

Right: **Spell 148** *The Seven Celestial Cows recline on shrine-shaped plinths with the standing Bull of Heaven. Behind them are the Four Rudders of Heaven which represent the four cardinal points, each protected by an udjat-eye, and the Four Sons of Horus. 10479/3*

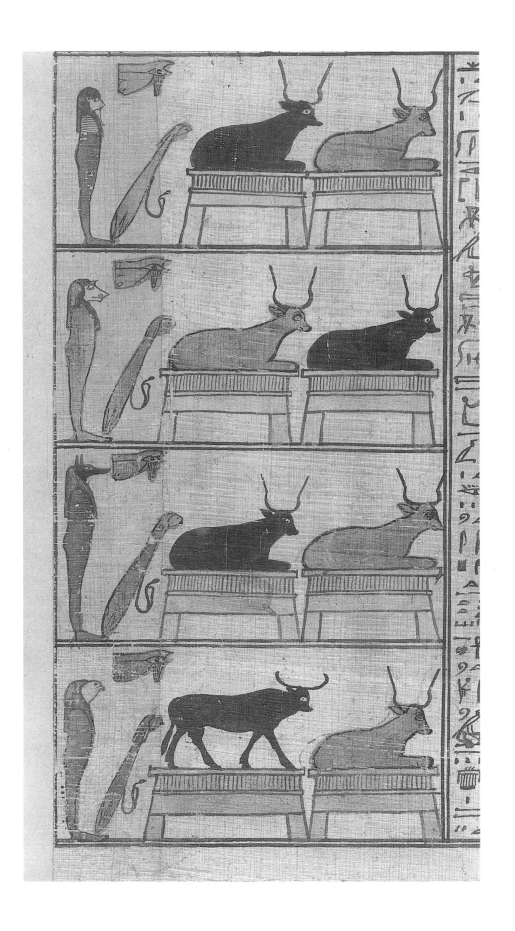

The seventh mound; green. The Mountain of the Rerek-snake. *N says:* As for this town of Ises, which is far out of sight, its breath is fire, and a snake in it is called 'Rerek'. It is seven cubits long over its back, and it lives on spirits, being provided with their power. Get back, Rerek in Ises, biting with your mouth and staring with your eyes! May your bones be broken, may your poison be powerless, for you shall not come against me, your poison shall not enter into me. Fall! Lie down! May your hot rage be in the ground, may your lips remain in the hole! The bull falls to the snake and the snake falls to the bull, but I am protected, for your head is cut off by Mafdet.

The eighth mound; green. The height Hahotep. *N says:* As for Hahotep, great and mighty, with waves over the water in which none have power, because so great is the terror of the height of its roar, the god in it is called 'High One of Hahotep'; it is he who guards it in order that none may come near it. I am this heron which is over the plateau which is not quiet, I bring the produce of the land to Atum at the time of enriching the crews of the gods. The terror of me has been put into those who are in charge of shrines, and the awe of me has been impressed on the owners of offerings. I will not be taken to the house of the Destroyer, which they desire for me, for I am the guide of the northern horizon.

The ninth mound; yellow. Ikesy-town and the Eye which captures. *N says:* As for Ikesy, which is hidden from the gods, of which the spirits are afraid to learn the name, from which none go in or out except that august god who is in his Egg, who puts the fear of him into the gods and the dread of him into the spirits: it opens with fire, and its breath is destruction to noses and mouths. He has made it against those who follow after him in order that they may not breathe the air except that august god who is in his Egg. He has done it against those who are in it in order that none may come near it except on the day of the great celebration. Hail to you, you august god who are in your Egg! I have come to you to be in your suite so that I may go in and out of Ikesy, that its doors may be opened to me, that I may breathe the air in it, and that I may have power through its offerings.

The tenth mound, which is on the plateau; yellow. *N says:* As for this town of Qahu which has taken possession of the spirits and which has power over the shades who eat what is fresh and gulp down corruption on account of what their eyes see, and who do not watch over the land, who are in their mounds: Put yourselves on your bellies until I have passed by you; no-one shall take my spirit, no-one shall have power over my shade, for I am a divine falcon and incense shall be burnt for me, offerings shall be presented to me, with Isis before me and Nephthys behind me; the road of the nau-snake, the bull of the sky, the bestower of powers, shall be cleared for me. I have come to you, you gods; save me and give me my powers for ever.

The eleventh mound; green. *N says:* As for that town which is in the realm of the dead, the body of which is secret, which has power over spirits from which none come out or go in through fear of revealing what is in it: The gods with him (its god) see it as a marvel, the dead with him see it in dread of him, except for those gods who are with him in his mystery as regards the spirits. O Idu-town, let me pass, for I am great of magic, with the knife which issued from Seth, and my legs are mine for ever. I have appeared in glory and am strong by means of that Eye of Horus which lifted up my heart after I was limp. One powerful in the sky and mighty on earth, I have flown up as a falcon, I have cackled as a goose, it has been granted to me to alight on the plateau of the lake, so that I stand on it and sit on it. I have appeared as a god, I have eaten of the provisions of Him of the Field of Offerings, I have gone down to the Bank of Reeds, I have opened the doors of Maat, I have thrown open the doors of the firmament, I have set up a ladder to the sky among the gods, for I am one of them. I have spoken as a goose until the gods have heard my voice, and I have made repetition for Sothis.

The twelfth mound; green. Isdjedet in the West. *N says:* As for that Mound of Wenet which is in front of Rosetjau, its breath is fire, and the gods cannot get near it, the spirits cannot associate with it; there are four cobras on it whose names are 'Destruction'. O Mound of Wenet, I am the greatest of the spirits who are in you, I am among the Imperishable Stars who are in you, and I will not perish, nor will my name perish. 'O savour of a god!' say the gods who are in the Mound of Wenet. If you love me more than your gods, I will be with you for ever.

The thirteenth mound; green. He who opens his mouth, a basin of water. *N says:* As for that Mound of Spirits over which no-one has power, its water is fire, its waves are fire, its breath is efficient for burning, in order that no-one may drink its water to quench their thirst, that being what is in them, because their fear is so great and so towering is its majesty. Gods and spirits see its water from afar, but they cannot quench their thirst and their desires are unsatisfied. In order that no-one may approach them, the river is filled with papyrus like the fluid in the efflux which issued from Osiris. May I have power over the water in the flood like that god who is in the Mound of Water. It is he who guards it from fear of the gods who would drink its water when it is removed from the spirits. Hail to you, you god in the Mound of Water! I have come to you that you may give me power over water and that I may drink of the flood, just as you did for that Great God for whom the Nile came, for whom herbage came into being, for whom green-stuff grew up when the same was given to the gods at his coming forth content. May you cause the Nile to come to me, may I have power over green-stuff, for I am your son for ever.

The fourteenth mound; yellow. The Mound of Kheraha. *N says:* As for that Mound of Kheraha which diverts the Nile to Busiris, which causes the Nile to come laden with barley, which guides it to the mouth of the eater, which gives god's-offerings to the gods and invocation-offerings to the spirits: The snake which belongs to it is in the caverns of Elephantine at the source of the Nile; it comes with the water and it halts at that plateau of Kheraha at its assembly which is above the flood in order that it may see in its hour in the silence of the night. O you gods of Kheraha, assembly which is above the flood, open your water-basins for me, throw open your waterways for me, that I may have power over water, that I may be satisfied with the flood, that I may eat grain, and that I may be satisfied with your provisions. Raise me up, that my heart may be happy, for you are the god who is in Kheraha. Your offerings shall be prepared for me, I shall be provided with the efflux which issued from Osiris, and I will never let go of it.

# —— SPELL 150 ——
[illustrated p.146]

## A SUMMARY LIST OF 'MOUNDS' WHICH DOES NOT ENTIRELY AGREE WITH SPELL 149

The Field of Rushes. The god who is in it is Re-Horakhty.
The Horns of Fire. The god who is in it is Lifter of Braziers.
The Very High Mountain.
The Mound of Spirits.
The Cavern. The god who is in it is Feller of Fish.
Iseset.
Hasret. The god who is in it is He who is on high.
The Horns of Qahu.
Idu. The god who is in it is Sothis.
The Mound of Wenet. The god who is in it is Destroyer of Souls.
The Horns of Water. The god who is in it is Greatest of the Mighty Ones.
The Mound of Kheraha. The god who is in it is the Nile.
The River of Flaming Fire.
Ikesy. The god who is in it is He who sees and takes.
The Beautiful West of the gods who live in it on shens-cakes and beer.

# —— SPELL 151 ——
[illustrated pp.146-7,148]

*Spell for the head of mystery*

*Hail* to you whose face is kindly, Lord of vision, one who is knit together for Ptah-Sokar and who is set on high for Anubis, to whom Shu has given the Supports, kindly face who is among the gods! Your right Eye is the Night-bark, your left Eye is the Day-bark, your eyebrows are the Ennead, your vertex is Anubis, the back of your head is Horus, your fingers are Thoth, your braided tress is Ptah-Sokar, and you are before N, who is happy with the Great God, whom he sees in you; lead him on fair roads that he may obstruct the confederacy of Seth for you, and make his enemies fall beneath him before the Great Ennead in the great Mansion of the Prince which is in Heliopolis. May you take a fair road into the presence of Horus, Lord of Patricians, O N.

Words spoken by Isis: I have come as your protection, O Osiris, with the north wind which issued from Atum. I have let your throat breathe, I have caused you to be a god, and I have placed your enemies under your sandals.

Words spoken by Nephthys: I have gone round about my brother Osiris N; I have come as your protection, and my protection will be about you for ever. Your call has been heard by Re, and vindication has been carried out for you, O son of Hathor, and your head will never be taken away. In peace! Arouse yourself!

FORMULA AT THE PRESENTATION OF A LIGHTED TORCH: O you who come to lasso, I will not let you lasso; O you who come to do harm, I will not let you do harm. I will harm you, I will lasso you, for I am N's protection.

THE PRESENTATION OF A DJED-PILLAR AMULET: O you who come seeking, reverse your steps; O you whose face is covered, I have illumined your covered place. I am he who stands behind the djed-pillar on the day when I should stand behind the djed-pillar, and I drive off the slayers, for I am N's protection.

ANOTHER PRESENTATION OF A TORCH: I am he who drags the sand to stop up the hidden place, I drive off him who would oppose himself to the torch of the necropolis. I have fired the necropolis, I have confused the path, for I am N's protection.

*Words spoken by* Anubis who presides over the god's booth, who is upon his mountain, Lord of the Sacred Land: I have come that I may spread my protection over N.

*Words spoken by* the living soul of N: I give praise in the sky to Re when he goes to rest in the western horizon of the sky.

*Words spoken by* the living soul and worthy spirit of N to Osiris. WHAT WAS TO HAVE BEEN SAID HAS BEEN OMITTED.

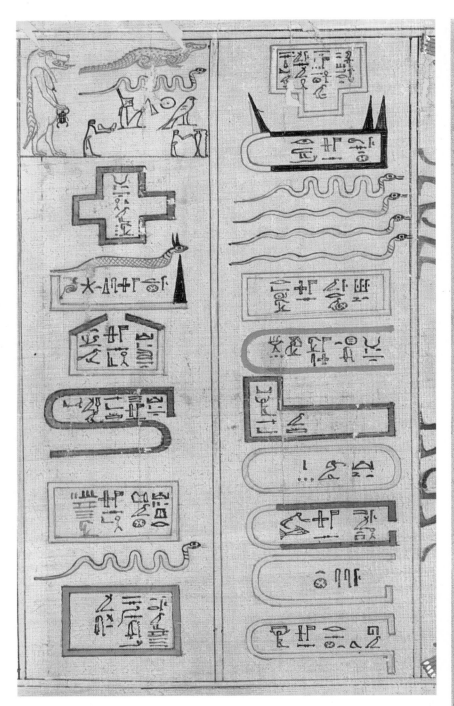

Above: **Spell 150** *A completely pictorial representation of the fifteen mounds of the Field of Rushes, named and attended by four snakes which perhaps represent the four cardinal points. 10009/1*

Right: **Spell 151** *A plan of the burial chamber represented as an elaborate booth, at the centre of which Anubis tends the mummy of Nakht, which lies on a lion-form bed, accompanied by Isis and Nephthys kneeling and holding signs of eternity. At each of the corners squats one of the Four Sons of Horus. Around the mummy, giving protection, are a djed-pillar, Anubis as a reclining jackal on a shrine and a squatting Thoth. 10471/20*

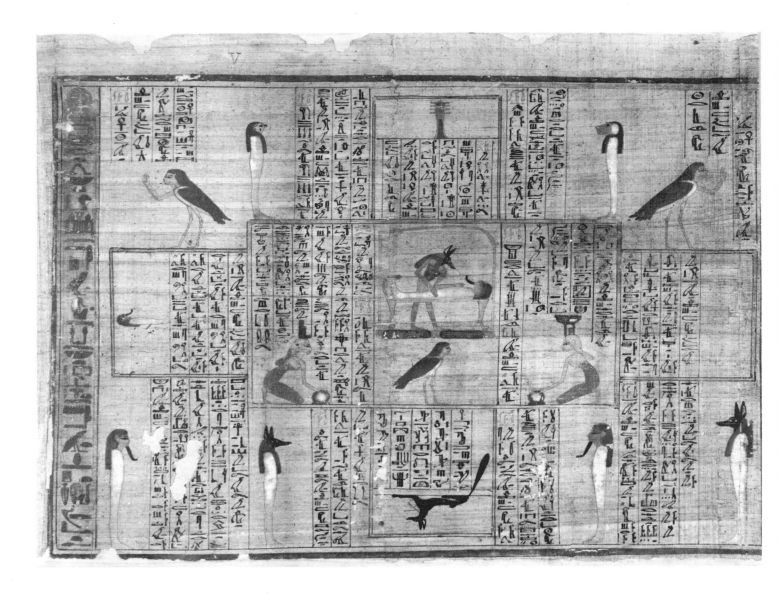

**Spell 151** *The burial chamber represented schematically with the mummy of Muthetepti at the centre lying in a booth attended by Anubis, with her human-headed soul nearby, while Isis and Nephthys kneel with shen-signs, symbolic of eternity. At each corner is one of the Four Sons of Horus and between them a djed-pillar, a lighted torch, a reclining jackal and a mummiform figurine, all giving protection. Also depicted are two shabti-figures, one with jackal's head, and Muthetepti's human-headed soul, shown twice, in adoration. 10010/5*

THE PRESENTATION OF A SHABTI. N says: O shabti, if I am summoned or counted of in the realm of the dead for any work, indeed obstacles are implanted there as a man at his duties, whether to make arable the fields, to flood the banks or to convey sand from West to East; 'Here am I,' you shall say.

*Words spoken by* Imsety: I am your son, O N. I have come that I may be your protection, and that I may make your house to flourish and endure, in accordance with the command of Ptah and in accordance with the command of Re.

*Words spoken by* Hapy: I have come that I may be your protection, O N: I have knit together your head and your members, I have smitten your enemies beneath you, and I have given you your head for ever.

*Words spoken by* Duamutef: I am your beloved son Horus, O N. I have come that I may protect my father Osiris from him who would harm you, and I lead him under your feet.

*Words spoken by* Qebehsenuef: I am Qebehsenuef, and I have come that I may be your protection, O N. I join your bones together for you, I collect your members for you, I bring your heart to you, I set it in its place in your body for you, and I have caused your house to flourish after you.

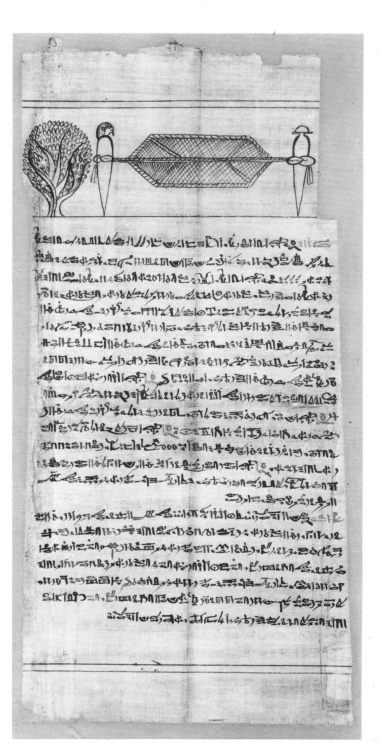

*Spell 153A Before a tree is pegged an open clap net of the type used to trap birds. One of the pegs is human-headed. The text is of Spell 182 and does not relate to the vignette. 10554/57*

## SPELL 152

[illustrated p.150]

*Spell for building a mansion on earth*

Geb is joyful when I hasten over him on his body, and men, the children of their fathers, give me praise when they see that Seshat brings the Destructive One.

Anubis has summoned me to build a mansion which is on earth, its foundation-plan is in Heliopolis, its circuit is in Kheraha, he who is pre-eminent in Letopolis is the scribe responsible for making new what belongs to it; men bring to it bowls of water, and the gangs (work at it). Thus said Osiris to the gods who are in his suite: 'Let us go and see the building of this mansion of this equipped spirit who today has come newly among you. Grant that he may be respected and give him the praise due to him who is favoured there, and you will see what I have done and spoken.'

Thus said Osiris to this god: 'Today he has come newly among you; it is Osiris who brings him herds, it is the south wind which brings him barley, it is the north wind which brings him emmer which the earth has ripened.'

The utterance of Osiris has announced me, he who was destroyed has turned himself over from upon his left side and has set himself upon his right side. Men, gods, spirits and the dead have seen, they spend their time in praise, and I am favoured thereby.

## SPELL 153A

[also illustrated p.151]

*Spell for escaping from the net*

O you who look backward, you with power in your heart, you fisherman who net at the river-bank and open up the earth: O you fishermen, children of your fathers, you takers of your catch, who go round about in the abode of the waters, you shall not catch me in this net of yours in which you catch the inert ones, you shall not trap me in this trap in which you trap the wanderers, the floats of which are in the sky and its weights on earth. I have escaped from its snare, and I have rejoiced as Henu; I have escaped from its clutch, and I have appeared as Sobk, I have used my arms for flying from you, even you who fish and net with hidden fingers.

I know the reel in it; it is the middle finger of Sokar.

I know the guard-beam in it; it is the shank of Shesmu.

I know the valve in it; it is the hand of Isis.

I know the cutter in it; it is the knife of Isis with which the navel-string of Horus was cut.

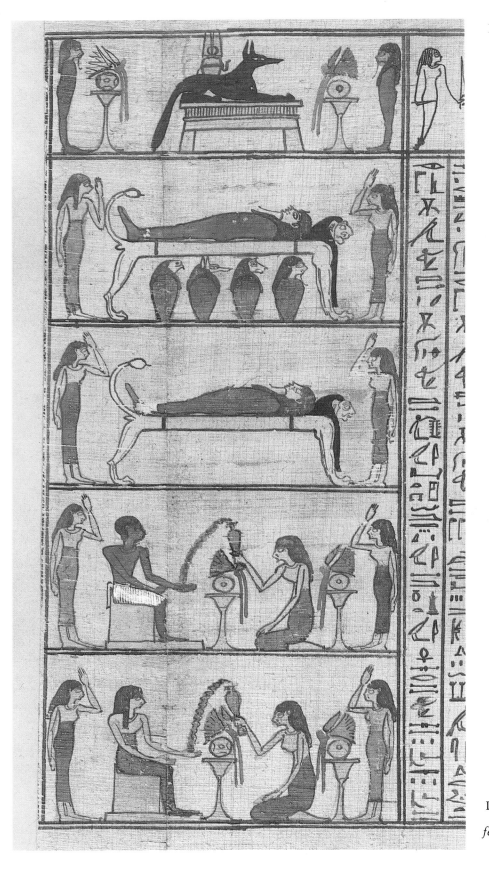

Right: *Spell 153A* *Nakht walks away unscathed from an open clap net.* 10471/15

Left: *Spell 152* *Hor and his wife seated separately behind offering-tables are mourned by standing female figures and given water by kneeling female figures.* 10479/2

I know the name of the floats in it and of its weight; they are the knee-cap and the knee of the Double Lion.

I know the name of its cords with which it catches fish; they are the sinews of Atum.

I know the names of the fishermen who use it; they are the Earth-gods, the forefathers of the Swallowers.

I know the names of its arms; they are the arms of the Great God who gives judgement in Heliopolis on the night of the half-monthly festival in the Mansion of the Moon ...

I know the name of the plateau on which it is pulled tight; it is the plateau of the firmament on which the gods stand.

I know the name of the agent who receives its fish; it is 'Marker of jars, the agent of the god'.

I know the name of the table on which he lays it; it is the table of Horus who sits alone in darkness and cannot be seen, of whom those who have not given him praise are afraid.

I have come and have appeared as a great one, I have governed the land, I have gone down to the earth in the two Great Barks, and the Great One has made presentation to me in the midst of the Mansion of the Prince. I have come as a fisherman, with my net and my reel in my hand, my knife in my hand, and my cutter in my hand; I go to and fro and I catch with my net.

I know the name of the reel which closes the mouth of the opening; it is the middle finger of Osiris.

I know the name of the fingers which hold it; they are the fingers which are on the hand of Re and the nails which are on the hand of Hathor.

I know the name of the cords which are on this reel; they are the sinews of the Lord of the Common Folk.

I know the name of its valve; it is the hand of Isis.

I know the name of its draw-rope; it is the draw-rope of the Eldest God.

I know the name of its netting; it is ... of the day.

I know the names of the fishermen who use it; they are the Earth-gods who are in the presence of Re.

I know the name of ...; they are everyone who is in the presence of Geb.

What you have brought and eaten, I have brought and eaten; you have swallowed what Geb and Osiris swallowed. O you who look behind you, O you who have power in your heart, fish and catch for him who opens the earth, O you fishers, children of your fathers, who entrap within Nefersenet, you shall not catch me in your net, you shall not entrap me in your net in which you catch the inert ones and entrap those who are throughout the earth, for I know it, I know it from its upper floats to its lower weights. Here am I, I have come with my reel in my hand, my peg in my hand, my valve in my hand and my knife in my hand; I have come and I have entered; I smite and I catch. Do you know that I know the name of the catcher of fledglings? I break his bow. I smite him and I put him in his place. As for the peg which is in my hand, it is the shank of Shesmu; as for the reel which is in my hand, it is the finger of Sokar; as for the valve which is in my hand, it is the hand of Isis; as for the knife which is in my hand, it is the decapitating sword of Shesmu.

Here am I; I have come. Here am I; I sit in the bark of Re, I ferry across the Lake of the Two Knives in the northern sky, I hear the words of the gods, I do as they do, I rejoice as they rejoice over my ka, I live on what they live on. I ascend on your ladder which my father Re made for me, and Horus and Seth grip my hands.

## —— Spell 153b ——

*Spell for escaping from the catcher of fish*

O you net-users, trappers and fishermen, O you children of your fathers, do you know that I know the name of that great and mighty net? 'The All-embracing' is its name.

Do you know that I know the name of its cords? They are the sinews of Isis.

Do you know that I know the name of the peg? It is the shank of Atum.

Do you know that I know the name of its reel? It is the finger of Shesmu.

Do you know that I know the name of its valve? It is the fingernail of Ptah.

Do you know that I know the name of its knife? It is the decapitating sword of Isis.

Do you know that I know the name of its weights? It is the iron in the midst of the sky.

Do you know that I know the name of the floats? They are the feathers of the Falcon.

Do you know that I know the name of its fishermen? They are baboons.

Do you know that I know the name of the plateau on which it is pulled tight? It is the Mansion of the Moon.

Do you know that I know the name of him who uses it for himself? He is the great prince who dwells in the eastern side of the sky.

The Great One shall not eat me, the Great One shall not swallow me, I shall not sit on my haunches by the water, for I have eaten and I have swallowed in his presence, and the food of the dead is in my belly.

I am a guinea-fowl, I am Re who emerged from the Abyss, my soul is a god. I am he who created Authority, and falsehood is my detestation. I am Osiris who created righteousness so that Re might live by it daily. I am prayed to as a bull, I am invoked in the Ennead in this my name of the guinea-fowl god. I came into being of myself in company with the Abyss in this my name of Khepri; I come into being in it daily, for I am the Lord of Light; I appear as Re, Lord of the East, and life is given to me at his risings in the East. I have come to the sky and I have sought out my throne which is in the East. They are the youths and elders who are in the fields who apportion the time when I am born in peace. I have eaten as Shu, I have swallowed as Shu, I have defecated as Shu; the Kings of Upper and Lower Egypt are in me, Khons is in me, the heads of the netters of fish are in me, while the warmth of the earth shall embrace you, you multitudes.

## —— Spell 154 ——
[illustrated p.154]

*Spell for not letting the corpse perish*

Hail to you, my father Osiris! I have come to you to the intent that you may heal my flesh; I am complete like my father Khepri, who is the like of one who does not perish. Come, that my breath may be stronger than yours, O Lord of Breath; where are the likes of him? May I endure longer than you, for I am fashioned as the possessor of a burial; may you permit me to go down into the earth for ever like that one who serves you and your father Atum, and his corpse will not perish; such is he who will not be destroyed. I have not done what you dislike; may your ka love me and not thrust me aside;

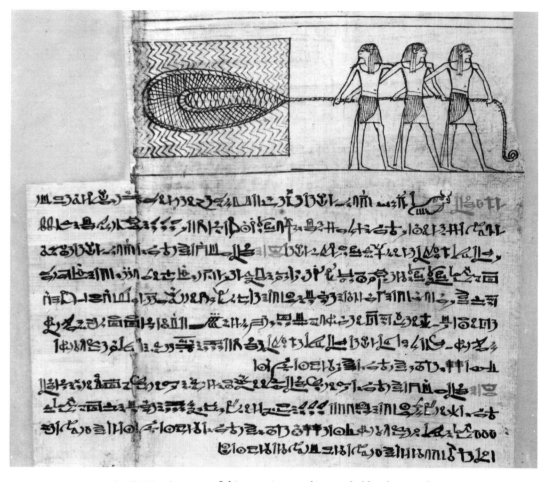

*Spell 153B An empty fishing net in a pool is trawled by three male deities standing on the bank. The text is a long address to Osiris, completely unrelated to the vignette.* 10554/58

take me after you. May I not become corrupt, being like that one who served you better than any god or any goddess, than any herds or any snakes who shall perish. May my soul ascend aloft after death; may it descend only after it has perished. Such is he who is decayed; all his bones are corrupt, his flesh is slain, his bones are softened, his flesh is made into foul water, his corruption stinks and he turns into many worms ... when he is sent to the Eye of Shu, whether as god, goddess, fowl, fish, snakes, worms and herds altogether, because they prostrated themselves to me when they recognised me; it is the fear of me which frightens them. Now every mortal is thus, one who will die whether (men), herds, fowl, fish, snakes or worms; those who live will die. May no worm at all pass by; may they not come against me in their various shapes; you shall not give me over to that slayer who is in his ..., who kills the body, who rots the hidden one, who destroys a multitude of corpses, who lives by killing the living, who carries out his business and who does what has been commanded to him. You

shall not give me over to his fingers, he shall not have power over me, for I am at your command, O Lord of the Gods.

Hail to you, my father Osiris! You shall possess your body; you shall not become corrupt, you shall not have worms, you shall not be distended, you shall not stink, you shall not become putrid, you shall not become worms. I am Khepri; I will possess my body for ever, for I will not become corrupt, I will not decay, I will not be putrid, I will not become worms, I will not be faint because of the Eye of Shu, I exist, I am alive, I am strong, I have awaked in peace, I have not decayed, there is no destruction in my viscera, I have not been injured, my eye has not rotted, my skull has not been crushed, my ears are not deaf, my head has not removed itself from my neck, my tongue has not been taken away, my hair has not been cut off, my eyebrows have not been stripped, no injury has happened to me. My corpse is permanent, it will not perish nor be destroyed in this land for ever.

153

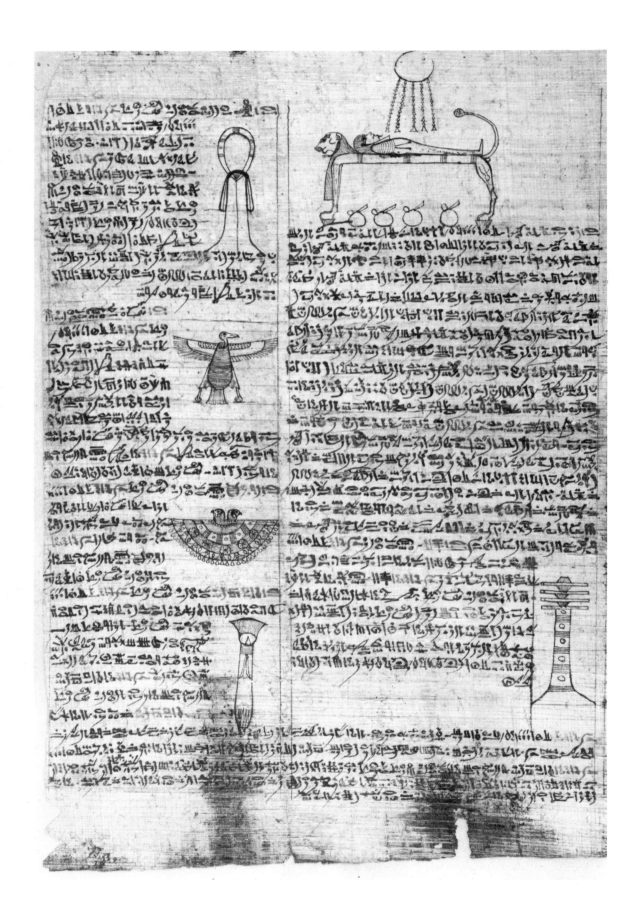

## SPELL 155
[illustrated opposite and p.158]

*Spell for a djed-pillar of gold*

Raise yourself, O Osiris, place yourself on your side, that I may put water beneath you and that I may bring you a djed-pillar of gold so that you may rejoice at it.

*To be said over* a golden djed-pillar embellished with sycamore-bast, to be placed on the throat of the deceased on the day of interment. As for him on whose throat this amulet has been placed, he will be a worthy spirit who will be in the realm of the dead on New Year's Day like those who are in the suite of Osiris. A matter a million times true.

## SPELL 156
[illustrated opposite and pp.156,157,158]

*Spell for a knot-amulet of red jasper*

You have your blood, O Isis; you have your power, O Isis; you have your magic, O Isis. The amulet is a protection for this Great One which will drive away whoever would commit a crime against him.

*To be said over* a knot-amulet of red jasper moistened with juice of the 'life-is-in-it' fruit and embellished with sycamore-bast and placed on the neck of the deceased on the day of interment. As for him for whom this is done, the power of Isis will be the protection of his body, and Horus son of Isis will rejoice over him when he sees him; no path will be hidden from him, and one side of him will be towards the sky and the other towards the earth.

A true matter; you shall not let anyone see it in your hand, for there is nothing equal to it.

## SPELL 157
[illustrated opposite and p.157]

*Spell for a golden vulture* to be placed on the neck of the deceased

Isis came, she halted at the town and sought out a hiding-place for Horus when he came out of his marshes ...

*Spells 154–160 Vignettes from an unnamed funerary papyrus. In the top right the sun streams rays over the mummy of the deceased which lies on a lion-form bed beneath which are bags of natron used during mummification (Spell 154). The other details show a djed-pillar, a knot-amulet, a golden vulture collar, a golden falcon collar and a papyrus-column amulet, illustrating equipment to be placed on the mummy to give protection. 10098/11*

awoke in a bad state and painted his eyes in the god's ship. It was commanded to him to rule the Banks, and he assumed the condition of a mighty warrior, for he remembered what had been done, and he engendered fear of him and inspired respect. His great mother protects him and erases those who come against Horus.

*To be spoken over* a golden vulture with this spell inscribed on it; it is to be set as a protection for this worthy spirit on the day of interment, as a matter a million times true.

## SPELL 158
[illustrated opposite]

*Spell for a golden collar to be placed on the throat of the deceased*

O my father, my brother, and my mother Isis, release me, look at me, for I am one of those who should be released when Geb sees them.

*To be spoken over* a golden collar with this spell inscribed on it; it is to be set on the throat of the deceased on the day of interment.

## SPELL 159
[illustrated opposite and p.157]

*Spell for a papyrus-column of green felspar to be placed on the throat of the deceased*

O you who have come forth today from the god's house, She whose voice is loud goes round about from the door of the Two Houses, she has assumed the power of her father, who is ennobled as Bull of the Nursing Goddess, and she accepts those of her followers who do great deeds for her.

*To be spoken over* a papyrus-column of green felspar with this spell inscribed on it; it is to be set on the throat of the deceased.

## SPELL 160
[illustrated opposite and p.161]

*Giving a papyrus-column of green felspar*

To me belongs a papyrus-column of green felspar which is not imperfect, and which the hand of Thoth supports, for he detests injury. If it is intact, then I will be hale; if it is uninjured, then will I be uninjured; if it is not struck, then I will not be struck. It is what Thoth has said which knits your spine together.

Welcome, O Elder of Heliopolis, greatest in Pe, to whom Shu has gone; he finds him in Shenmu in this his name of 'Green Felspar'. He has taken his place opposite the Great God, and Atum is satisfied with his Eye, so that my members will not be damaged.

## —— Spell 161 ——
[illustrated p.159]

*Spell for breaking an opening into the sky* which Thoth made for Wennefer when he broke into the solar disc

Re lives, the tortoise is dead, the corpse is interred and N's bones are reunited.

Re lives, the tortoise is dead, and he who is in the sarcophagus and in the coffin is stretched out.

THE TWO REMAINING PARAGRAPHS CONTINUE THE REFRAIN 'RE LIVES, THE TORTOISE IS DEAD', BUT OTHERWISE ARE UNINTELLIGIBLE. A 'RUBRIC' IN BLACK FOLLOWS:

As for any noble dead for whom this ritual is performed over his coffin, there shall be opened for him four openings in the sky, one for the north wind – that is Osiris; another for the south wind – that is Re; another for the west wind – that is Isis; another for the east wind – that is Nephthys. As for each one of these winds which is in its opening, its task is to enter into his nose. No outsider knows, for it is a secret which the common folk do not yet know; you shall not perform it over anyone, not your father or your son, except yourself alone. It is truly a secret, which no-one of the people should know.

## —— Spell 162 ——
[illustrated p.160]

*Spell to cause to come into being a flame beneath the head of a spirit*

Hail to you Lord of Might, tall of plumes, owner of the

Above: *Spells 155, 156, 29ʙ and 166* Ani's djed-pillar amulet, knot-amulet, heart amulet and headrest amulet. 10470/33

Right: *Spell 161* Thoth, shown four times, is about to pull open the barrier which blocks the four winds. 10479/11

Wereret-crown, whose possession is the flail. You are lord of the phallus, strong when dawning, a light never ceasing to dawn. You are possessor of (different) forms, rich in hues, one who hides in the Sacred Eye until his birth. You are one powerful of bellow in the Ennead, a mighty runner, swift of steps. You are a powerful god who comes to the aid of one who asks for it, who saves the wretched from affliction. Come at my voice, I am the ihet-cow; your name is in my mouth and I shall utter it: *Penhaqahagaher* is your name, *Iuriuiaqrsainqrbaty* is your name, tail of the lion-ram is your name, *Kharsati* is your name: I adore your name. I am the ihet-cow, hear my voice today. You have set the flame under the head of Re and he is in the divine Netherworld in Heliopolis. May you cause him to appear like one who is on earth: he is your soul, do not forget him. Come to the Osiris N. Cause to come into being a flame beneath his head for he is the soul of that corpse which rests in Heliopolis, Atum is his name, *Barkatitjawa* is his name. Come, cause him to be like one in your following, for he is such a one as you.

Words to be spoken over a statuette of an ihet-cow made of fine gold and placed at the throat of the deceased; also a drawing of it on a new papyrus scroll placed under his head. A great quantity of flames will envelop him completely like one who is on earth. A very great protection which was made by the ihet-cow for her son Re when he set. His place will be enclosed by a blaze and he will be a god in the realm of the dead and will not be repulsed from any portal of the Netherworld in very truth. You shall say as you place this goddess at the throat of the deceased 'O you most hidden of hidden gods in heaven, regard the corpse of your son; keep him safe in the realm of the dead. This is a book of great secrecy – let no-one see it for that would be an abomination. But the one who knows it and keeps it hidden shall continue to exist. The name of this book is "Mistress of the hidden temple".'

## ——— Spell 163 ———
[illustrated p.163]

*Spells taken from another book, added to the book of coming forth by day. Spell for preventing a man's corpse from putrefying in the realm of the dead in order to rescue him from the eater of souls who imprisons in the Netherworld and to prevent accusations of his crimes upon earth being imputed to him; to cause his flesh and bones to be safe from maggots and every god who mutilates in the realm of the dead and to allow him to come and go as he wants and to do everything which is in his heart without being restrained.*

Words to be spoken over a snake with two legs, a sun-disc and two horns; over two Sacred Eyes, each with two legs and wings. In the pupil of one is the figure of Him whose arm is raised and a head of Bes with two plumes, whose back is like a falcon's. In the pupil of the other is a figure of Him whose arm is raised and a head of Neith with two plumes, whose back is like a falcon's. Drawn in dried myrrh mixed with wine, repeated with green stone of Upper Egypt and water from the well west of Egypt on a green bandage with which all a man's limbs are enveloped.

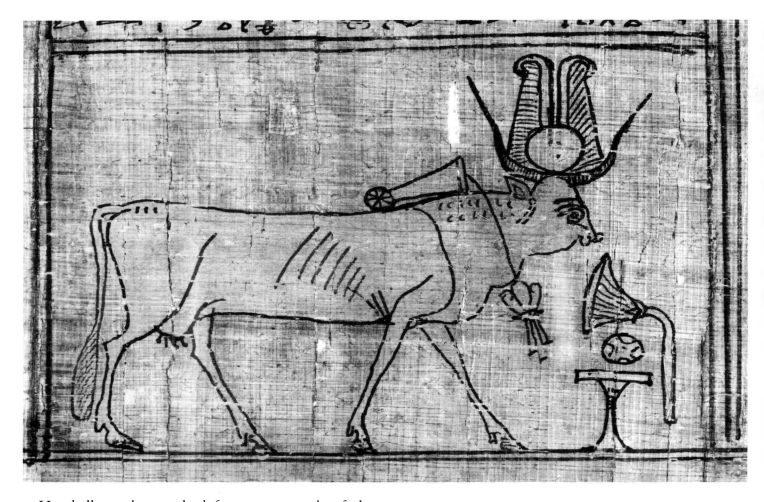

He shall not be repulsed from any portals of the Netherworld; he shall eat and drink, defecate from the hinder-parts as when he was on earth. No complaint shall be raised against him nor the hand of an enemy profit against him for ever.

If this text is used on earth he will not be exposed by the messengers who attack those who commit wrong in all the earth. His head shall not be cut off, he shall not be destroyed by the knife of Seth. He shall not be carried off to any prison. But he shall enter the tribunal and come forth justified. He shall be preserved from the fear of wrong-doing which exists in all the earth.

## ── SPELL 164 ──
[illustrated p.163]

*Another spell*

To be said over (a figurine of) Mut having three heads: one being the head of Pakhet wearing plumes, a second being a human head wearing the Double Crown, the third being the head of a vulture wearing plumes. She also

*Spell 162 Behind an offering-table topped by a lotus stands the ihet-cow wearing a sun-disc and plumes, with a Bat-amulet about her neck. 9946/6*

has a phallus, wings and the claws of a lion. Drawn in dried myrrh with fresh incense, repeated in ink upon a red bandage. A dwarf stands before her, another behind her, each facing her and wearing plumes. Each has a raised arm and two heads, one is the head of a falcon, the other a human head.

Wrap the breast therewith: he shall be a god among gods in the realm of the dead. He shall not be repulsed for ever. His flesh and bones shall be sound like one who does not die. He shall drink water from the river; land shall be given to him in the Field of Rushes; a star of the sky shall be given to him. He shall be preserved from the serpent, the hot-tempered one who is in the Netherworld. His soul shall not be imprisoned. The djeriu-bird shall rescue him from the one at his side and no maggot shall eat him.

*Spell 160 Thoth hands over to Nebseny a rectangular plaque,
presumably carved with a papyrus-column. 9900/10*

## ——— SPELL 165 ———
[illustrated p.164]

*Spell for mooring and not letting the Sacred Eye be
injured, for maintaining the corpse and drinking water*

To be said over a divine image with raised arm, plumes
on his head, his legs apart, his middle a scarab; drawn
with lapis-lazuli and water of gum. Also an image whose
head is human, his arms hanging down, the head of a
ram on his right shoulder, another on his left shoulder.
Draw on a single bandage level with his heart the image
of Him with raised arm; draw the other image over his
breast without letting Sugady who is in the Netherworld
have knowledge of it. He shall drink water of the river;
he shall shine like a star in the sky.

## ——— SPELL 166 ———
[illustrated p.158]

*Spell for a headrest*

May the pigeons awaken you when you are asleep, O N,
may they awaken your head at the horizon. Raise yourself, so that you may be triumphant over what was done
against you, for Ptah has felled your enemies, and it is
commanded that action be taken against those who
would harm you. You are Horus son of Hathor, the
male and female fiery serpents, to whom was given a
head after it had been cut off. Your head shall not be
taken from you afterwards, your head shall not be taken
from you for ever.

## SPELL 167

[illustrated p.165]

*Spell for bringing a Sacred Eye by N*

Thoth has fetched the Sacred Eye, having pacified the Eye after Re had sent it away. It was very angry, but Thoth pacified it from anger after it had been far away. If I be hale, it will be hale, and N will be hale.

## SPELL 168

[illustrated pp.166,167,168-9]

Those who lift up their faces to the sky in the bow of the Bark of Re will permit N to see Re when he rises. *A bowl is offered to them on earth by N,* a possessor of gifts in the West within the Field of Offerings.

Those who lift up their faces to the sky in the bow of the Bark of Re will permit Osiris to see Re when he rises. *A bowl is offered to them on earth by N,* a follower of the Great God, the Lord of the beautiful West.

Those who drive Re will cause bread to pass to N as to the suite of Re when he goes to rest. *A bowl will be offered to them on earth by N,* who comes to Horus, Lord of the Mountain-top.

The bearers of gifts will cause N to be like those who are in the Netherworld. *A bowl will be offered to them on earth by N,* who goes out and comes in with Re for ever.

The inert ones will permit N to enter into the Hall of Justice. *A bowl will be offered to them on earth by N,* as a possessor of gifts in the beautiful West.

The snakes will permit N to follow Re into his bark. *A bowl will be offered to them on earth by N,* who travels freely with the gods of the Netherworld.

The bearers of offerings who give offerings to the gods will give offerings and provisions to N in the realm of the dead. *A bowl will be offered to them on earth by N.* May they not stand up against the soul at the portal.

*The gods of the eighth cavern of the Netherworld whose shapes are mysterious, who breathe the air.*

The gods who are in their shrines which are about the Abyss. May they let N drink. *A bowl will be offered to them on earth by N;* may his soul live and may his corpse be intact in the realm of the dead.

The gods who are in the suite of Osiris. May they grant that N be at rest with his mummy. *A bowl is offered to them on earth by N,* in the presence of the Great God who dwells in his bark.

He who stands up. May he permit N to worship Re when he rises. *A bowl is offered to them on earth by N;* he shall be in charge of the braziers.

He who is hidden. May he make N strong in the hall of Geb. *A bowl is offered to them on earth by N,* who

knows the secrets of the Lords of the Netherworld.

He who is mysterious. May he permit N's corpse to be strong and intact on earth and in the realm of the dead. *A bowl is offered to them on earth by N,* being a possessor of movement in the realm of the dead and in Rosetjau.

He who is concealed. May he give bread and beer to N with you in the House of Osiris. *A bowl is offered to them on earth by N,* who enters into the secrets of the Lords of the Netherworld.

The mysterious one of Osiris. May he cause N to be a possessor of movement in the sacred place. *A bowl is offered to them on earth by N,* who becomes the owner of a throne in the realm of the dead.

Sherem. He shall not let evil draw near to N in the realm of the dead. *A bowl is offered to them on earth by N,* a soul who hears the words of the gods.

The Usher. May he permit N to see Re when he rises and sets. *A bowl is offered to them on earth by N.* May his members live and his body be hale for ever.

The Dark One. May he make N to be a spirit on earth and to be strong in the West. *A bowl is offered to them on earth by N,* whose legs have power as a possessor of a throne in the West.

The Eyeless One. May he permit N to be among those who are in charge of braziers. *A bowl is offered to them on earth by N,* who belongs to the Standing One who is in the Netherworld.

The Embalmers. May they permit N to be in the presence of the Great God, Lord of the West. *A bowl is offered to them on earth by N,* who becomes a possessor of arms and one who is stouthearted in the realm of the dead.

The Males whose arms are hidden. May they permit N to be with them for ever in the realm of the dead. *A bowl is offered to them on earth by N,* who will attain to the throne of Osiris.

The Females whose arms are hidden. May they grant that N be hale and that his offerings endure in his presence. *A bowl is offered to them on earth by N;* he is the two-horned one who hears the words of the gods.

He whose body is hidden. May he grant to N righteousness with Re who is in his Ennead. *A bowl is offered to them on earth by N,* as the possessor of a phallus who takes women for ever.

The souls who go forth. May they judge the speech of N among the gods who are with them. *A bowl is offered to them on earth by N* among the living, the lords of eternity.

Those who belong to ... May they grant that N have power through his offerings on earth like all the gods. *A bowl is offered to them on earth by N,* who benefits from provisions in the realm of the dead.

Those who receive. May they permit N to enter into

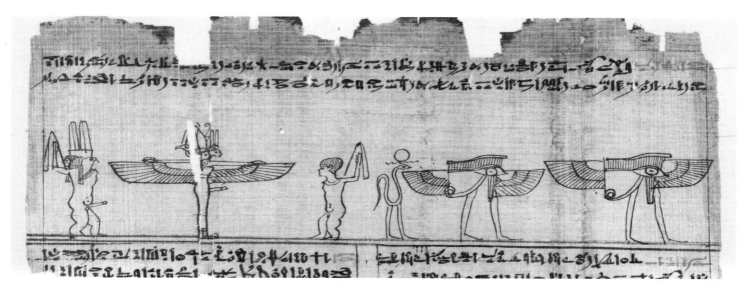

*Spells 163 and 164 On the left is a winged female ithyphallic figure with three heads, that of a vulture, a woman and a lioness, standing between two dwarfs. One is ithyphallic, has a human and a falcon's head, wears plumes and carries a flail; the other is human-headed and carries a flail (Spell 164). On the right are two winged udjat-eyes on human legs followed by a serpent with legs, wearing horns and a sun-disc. 10257/21*

all the secret places of the Netherworld. *A bowl will be offered to them on earth by N*, who shall have power over offerings upon earth as a possessor of braziers.

The female inert ones. May they grant that N be with the Great God as the possessor of a phallus. *A bowl is offered to them on earth by N*, so that he who is in the secret place in darkness may have light.

Osiris-Anubis. May he grant that N be a possessor of a throne in the Sacred Land. *A bowl is offered to them on earth by N*, who passes the threshold of the portal of Osiris.

*The gods of the tenth cavern in the Netherworld, who cry aloud and whose mysteries are holy.*

Those who belong to the sunshine. May they give light to N in darkness. *A bowl is offered to them on earth by N*, who worships the Great God in his place every day.

Those who take hold. May they grant that N be acclaimed. *A bowl is offered to them on earth by N*, on the day of driving off the great encircling serpent.

The Nine Gods who guard those who are in (the cavern). May they grant the breath of life to N on earth and in the realm of the dead. *A bowl is offered to them on earth by N*, whose hand is extended and who repels him who comes.

The Nine Gods whose arms are hidden. May they grant that N be a spirit like the worthy spirits. *A bowl is offered to them on earth by N*, whose head is hale on earth and in the realm of the dead.

The Hidden Goddess. May she grant that N's soul be strong and his corpse intact like the gods who are in the Netherworld. *A bowl is offered to them on earth by N*; may his soul rest in the place where it desires to be.

The souls of the gods who have become the members of Osiris. May they grant that N have peace. *A bowl is offered to them on earth by N*, who receives his place on earth and in the realm of the dead.

Those who worship Re. N shall not be driven off from any of the portals of the Netherworld. *A bowl is offered to them on earth by N* when he goes out into the day and is cool in the cool place.

Those whose faces are warlike. May they grant that N be cool in the place of heat. *A bowl is offered to them on earth by N*; may he sit in front in the presence of the Great God.

*The gods of the eleventh cavern, covered, ... hidden, secret.*

The Python. May she grant that N be hale before the Great God who is in the Netherworld. *A bowl is offered to them on earth by N*, who shall come into being as Khepri in the West.

The Soul of the West. May he grant invocation-offerings of bread and beer, oxen and fowl to N on earth and in the realm of the dead. *A bowl is offered to them on earth by N*, a possessor of a throne whose heart is content on the mountain of the realm of the dead.

The Souls of Earth. May they grant triumph to N over his enemies in sky and earth. *A bowl is offered to them on earth by N*, who keeps silence regarding all that he has seen.

Those who make offerings. May they grant that N be like the crew (of the solar bark) in the sky. *A bowl is offered to them on earth by N*; may he go in by the secret portal.

**Spell 165** *An ithyphallic male figure, with a scarab for a body, wearing plumes and carrying a flail walks before a human figure with two rams' heads.* 10257/22

The Nine Gods who rule the West. May they permit N to go in by the great secret portal of Osiris. *A bowl is offered to them on earth by N,* who is dominant over the Lords of the Netherworld.

The Nine Gods who are in the suite of Osiris. May they grant that N have power over his enemies. *A bowl is offered to them on earth by N;* may he become a worthy soul from day to day.

Iqeh. May he grant that N be in the presence of Re and that he may cross the sky for ever. *A bowl is offered to them on earth by N,* for he is in the following of Him who dwells in the Place of Embalmment, Lord of the Sacred Land.

The Embalmer of Osiris. May he grant that N's soul shall live; he shall not die again for ever. *A bowl is offered to them on earth by N;* mourning shall be decreed for him and for his god.

The Nine Watchers. May they grant wakefulness to N; he shall never be destroyed. *A bowl is offered to them on earth by N,* who is vindicated before Osiris, Lord of the Faiyum.

The Nine Mourners. May they grant mourning for N like what was done for Osiris. *A bowl is offered to them on earth by N* when his soul ascends among the spirits.

He whom Re summoned. May he summon N to Re and his Ennead. *A bowl is offered to them on earth by N* whose soul comes into the secret place and goes up from the earth.

Iqen. May he drive away all evil from N for ever. *A bowl is offered to them on earth by N,* who comes in peace and is vindicated.

Those who are with Her whose head is red. May they permit N to go in and out and to stride forward like the Lords of the Netherworld. *A bowl is offered to them on earth by N* when he goes in and out of the portal of the Netherworld.

She whose head is red. May she grant that N have power over the waters. *A bowl is offered to them on earth by N* as one who strides freely up the great stairway.

The Coiled Serpent. May she grant that N be holy in the Netherworld for ever. *A bowl is offered to them on earth by N,* as a worthy soul who is in his cavern.

Those who are with the Coiled Serpent. May they permit N to stride forward freely in the sacred place. *A bowl is offered to them on earth by N,* and he shall be in the presence of the Followers of Horus.

The Nine Gods who hide Osiris. May they grant that N dwell in the place which he desires. *A bowl is offered to them on earth by N,* and he shall be among the Lords of Righteousness.

The Destroyer. May he clear N's vision that he may see the Sunshine-god. *A bowl is offered to them on earth by N,* so that he may be in the following of the serpent-guardian of the West.

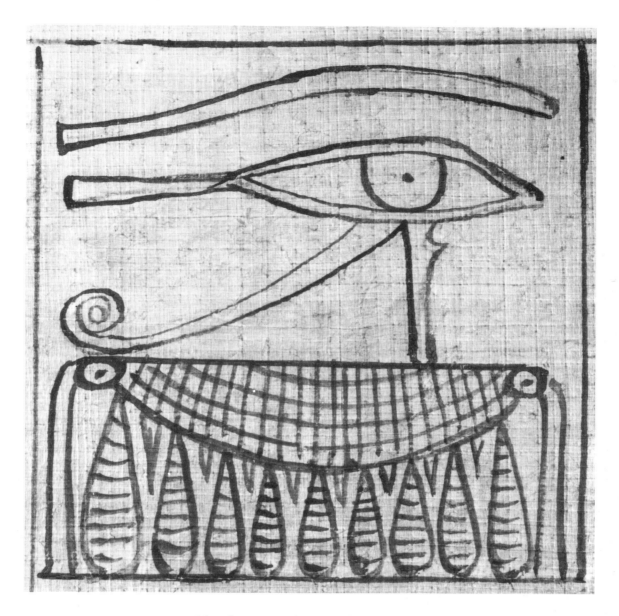

*Spell 167* The udjat-eye stands on an elaborate collar which is the hieroglyphic sign for 'gold'. 9900/22

*The gods of the twelfth cavern of the Netherworld; the gods are united in front of those who guide.*

He of the river-bank. May he grant that N be Lord of the Island of the Just. *A bowl is offered to them on earth by N* as a possessor of offerings in the Field of Rushes.

The gods who are in the region of the Netherworld. May they give justice to N in the Hall of Justice. *A bowl is offered to them on earth by N;* may he plough in the Field of Offerings.

The gods who are with the Coiled Serpent. May they grant that N be in the place which his ka desires, and he will be there. *A bowl is offered to them on earth by N,* who will come into being at the word of the Lord of the West.

The gods who are on the earth. May they give an island to N in the Field of Rushes. *A bowl is offered to them on earth by N;* may he dwell in the place where he desires to be.

He who is in charge of the earth. May he make a grant of land to N in the Field of Offerings. *A bowl is offered to them on earth by N;* may amulets protect him like the Lords of the Netherworld.

The gods who are in the earth. May they give food-offerings, provisions and a portion of meat to N in the realm of the dead. *A bowl is offered to them on earth by N,* when he sets in Manu.

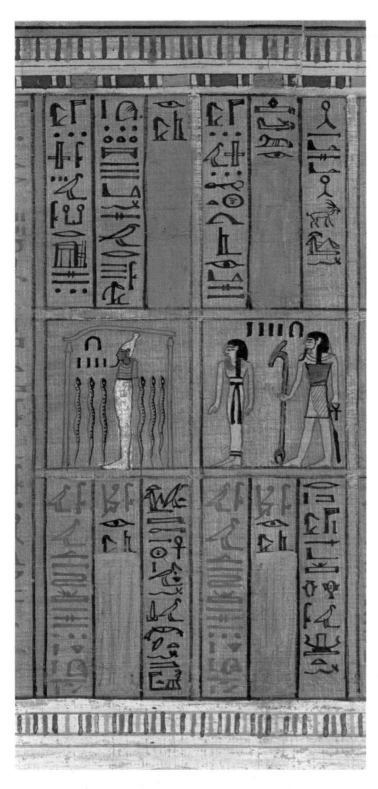

Those who are in charge of the secret things which are in the earth. May they place their walls about N, like what is done for the Inert One. *A bowl is offered to them on earth by N* when he goes in and out of the realm of the dead.

The gods who are in the coils of the Serpent. May they cause the sun-disc to look on N. *A bowl is offered to them on earth by N* as a mighty spirit in his firmament.

Yuba. May he grant that N rest in the West. *A bowl is offered to them on earth by N* when going in and out of the West more than anyone.

## —— SPELL 169 ——

*Spell for erecting a bier*

You are the Lion, you are the Double Lion, you are Horus the protector of his father, you are the fourth of these four mighty gods who belong to those who make acclamation and who make shouting, who bring water by means of their power of ... Raise yourself upon your right side, lift yourself upon your left side, for Geb will open for you your blind eyes, he will straighten your bent knees, and there will be given to you your heart which you had from your mother, your heart which belongs to your body. Your soul is bound for the sky, your corpse is beneath the ground; there is bread for your belly, water for your throat and sweet air for your nose. Those who are in their tombs will be kindly to you, those who are in their coffins will be open to you, they will bring to you your members when you are re-established in your original shape. You shall go up to the sky, the cord shall be knotted for you in the presence of Re, you shall close the net in the river, you shall drink water from it, you shall walk on your feet, you shall not walk upside down. You shall ascend to those who are above the earth, you shall not go out to those who are under the walls; your walls which belong to you, being what your city god made for you, will not be thrown down.

You are pure, your front is pure, your back parts are clean by means of natron, fresh water and incense, and you are pure by means of milk of Apis, by beer of Tjenmyt, and by natron which dispels the evil on you. Tefnut the daughter of Re will feed you in the presence of her father Re; She of the Valley will knit you together as at the burial of her father Osiris, you will bite on something sweet which he gives to you there. Your three portions are above with Re, of barley of Ibu; your four portions are below with Geb, of barley of Upper Egypt; it is the citizens who bring to you Him of the Field of Offerings, and he is set before you. You shall go forth with Re, you shall have power through Re, you shall

*Spell 168 In the Ninth Cavern an enshrined mummiform figure wearing the White Crown and flanked by vertical snakes is accompanied by the figure fourteen. Behind stand a woman and a god who carries a was-sceptre and an ankh, also accompanied by the figure fourteen. 10478/6*

*Spell 168 Some of the inhabitants of the Caverns of the Underworld. In the Eighth Cavern a god carries a child on his shoulder accompanied by the figure four, meaning there are four such figures; a woman lies prone with her hands to a falling lock of hair – again there are four such figures. 10478/6*

have power in your legs at all seasons and at any hour.

You shall not be examined, you shall not be imprisoned, you shall not be watched, you shall not be fettered, you shall not be put in the cell for rebels, the sand shall be removed from your face. Beware of him who is heavy against you, let none oppose you; beware that you do not go forth. Take your garment, your sandals, your staff, your loin-cloth and all your weapons, so that you may cut off the heads and sever the necks of those rebellious enemies who draw near when you are dead. 'Do not go near' is the word of the Great God to you, even he who brings himself on the day of coming into being. The Falcon rejoices at you, the Goose cackles at you, the doors of the sky are opened by Re, the earth is thrown open for you by Geb, because your power is so great and the knowledge of your name is so effective. It is opening up the West for this worthy soul, it is speech which is pleasing to the heart of Re and satisfactory to the heart of his tribunal which watches over men. May the Double Lion lead to the place where N has made his ka content.

O N, entrap all those who would harm you, for you

have life, your soul has health, your corpse is long-enduring, you see the flame, you breathe the air, your vision is clear in the House of Darkness which is set in the entrance (of the sky), without seeing a storm. You serve the ruler of the Two Lands, you refresh yourself at the meru-tree in the presence of him whose magic is mighty, while Seshat sits before you, Sia protects your body, the Ox-herd milks for you his herd which follows Sekhat-Hor. May you raise yourself at the opening of the waters of Kheraha, may the great ones of Pe and Dep praise you, may you gaze on Thoth the representative of Re in the sky, may you go up and enter into the pillared hall, may the Rivals make report to you. Your ka is with you because of your joy of heart at your existing. Your happy ... awaken you, the Ennead makes your heart glad; four loaves are issued to you in Letopolis, four loaves in Hermopolis and four loaves in Heliopolis upon the altar of the Lady of the Two Lands. May the night of stars awaken you, may the Lords of Heliopolis refresh you, may food be in your mouth, for your feet shall not go astray, your limbs shall have life, you shall grasp a whip in Abydos; you shall guide the collection of the great ones, the full muster of those who are in charge of the company at the jubilee of Osiris at the morning of the Wag-festival, and of the masters of the mysteries. You shall be adorned with gold, your vestment being of fine linen, Hapi shall surge over your breast, the seter-plant will be beneficial to you, being carved on your

*Spell 168* Four representations of the sun-god: three squat within cabins on boats – one falcon-headed, one scarab-headed and one ram-headed – the fourth is enthroned and falcon-headed, embraced

*by an animated sun-disc which emerges from the symbol for the sky. Beneath are some of the curious inhabitants of the Caverns of the Underworld. 10010/2*

offering-stone, and you shall drink beside the Lake of the Two Knives. The gods who are yonder shall favour you, you shall ascend to the sky with the gods who present Truth to Re, you shall be inducted into the presence of the Ennead, and you shall be made like one of them. Yours is the khar-goose, son of the ro-goose, and you shall offer it to Ptah South-of-his-Wall.

## —— Spell 170 ——

*Spell for assembling a bier*

O N, I have given you your flesh, I have gathered your bones together for you, I have collected your members for you, I have thrown off for you the earth which was on your flesh, for you are Horus within the Egg. Raise yourself that you may see the gods, extend your arm towards the horizon, to the pure place where you desire to be. May men serve you there, may acclamation be made for you, with what is issued from the altar. Horus will raise you up at his appearings, just as he did for Him who was in the Pure Place.

O N, Anubis who is on his mountain will raise you up and will make your bandages strong.

O N, Ptah-Sokar will give you an arm with its temple adornments.

O N, Thoth himself will come to you with the book of the sacred words, and he will set your hand on the horizon, at the place which your ka desires; he it was who helped you, O Osiris, on that night of death. May your White Crown be firm on your brow, for Shesmu is with you, and he will present you with the choicest of fowl.

O N, raise yourself on your bier that you may go forth. Re will raise you up in the horizon, to the bank of rowers which is in his Bark.

O N, Atum, father of the gods, will cause you to endure for ever.

O N, Min of Coptos will raise you up so that gods of the shrine may worship you.

O N, how happy a thing it is that you should cross in peace to your house for eternity, your tomb for everlasting! May you be greeted in Pe and Dep in the shrine which your ka desires, for your place is pre-eminent and your power is great. The great bier will raise you up to the Wild Bull whom the gods embrace, for you are a god who begot those who exist, whose shape is better than those of the gods. Your brilliance is greater than that of the spirits, your power is mightier than that of those who are yonder.

O N, Ptah South-of-his-Wall will raise you up and will advance your position above that of the gods.

O N, you are Horus, son of Isis, whom Ptah begot,

whom Nut created; may you shine like Re in the horizon when he illumines the Two Lands with his beauty. The gods say to you: 'Welcome! Cross over that you may see your possessions in your house for eternity.' Renenutet will raise you up, even she whom Atum impregnated in the presence of the Ennead.

O Nut, I am the heir of the sky, the companion of Him who created his light; I went forth from the womb when I was orphaned of my father without having the wisdom to answer for my deeds.

## —— Spell 171 ——

*Spell for donning a pure garment*

Atum, Shu, Tefnut, Geb, Nut, Osiris, Isis, Seth, Nephthys, Horakhty, Hathor, the Great Mansion, Khepri, Mont the Lord of Thebes, Amun the Lord of the thrones of the Two Lands, the Great Ennead, the Lesser Ennead, the gods and goddesses who are in the Abyss, Sobk of Crocodilopolis, Sobk in all his many names in every place of his where his soul desires to be; the southern gods and the northern gods, those who are in the sky and those who are on earth: may you give this pure garment to the worthy spirit N; may you grant that it be beneficial to him; may you remove the evil which is on him. As for this pure garment for N, may it be allotted to him for ever and ever, and may you remove the evil which is on him.

## —— Spell 172 ——

*Here begin the spells of praising which are made in the realm of the dead*

I am purified with natron, I chew natron, incense ... I am pure, and pure are the recitations which come forth from my mouth. They are more pure than the fins and scales of the fish in the river, more than the image belonging to the Mansion of Natron; my recitations are pure. How happy am I! Ptah praises me, He who is South-of-his-Wall praises me, every god praises me and every goddess praises me (and they say): 'Your beauty is that of a calm pool, like a quiet water; your beauty is that of a hall of festival wherein every god is extolled; your beauty is like the column of Ptah, indeed like the shaft of Re.' May there be made for me a column for Ptah and a metal jar for Him who is South-of-his-Wall.

*See, you are doubly mourned.* First stanza. See, you are lamented, you are glorified, you are exalted, you are a spirit, you are mighty. Rise up, for you are indeed risen! Rise up against those who would harm you, male or female, for your enemies are fallen; Ptah has felled your enemies, and you are victorious over them, you have power over them. Your words are heard, orders are carried out for you, for you are risen and vindicated in the tribunals of every god or goddess.

*See, you are doubly mourned.* Second stanza. Your head, O my lord, is adorned with the tress of a woman of Asia; your face is brighter than the Mansion of the Moon; your upper part is lapis-lazuli; your hair is blacker than all the doors of the Netherworld on the day of darkness, your hair is bestrewn with lapis-lazuli; the upper part of your face is as the shining of Re; your visage is covered with gold and Horus has inlaid it with lapis-lazuli; your eyebrows are the two sisterly Serpents, and Horus has inlaid them with lapis-lazuli; your nose is in the odour of the place of embalming, your nostrils are like the winds of the sky; your eyes behold Bakhu; your eyelashes are firm every day, being coloured with real lapis-lazuli; your eyelids are the bringers of peace, and their corners are full of black eye-paint; your lips give you truth, they repeat truth to Re and make the gods content; your teeth are those of the Coiled Serpent, with which the Two Horuses play; your tongue is wise and sharp when you speak to the kites of the field; your jaw is the starry sky; your breasts are firm in their place when they traverse the western desert.

*See, you are doubly mourned.* Third stanza. Your neck is adorned with gold and also with fine gold; your throat is great, your windpipe is Anubis; your vertebrae are the Two Cobras; your back is overlaid with gold and also with fine gold; your lungs are Nephthys; your face is Hapi and his flood; your buttocks are eggs of cornelian; your legs are strong in walking; you are seated on your throne, and the gods have given you your eyes.

*See, you are doubly mourned.* Fourth stanza. Your gullet is Anubis; your body is extended with gold; your breasts are eggs of cornelian which Horus has inlaid with lapis-lazuli; your arms glitter with faience; your shoulders are firm in their places; your heart is happy every day; your heart is the work of the two Mighty Ones; your thighs worship the lower stars, your belly is the peaceful sky; your navel is the Morning Star which makes judgement and promises light in darkness, and whose offerings are the "life-is-in-it' plant; it worships the Majesty of Thoth. I love its beauty in my tomb which my god decreed for me in the pure place where I desire to be.

*See, you are doubly mourned.* Fifth stanza. Your arms are a waterway at the fair season of inundation, a waterway which the Children of Water have covered; your knees are enclosed with gold; your breast is a thicket of the swamps; the soles of your feet are firm every day; your toes guide you on fair paths, O N; your hands are the reeds in the water-basins; your fingers are picks of gold and their nails are knives of flint in the faces of those who would harm you.

*See, you are doubly mourned.* Sixth stanza. You don the pure garment, you discard the thick cloth, you rise up from the bier, the foreleg is cut off for your ka, O N, the heart is for your mummy, you receive the loin-cloth of fine linen from the hands of the messenger of Re; you eat bread upon a cloth woven by Tayt herself; you eat the foreleg, you devour the haunch. Re glorifies you in his pure abode; you wash your feet in bowls of silver fashioned by the craft of Sokar, while you eat the shens-bread which was issued from the altar; the two God's-Fathers make presentation, and you eat persen-bread prepared in the cooking-vessel of the storehouse; in the fear of your heart you chew onions from your offering-stone; the nurse-baboons prepare for you the provisions and food of the Souls of Heliopolis, who themselves bear food to you; fowl and fish are promised to you to be at your feet in the portals of the Great Mansion. You raise up Orion, your hinder-parts reach to the sky; and her hands are on you. That is what Orion said, even he the son of Nut who bore the gods. The two Great Gods of the sky said the one to the other: 'Take on your shoulder him whom I have brought on my shoulder and let us help N on this happy day. May he be glorified, may he be remembered, even he who will be in the mouths of all children.' Raise yourself and listen to your praises in the mouths of all your household.

*See, you are doubly mourned.* Seventh stanza. May Anubis embalm you, for he has acted on behalf of one whom he has favoured. May the Greatest of the Seers make presentation of his clothing when you go to bathe in the Lake of Perfection, for he is the butler of the Great God. May you make offerings in the Upper Houses, may you propitiate the Lords of Heliopolis, may you present to Re water in a vase and two large jars of milk. May your offering be raised up on the altar; may your feet be washed on a stone of ... on the slab of the God of the Lake; may you ascend and see Re on the supporting posts of the sky, on the head of Pillar-of-his-Mother, and on the shoulders of Wepwawet; may he open a path for you that you may see the horizon, the pure place where you desire to be.

*See, you are doubly mourned.* Eighth stanza. Offerings are divided up for you in the presence of Re. You have your front part, you have your back part, being what Horus and Thoth decreed for you. They have summoned you, and you see that whereby you become a spirit. It is caused that the god goes up to you in the neighbourhood of the Souls of Heliopolis; may you proceed on the paths, great in your dignity of one who receives the offerings of your father who was before you, being clad in fine linen every day and being guided by the god to the portals of the Great Mansion.

*See, you are doubly mourned.* Ninth stanza. As for N, there is air for him, air for his nose, air for his nostrils; a thousand geese, and fifty baskets of everything good and pure. Your enemies have fallen and shall exist no longer, O N.

# —— SPELL 173 ——

The greetings of Horus to his father when he went in to see his father Osiris when he went up into the great pure place, so that Re might see him as Wennefer, Lord of the Sacred Land; they embraced each other in order that he might be a spirit thereby in the realm of the dead.

Worship of Osiris, Foremost of the Westerners, the Great God, Lord of Abydos, King of Eternity and Ruler of Everlasting, the august god in Rosetjau, by N.

I give you praise, O Lord of the Gods, sole god who lives on truth – so says your son Horus. I have come to you that I may greet you, and I have brought truth to you at the place where your Ennead is; may you grant that I be among those who are in your suite and that I may fell all your enemies, for I have perpetuated your offerings on earth for ever.

Ho Osiris! I am your son Horus, and I have come to you that I may greet you, my father Osiris.

Ho Osiris! I am your son Horus; I have come, having felled your enemies for you.

Ho Osiris! I am your son Horus; I have come that I may remove all evil which is on you.

Ho Osiris! I am your son Horus; I have come that I may slay for you him who mutilated you.

Ho Osiris! I am your son Horus; I have come, having thrust my hand against those who rebelled against you.

Ho Osiris! I am your son Horus; I have come, having brought to you the confederacy of Seth with their bonds on them.

Ho Osiris! I am your son Horus; I have come, having brought Upper Egypt to you and having bound Lower Egypt together for you.

Ho Osiris! I am your son Horus; I have come, having perpetuated god's-offerings for you in Upper and Lower Egypt.

Ho Osiris! I am your son Horus; I have come, having cultivated fields for you.

Ho Osiris! I am your son Horus; I have come, having flooded the river-banks for you.

Ho Osiris! I am your son Horus; I have come, having ploughed up the lands for you.

Ho Osiris! I am your son Horus; I have come, having constructed canals for you.

Ho Osiris! I am your son Horus; I have come, having cut irrigation channels for you.

Ho Osiris! I am your son Horus; I have come, having made for you a massacre of those who rebelled against you.

Ho Osiris! I am your son Horus; I have come, having made wild bulls and herds into butchery for you.

Ho Osiris! I am your son Horus; I have come, having made provision for you.

Ho Osiris! I am your son Horus; I have come, having brought to you ...

Ho Osiris ! I am your son Horus; I have come, having killed for you ...

Ho Osiris! I am your son Horus; I have come, having struck down calves for you.

Ho Osiris! I am your son Horus; I have come, having wrung the necks of geese and ducks for you.

Ho Osiris! I am your son Horus; I have come, having lassoed your enemies for you with their own ropes.

Ho Osiris! I am your son Horus; I have come, having got rid of your enemies for you down a drain-pipe.

Ho Osiris! I am your son Horus; I have come, having brought you fresh water from Elephantine so that you may be refreshed with it.

Ho Osiris! I am your son Horus; I have come, having brought you all kinds of fresh vegetables.

Ho Osiris! I am your son Horus; I have come, having perpetuated your offerings on earth like Re.

Ho Osiris! I am your son Horus; I have come, having prepared your bread of red emmer in Pe.

Ho Osiris! I am your son Horus; I have come, having prepared your beer from white shert-grain in Dep.

Ho Osiris ! I am your son Horus; I have come, having cultivated barley and emmer for you in the Field of Rushes.

Ho Osiris! I am your son Horus; I have come, having reaped them there for you.

Ho Osiris! I am your son Horus; I have come that I may glorify you.

Ho Osiris! I am your son Horus; I have come that I may cause you to be a soul.

Ho Osiris! I am your son Horus; I have come that I may make you strong.

Ho Osiris! I am your son Horus; I have come that I may cause ...

Ho Osiris! I am your son Horus; I have come that I may cause ...

Ho Osiris! I am your son Horus; I have come that I may make you respected.

Ho Osiris! I am your son Horus; I have come that I may cause you to be feared.

Ho Osiris! I am your son Horus; I have come that I may give you your eyes and the plumes on your head.

Ho Osiris! I am your son Horus; I have come that I may cause Isis and Nephthys to make you enduring.

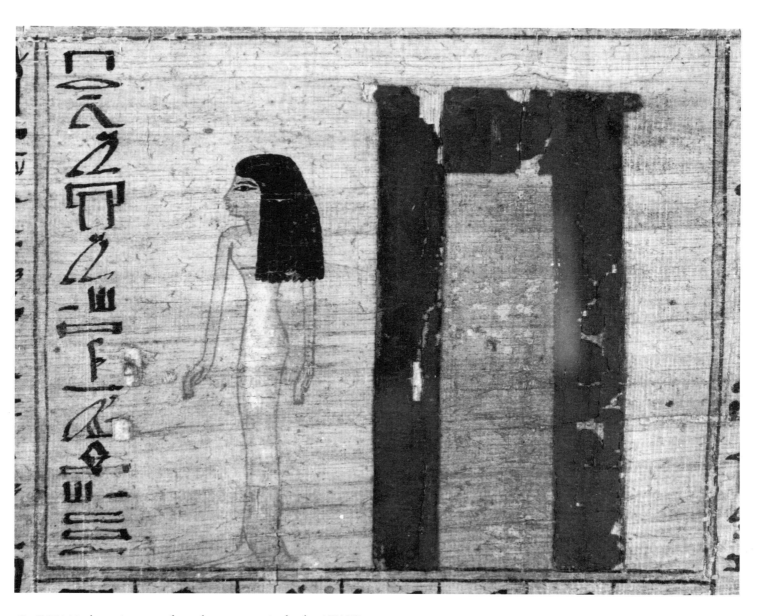

*Spell 174 Muthetepti emerges from the great gate in the sky.* 10010/3

Ho Osiris! I am your son Horus; I have come, having filled the Eye of Horus with unguent for you.

Ho Osiris! I am your son Horus; I have come, having brought you the Eye of Horus so that your face may be provided with it.

## ——— SPELL 174 ———

*Spell for letting a spirit go out from the great gate in the sky*

Your son has acted on your behalf, and the great ones tremble when they see the sword which is in your hand when you ascend from the Netherworld. Hail to you, O Wise One! Geb has created you, the Ennead has borne you. Horus is pleased with his Eye, Atum is pleased with his years, the gods of West and East are pleased with the Great Goddess who came into being in the arms of Her who bore the god.

I am reborn, I see, I behold, I will be yonder, I am

raised up on my side, I make a decree, I hate sleep, (I detest) limpness, and I who was in Nedit stand up. My bread is prepared in Pe, I receive the sceptre in Heliopolis; it was Horus who commanded that I his father be helped. As for the Lord of Storm, the slavering of Seth is forbidden to him.

I will raise up Atum, for my words are great; I have issued from between the thighs of the Ennead, I was conceived by Sakhmet, it was Shesmetet who bore me, a star brilliant and far-travelling, who brings distant products to Re daily. I have come to my throne upon the Vulture and the Cobra, I have appeared as a star.

O you two fighters, tell the Noble One, whoever he may be, that I am this lotus-flower which sprang up from the earth. Pure is he who received me and prepared my place at the nostril of the Great Power. I have come into the Island of Fire, I have set right in the place of wrong, and I am he who guards the linen garments which the Cobra guarded on the night of the great flood. I have appeared as Nefertum, the lotus at the nostril of Re; he issues from the horizon daily, and the gods will be cleansed at the sight of him.

I am he who is vindicated with the kas, who unites hearts, who is in charge of wisdom, a great one under the god, namely Sia who is at the right hand of Re. I have come to my place among the doubles, I unite hearts because of the wisdom of the Great Goddess, I have become Sia, the god at the right hand of Re. O you who are protected by my hand, it is I who say what is in the heart of the Great Goddess in the Festival of Red Linen. I am Sia who is at the right hand of Re, the haughty one who presides over the Cavern of the Abyss.

## —— SPELL 175 ——

*Spell for not dying again*

O Thoth, what is it that has come about through the Children of Nut? They have made war, they have raised up tumult, they have done wrong, they have created rebellion, they have done slaughter, they have created imprisonment, they have reduced what was great to what is little in all that we have made; show greatness, O Thoth! – so says Atum. You shall not witness wrong-doing, you shall not suffer it! Shorten their years, cut short their months, because they have done hidden damage to all that you have made. I have your palette, O Thoth, I bring your inkpot to you; I am not among those who have done hidden damage, and none will work harm on me.

*Thus says N:* O Atum, how comes it that I travel to a desert which has no water and no air, and which is deep, dark and unsearchable ?

ATUM: Live in it in content!

N: But there is no love-making there!

ATUM: I have given spirit-being instead of water, air and love-making, contentment in place of bread and beer – so says Atum. Do not be sorry for yourself, for I will not suffer you to lack.

N: But every god has taken his place in the Bark of Millions of Years!

ATUM: Your seat now belongs to your son Horus – so says Atum – and *he* will despatch the Elders, he will rule from your seat, he will inherit the throne which is in the Island of Fire.

N: Command that I may see his equal, for my face will see the face of the Lord of All. What will be the duration of my life? – so said he.

ATUM: You shall be for millions on millions of years, a lifetime of millions of years. I will despatch the Elders and destroy all that I have made; the earth shall return to the Abyss, to the surging flood, as in its original state. But I will remain with Osiris, I will transform myself into something else, namely a serpent, without men knowing or the gods seeing. How good is what I have done for Osiris, even more than for all the gods! I have given him the desert, and his son Horus is the heir on his throne which is in the Island of Fire; I have made what appertains to his place in the Bark of Millions of Years, and Horus is firm on his throne in order to found his establishments.

N: But the soul of Seth will travel further than all the gods.

ATUM: I have caused his soul which is in the bark to be restrained, so that the body of the god may be afraid.

N: O my father Osiris, do for me what your father Re did for you, so that I may be long-lived on earth, that my throne may be well founded, that my heir may be in good health, that my tomb may be long-enduring, and that these servants of mine may be on earth; let my enemies be split open, may the Scorpion be on their bones, for I am your son, O my father Re; do this for me for the sake of my life, welfare and health, for Horus is firmly established on his throne, and let my lifetime come to attain to the blessed state.

## —— SPELL 176 ——

*Spell for not dying again*

I abhor the eastern land, I will not enter the place of destruction, none shall bring me offerings of what the gods detest, because I pass pure into the midst of the Milky Way, one to whom the Lord of All granted his power on that day when the Two Lands were united in the presence of the Lord of Things.

As for him who knows this spell, he will be a worthy spirit and he will not die again in the realm of the dead.

## —— SPELL 177 ——

*Spell for raising up a spirit and causing a soul to live in the realm of the dead*

*N:* O Nut, Nut, I have cast my father to the earth, with Horus behind me. My wings have grown into those of a falcon, my plumes are those of a sacred falcon, my soul has brought me and its words have equipped me.

*Nut:* You have opened up your place among the stars of the sky, for you are the Lone Star of the sky; see, O N, fair are the orders which you give to the spirits, for you are a Power; you will not go hungry, you are not among them and you will not be among them. See, upon your head as a soul are horns as of a wild bull, for you are a black ram which a white ewe bore, one who sucked from the four teats. The blue-eyed Horus comes to you; the red-eyed Horus, violent of power, waits for you. He meets his soul, his messengers go, his couriers run, they come to him who is supported above the West; this one goes from you of whom it is said: 'The god who speaks to the Field of the Gods.' Your name is vindicated in the presence of the gods, the Ennead raise you up with their hands, the god speaks to the Field of the Gods. Be strong at the door of the kas of the horizon-dwellers, for their doors shall be opened to you, they shall praise you and you shall have power over them ... they go forth and lift up their faces, so that they see you before the Great God. Min ... your head. Someone stands behind you, and you have power; you shall neither perish nor be destroyed, but you shall act among men and gods.

## ——— SPELL 178 ———

*Spell for raising the corpse*, for having power in the eyes and ears and for making the head firm when it has been set in its proper place

Take to yourself the Eye of Horus for which you have asked, namely a funeral meal.

Rejoice, O you who use the hoe! Lift up the heart so as to cleanse the breast, that you may swallow the bright Eye of Horus which is in Heliopolis and drive out what is in the belly of Osiris ... N shall not be hungry, he shall not be thirsty, for Ha has saved him and removed his hunger, and hearts are filled, are filled.

O you who are in charge of food and attend to supplies of drink, N is commended to the House of Bread ... Re himself commended him; Re commends him to those who are in charge of food-supplies for this year. They seize and give to him barley and emmer, for this bread of his belongs to the Great Bull. May you give to N five loaves in the temple, for three loaves are in the sky with Re and two loaves are on earth with the Enneads. Nun departs and sees Re, and it goes well with N on this happy day. N is under the command of Shu and Isis and is united happily with his god. They give bread and beer to N, and they make for him everything good and pure on this happy day.

A meal for the guide who travels, a meal of the Eye of Horus! A meal for all who go in and see the god! May you have power over water, may your shin of beef be on the altar of roast meat – four handfuls of water – according to the command of Osiris for N; Shu has ordered meals for N. That is your bread and beer.

Awake, O Judge! Be high, O Thoth! Awake, you sleepers! Rouse up, O you who are within! Offerings shall be given to you in the presence of Thoth, the Great One who went up from the Nile, and of Wepwawet who issued fom Tamarisk-town. N's mouth is pure, the Ennead has censed N's mouth, and truly pure are his mouth and the tongue which is in his mouth. What N detests is faeces, he rejects urine, even as Seth rejected it. O you two Companions who cross the sky, namely

(Re and) Thoth, take N with you, that he may eat of what you eat, that he may drink of what you drink, that he may sit on what you sit on, that he may be strong by means of that whereby you are strong, that he may sail in that wherein you sail. N's booth is plaited with rushes, N's drink-supply is in the Field of Offerings, his food-supplies are with the gods, and N's water is the wine of Re; he goes round about the sky and travels like Thoth.

N detests hunger, and he will not eat it; he detests thirst. Bread is given to him by the Lord of Eternity, who makes an order for him. N was conceived in the night, he was born in the morning, he belongs to those who are in the suite of Re, who are before the Morning Star; he has brought to you the bread which he has found.

The Eye of Horus drips upon the bush of the djenu-plant, the Foremost of the Westerners comes for him and brings provisions to Horus who presides over the houses. What he lives on, N lives on; what he drinks of, N drinks of; the shin of beef is on the altar of the roast meat, and N is vindicated, even he who is favoured by Anubis who is on his mountain.

Ho N! Such is your good repute in which you were held on earth; you are alive and young every day. Your vision is cleared, you are the Lord of the Horizon, and he gives you bread in its due hour, and his nightly portion. Horus has protected you, he has destroyed the jaws of your enemies, he has arrested the thief at the door of his lair.

Ho N! you have no enemies in the Mansion of the Great One, the balance is true as regards your deeds ... for Osiris, Lord of Provisions for the West. May you go in at will, may you see the Great God in his shape; may there be given to you life for your nose and triumph over your enemies.

Ho N! Your detestation is lies, and the Lords of Offerings will be gracious to you on that night of silence and weeping. Sweet life is given to you from the mouths of the Ennead, and Thoth is pleased about it. May you be triumphant over your enemies, O N; Nut has spread herself over you in her name of Her of Shetpet, and she will cause you to be in the suite of the Great God. You have no enemies, and she will save you from all things evil in her name of 'Great Well', for you are the greatest of her children.

O you who are in charge of the hours, who are before Re, make a path for N that he may pass within the circle of Osiris, Lord of Ankh-tawy, living for ever.

O N, be happy in the suite of Nefertum, the lotus-bloom at the nose of Re ... cleansed in the presence of the gods, that you may see Re for ever.

# ——— SPELL 179 ———

*Spell for leaving yesterday and coming into today, which he asks for himself and his members*

My demise was granted yesterday, I have returned today, I have gone forth in m] own shape; I am tousled, having issued from my imet-tree; M am dishevelled, having gone forth with my sceptre; I am Lord of the Wereret-crown, a third to Nehebkau; I am the Red One whose eye is protected. I died yesterday, I returned today, and a path has been made for me by the door-keeper of the great arena. I have gone out into the day against my enemy, and I have power over him; he has been given over to me and he will not be taken from me, for an end will be put to him under me in the tribunal, Osiris being in his shroud ... I am a possessor of blood on the day of coming into being, I am a possessor of knives and I will not be robbed; a path is prepared for me, I am the embalmer-scribe of Her who is in date-wine, and there is brought to me what appertains to the great Red Crown. The great Red Crown has been given to me, and I go out into the day against yonder enemy of mine so that I may fetch him, for I have power over him; he has been given over to me and he shall not be taken from me, for an end will be put to him under me in the tribunal. I will eat him in the Great Field upon the altar of Wadjet, for I have power over him as Sakhmet the Great. I am a possessor of being, to me belongs the shape of every god when they go round about ...

# ——— SPELL 180 ———

Spell for going out into the day, worshipping Re in the West, giving praise to those who are in the Netherworld; opening a path for a worthy spirit who is in the realm of the dead, granting him his movements, extending his strides, going in and out of the realm of the dead, and taking shape as a living soul.

O Re, you who go to rest as Osiris with all the appearings in glory of the spirits and gods of the West; you are the hidden one of the Netherworld, the holy soul at the head of the West, Wennefer who shall exist for ever and ever.

How well provided are you, O Dweller in the Netherworld! Your son Horus is pleased about you, and he has taken over the governance; may you permit him to appear to those who are in the Netherworld, even he the great star who brings what is his to the Netherworld, and who traverses the place where they are as the son of Re who went forth from Atum.

How well provided are you, O Dweller in the Netherworld! Your stepped throne is in the midst, O Your Majesty the King who rules the Silent Land, great prince of the Wereret-crown, Great God whose throne is secret, Lord of judgement who is over his tribunal.

How well provided are you, O Dweller in the Netherworld! How content are you!

How well provided are you, O Dweller in the Netherworld! The mourners are dishevelled because of you, they clap their hands because of you, they cry out because of you, they lament because of you, they weep because of you. But your soul is joyful, your corpse has power, the souls of Re are on high in the West ... souls when they are set on high in the cavern of the Netherworld, because of the souls of Re who is in the Netherworld in the person of the soul of the Angry One, who rests in the person of his soul.

O Osiris, I am a servant of your chapel which is in the middle of your temple. May you give orders that you grant to me appearance in glory to those who are in the Netherworld, the great star who brings what is his to the Netherworld, who travels over what is in it, the son of Re who issued from Atum. I rest in the Netherworld, I have power in the darkness, I go in and out of it. The arms of Tatenen are what receive me and raise me up. O you who are at peace, give me your arms, for I know the spells for guidance; guide me.

Praise to you who are at peace; give praise joyfully. O Re, be praised through me like Osiris. I have perpetuated your offerings for you, that you may have power through your gifts, just as Re decreed for me. I am the guardian, I am his heir upon earth. Prepare a path for me, O you who are at peace; see, I enter into the Netherworld, I open up the beautiful West, I make firm the staff of Orion and the wig-cover of Him whose name is hidden. Look at me, O you who are at peace, you gods who guide Him of the Netherworld. See, I take my powers, having appeared as master of the mysteries; save me from the whipping-posts and the ropes of the whipping-posts; you shall not bind me to your whipping-posts, you shall not give me over to the place of punishment.

I am the heir of Osiris, I have received his wig-cover in the Netherworld; look at me, for I have appeared in glory in coming forth from your body, I have become his father, and he applauds. Look at me, rejoice over me, for behold, I am on high, I have come into being, one who provides his own shape; open a path to my soul, stand at your proper places, let me be at peace in the beautiful West, open a place for me among you. Open your paths, draw back your bolts. O Re who guides this land, you are the guide of souls, you are the leader of the gods. I am the keeper of the gate, who ushers in those who are to be ushered in; I am one who guards the portals and who sets the gods in their places; I am one who is in his proper place in the Netherworld; I am the surveyor who is in charge of the surveyors; to me belong

*Spell 183* The ibis-headed Thoth offers the signs for 'all life and dominion' to an unseen Osiris. 9901/2

*Spell 182* The mummy of Muthetepti lies in a shrine on a lion-form bed beneath which are containers. At her head stand Nephthys, Imsety and Qebehsenuef, at her foot Isis, Hapy and Duamutef. Above and below sit or stand protective deities brandishing snakes and lizards – symbols of regeneration – and knives. 10010/3

the limits of the Netherworld; I am one who is at peace in the Silent Land, I have made for myself offerings in the West with the souls who are among the gods. I am the guardian of Re, I am the mysterious phoenix, I am one who goes in that I may rest in the Netherworld, and who ascends peacefully to the sky. I am Lord of the Celestial Expanses, I travel through the lower sky in the train of Re; my offerings in the sky are in the Field of Re, my gifts on earth are in the Field of Rushes. I traverse the Netherworld after the manner of Re, I give judgement like Thoth, I walk and am glad, I run at my own pace in my dignity of one whose affairs are secret, my shape is that of the double god Horus-Seth. I am in charge of the gifts to the gods of the Netherworld, one who gives food-offerings to the spirits; I am one stout of heart, smiting my enemies. O you gods and spirits who are before Re and who follow after his soul, usher me in at your usherings, for you are those who guide Re, who usher in those who are in the sky, and I am a soul who is holy in the West.

## —— Spell 181 ——

*Spell for going into the tribunal of Osiris* and the gods who govern the Netherworld, who guard their gates, who make report concerning their courts, who keep the doors of the portals of the West; for taking shape as a living soul, worshipping Osiris, and becoming an Elder of the tribunal.

Hail to you, Foremost of the Westerners, Wennefer, Lord of the Sacred Land! You have appeared in glory like Re, and behold, he has come to see you and to rejoice at seeing your beauty.

> His sun-disc is your sun-disc;
> His rays are your rays;
> His crown is your crown;
> His greatness is your greatness;
> His appearings are your appearings;
> His beauty is your beauty;
> His majesty is your majesty;
> His savour is your savour;
> His extent is your extent;
> His seat is your seat;
> His throne is your throne;
> His heritage is your heritage ;
> His panoply is your panoply;
> His destiny is your destiny;
> His West is your West;
> His goods are your goods;
> His wisdom is your wisdom;
> His distinction is your distinction;
> He who should protect himself does indeed
>     protect himself –
> And vice versa.

> He will not die and you will not die;
> He will triumph over his enemies
> And you will triumph over your enemies;
> Nothing evil will come into being against him,
> And nothing evil will come into being against
>     you for ever and ever.

Hail to you, Osiris, son of Nut, possessor of horns, whose Atef-crown is tall, to whom the Wereret-crown and crook have been given in the presence of the Ennead; the awe of whom Atum created in the hearts of men, gods, spirits and the dead; to whom the crook was given in Heliopolis; great of shape in Busiris; Lord of Fear in the Two Mounds, greatly dreaded in Rosetjau; Lord of fair remembrance in the Castle, who greatly appeared in glory in Abydos; to whom vindication was given in the presence of the Ennead; who protects the great powers; the dread of whom pervades the land; on whom men wait, the Elders being on their mats. Monarch of the gods of the Netherworld, great Power in the sky who rules the living, King of those who are yonder, who glorifies thousands in Kheraha, at whom the sun-folk rejoice; possessor of choice morsels in the Upper Houses, for whom a shin of beef is prepared in Memphis; for whom the night-ritual is performed in Letopolis.

You are a Great One whose strength is mighty, and your son Horus is your protector; he will remove all evil which is on you. Your flesh is knit together for you, your members are recreated for you, your bones are reassembled for you, and there is brought to you ... Rise up, Osiris; I have given you my hand and have caused you to stand up living for ever. Geb has wiped your mouth for you, the Great Ennead calls on you ... when they travel protected to the gate of the Netherworld. Your mother Nut has put her arms about you that she may protect you, and she will continually guard you, even you the high-born. Your sisters Isis and Nephthys will come to you, they will enfold you with life, prosperity and health, and you will be glad through them; they (will rejoice) over you through love of you. They will enclose everything for you within your arms; the gods, the lords of kas will care for you, and they will worship you for ever.

Happy are you, O Osiris! You have appeared in glory, you have power, you are a spirit; you have made your shape everlasting, and your face is that of Anubis. Re rejoices over you and he is well disposed towards your beauty. You have seated yourself on your pure throne which Geb, who loves you, made for you; you receive him in your arms in the West, you cross the sky daily, you convey him to his mother Nut when he goes to rest daily in the West in the Bark of Re, together with Horus who loves you. The protection of Re is your safeguard, the power of Thoth is behind you, and the spells of Isis pervade your members.

I have come to you, O Lord of the Sacred Land, Osiris Foremost of the Westerners, Wennefer who will exist for ever and ever. My heart is true, my hands are clean, I bring a meal to its owner and offerings to him who made them. I have come here to your towns, I have done what is good on earth, I have smitten your enemies for you as bulls, I have slain cattle for you, and I cause them to fall on their faces before you. I have purified your pure place, I have cleansed your lustral basin, I have wrung the necks of birds upon your altar for the benefit of your soul, of your powers, and of the gods and goddesses who are in your suite.

As for him who knows this book, nothing evil shall have power over him, he shall not be turned away at the gates of the West; he shall go in and out, and bread and beer and all good things shall be given to him in the presence of those who are in the Netherworld.

## —— SPELL 182 ——
[illustrated pp.178-9]

*Book for the permanence of Osiris, giving breath to the Inert One in the presence of Thoth, and repelling the enemy of Osiris,* who comes yonder in his various shapes; the safeguarding, protection and defence in the realm of the dead which Thoth himself has carried out in order that the sunlight might rest on him every day.

I am Thoth the skilled scribe whose hands are pure, a possessor of purity, who drives away evil, who writes what is true, who detests falsehood, whose pen defends the Lord of All; master of laws who interprets writings, whose words establish the Two Lands.

I am the Lord of Justice, one truly precise to the gods, who judges a matter so that it may continue in being; who vindicates him whose voice is hushed; who dispels darkness and clears away the storm. I have given the sweet breath of the north wind to Osiris Wennefer as when he went forth from the womb of her who bore him; I cause Re to go to rest as Osiris, Osiris having gone to rest at the going to rest of Re; I cause him to go in to the secret cavern in order to revive the heart of the Inert One, the Holy Soul at the head of the West. Acclamation for the Inert One, Wennefer the son of Nut!

I am Thoth, the favoured of Re; Lord of strength who ennobles him who made him; great of magic in the Bark of Millions of Years; master of laws who makes the Two Lands content; whose power protects her who bore him; who gets rid of noise and quells uproar; who does what Re in his shrine approves.

I am Thoth who made Osiris triumphant over his enemies.

I am Thoth who foretells the morrow and foresees the future, whose act cannot be brought to naught; who guides sky, earth and the Netherworld; who nourishes the sun-folk. I give breath to him who is in the secret places by means of the power which is on my mouth, and Osiris is triumphant over his enemies.

I have come to you, O Lord of the Sacred Land, Osiris the Bull of the West, and I have made you flourishing for ever, I grant eternity as a protection for your members.

I have come to you bearing the amulet which is in my hand, my protection for the daily course. Protection and life are about him, namely this god who guards his ka, King of the Netherworld, Ruler of the West, who takes possession of the sky in vindication, whose Atef-crown is firm, who appears in the White Crown, having grasped the crook and the flail; whose power is great and whose Wereret-crown is mighty. He has assembled all the gods, for love has pervaded their bodies for Wennefer, who shall exist for ever and ever.

Hail to you, Foremost of the Westerners, who re-fashioned mankind, who comes as one rejuvenated in his time, better than he was formerly! Your son Horus is your protector, in the function of Atum; your face is potent, O Wennefer. Raise yourself, O Bull of the West, be firm as you were firm in the womb of your mother Nut. She enfolds you, even you who issued from her; may your heart be firm in its place, may your heart be like it was before, may your nose endure with life and dominion, you being alive, renewed and young like Re every day. Great, great in triumph is Osiris – may he endure in life.

I am Thoth; I have pacified Horus, I have calmed the Rivals in their time of raging; I have come and have washed away the blood, I have calmed the tumult and have eliminated everything evil.

I am Thoth; I have performed the night-ritual in Letopolis.

I am Thoth; I have come today from Pe and Dep, I have conducted the oblations, I have given bread-offerings as gifts to the spirits, I have guarded the elbow of Osiris whom I embalmed and I have sweetened his odour like a pleasant smell.

I am Thoth; I have come today from Kheraha, I have knotted the cord and have put the ferry-boat in good order, I have fetched East and West, I am uplifted on my standard higher than any god in this my name of Him whose face is on high; I have opened those things which are good in this my name of Wepwawet; I have given praise and have made homage to Osiris Wennefer, who shall exist for ever and ever.

***Spell 185*** *The deceased and his wife stand with arms raised in adoration before a heaped offering-table and a shrine topped by an archaic falcon in which sits Osiris. Unusually, the god is not depicted wrapped like a mummy. Behind him stands Isis; before him is the imywet-fetish of Anubis.* 10478/1

# SPELL 183
[illustrated p.178]

*Worshipping* Osiris, giving praise to him and homage to Wennefer, doing obeisance to the Lord of the Sacred Land, exalting Him who is on his sand, by N. *He says:* I have come to you, O Son of Nut, Osiris, Ruler of Eternity; I am in the suite of Thoth, and I am joyful because of all that he has done. He brings to you sweet air for your nose, life and dominion for your face, and fair is the north wind which goes forth from Atum to your nostrils, O Lord of the Sacred Land. He causes the sun to shine on your breast, he illumines the dark way for you, he removes the evil which is on your body by means of the power which is on his mouth. He has pacified the Rival Gods for you, he has stopped the raging and the tumult for you, he has made the Rivals well-disposed to you, and the Two Lands are peacefully reconciled before you; he has driven anger from their hearts for you, and they fraternise with each other. Your son Horus is vindicated in the presence of the entire Ennead; the kingship over the land has been given to him, and his uraeus pervades the entire land. The throne of Geb has been allotted to him, and the potent office of Atum has been confirmed in writing in a testament which has been engraved on a block of sandstone, according as your father Ptah-Tatenen commanded from upon the great throne. His brother has been set for him upon the Supports of Shu, raising up water to the mountains in order to make flourishing what comes out on the desert and the fruit which comes forth on the flat-land, and he gives produce by water and by land. The gods of the sky and the gods of the earth have entrusted the earth to your son Horus, and they follow to his court; all that he has decreed is in their sight, and they perform it immediately.

Your heart is happy; your heart, O Lord of the Gods, possesses all joy. The Black Land and the Red Land are at peace, and they serve your uraeus; the shrines are made firm in their places, towns and nomes are established by name. They make presentation to you with god's-offerings; men make offering to your name for ever; men call out praises to you because of your name; men present libations to your ka and invocation-offerings to the spirits who are in your suite; water is poured over halved bread-cakes for the souls of the dead in this land. Every design of yours is as effective as in its former state; appear, O Son of Nut, as the Lord of All in his glorious appearings, for you are living, permanent, young and real. Your father Re has made your body hale, your Ennead give you praise; Isis is with you and will not forsake you, and there will be no more felling of your enemies. The lords of all the lands worship your beauty like Re when he shines at dawn. You appear as one upraised on his standard, and your beauty is exalted and widespread. The kingship of Geb has been given to you, for he is your father who created your beauty. It was your mother Nut who bore the gods who brought your body into being, who bore you as the greatest of the Five Gods, who made the White Crown firm on your head, and you grasped the crook and the flail while you were yet in the womb, before you had come forth on earth. You have appeared as Lord of the Two Lands, and the Atef-crown of Re is on your brow; the gods come to you bowing down, and the fear of you pervades their bodies; they see you in the dignity of Re, and the dread of Your Majesty is in their hearts. Life is with you, food follows after you, and Truth is presented before you.

May you let me be in Your Majesty's suite as when I was on earth; may my soul be summoned, and may it find you beside the Lords of Truth. I come from the city of the god, the primeval region; soul, ka and spirit are what is in this land. Such is its god, namely the lord of Truth, possessor of provisions, rich in precious things, he to whom every land is drawn. Upper Egypt comes downstream to Lower Egypt with wind and oar to make it festive with gifts, in accordance with what its god commanded; as for anyone who rests within it, he will never have to express a wish. Happy is he who does what is right for the god in it; he will grant old age to him who does it until he reaches the blessed state, and the end of this is a happy burial in the Sacred Land.

I come to you with my hands bearing Truth, and my heart has no lies in it. I place Truth before you, for I know that you live by it. I have done no wrong in this land, and no man will suffer loss of his possessions.

I am Thoth, the skilled scribe whose hands are pure, the Lord of purity who drives away evil; who writes what is true, who detests falsehood, whose pen defends the Lord of All; master of laws who interprets writings, and whose words have settled the Two Lands.

I am Thoth, Lord of Justice, who vindicates him whose voice is hushed; protector of the poor man who has suffered loss of his property; who dispels darkness and clears away the storm. I have (given) breath to Wennefer, even the fair breeze of the north wind, as when he came forth from his mother's womb. I have caused him to enter into the secret cavern in order to revive the heart of the Inert One, Wennefer the son of Nut, the vindicated Horus.

# SPELL 185
[illustrated pp.182-3,186]

Giving praise to Osiris, doing homage to the Lord of Eternity, propitiating the god with what he desires, speaking truth to him who knows its lord.

Hail to you, you august, great and potent god, prince for ever, foremost of place in the Night-bark, great of glorious appearings in the Day-bark, to whom is given acclamation in sky and earth, whom the patricians and the common folk extol! Great is the awe of him in the hearts of men, spirits and the dead; his powers were granted in Mendes, the awe of him in Heracleopolis, his sacred images are placed in Heliopolis and many are his shapes in the Pure Place.

My heart comes to you bearing Truth, my heart has no falseness. May you grant that I be among the living, and that I fare downstream and upstream in your suite.

## —— Spell 186 ——
[illustrated pp.186-7]

### Text accompanying a picture of the goddess Hathor

Hathor, Lady of the West; She of the West; Lady of the Sacred Land; Eye of Re which is on his forehead; kindly of countenance in the Bark of Millions of Years; a resting-place for him who has done right within the boat of the blessed; who built the Great Bark of Osiris in order to cross the water of truth.

## —— Spell 187 ——

*Spell for going in to the Ennead*

Hail to you, Ennead of Re! I have come to you, for I am in the suite of Re; prepare a path for me that I may pass among you, for I will not be turned away because of what I have done this day.

## —— Spell 188 ——

*Sending a soul, building tomb-chambers, and going out into the day among men*

In peace, O Anubis! It goes well with the son of Re at peace with my Sacred Eye; may you glorify my soul and my shade, that they may see Re by means of what he brings. I ask that I may come and go and that I may have power in my feet so that this person may see him in any place where he is, in my nature, in my wisdom, and in the true shape of my equipped and divine spirit. It shines as Re, it travels as Hathor. Therefore you have granted that my soul and my shade may walk on their feet to the place where this person is, so that he may stand, sit and walk, and enter into his chapel of eternity, because I am

one of the entourage of Osiris, who goes by night and returns by day, and no god can be created when I am silent.

## —— Spell 189 ——

*Spell for preventing a man from going upside down and from eating faeces*

What I doubly detest, I will not eat; what I detest is faeces, and I will not eat it; excrement, I will not consume it. It shall not fall from my belly, it shall not come near my fingers, and I will not touch it with my toes.

'What will you live on', say the gods and spirits to me, 'in this place to which you have been brought?'

'I will live on seven loaves which have been brought to me; four loaves are with Horus and three loaves with Thoth.'

'Where is it granted to you to eat?' say the gods and spirits to me.

'I will eat under that sycamore of Hathor, for I have placed my portions there for her minstrels. My fields have been assigned to me in Busiris, my green plants are in Heliopolis, and I will live on bread of white emmer and beer of red barley; there shall be given to me my father's and my mother's families, and my door-keeper in respect of my land.'

Open to me; may there be space for me, make a path for me, that I may dwell as a living soul in the place which I desire, and I will not be subdued by my enemies. I detest faeces and will not eat it, I have not gone infected into Heliopolis. Be far from me, for I am a bull whose throne is provided; I have flown up as a swallow, I have cackled as a goose, I have alighted on the beautiful tree which is in the middle of the island in the flood. I have gone up and have alighted on it, and I will not suffer neglect; as for him who dwells under it, he is a great god.

What I detest, I will not eat; what I detest is faeces, and I will not eat it; what my ka detests is faeces, and it shall not enter into my body, I will not approach it with my hands, I will not tread on it with my sandals. I will not flow for you into a bowl, I will not empty out for you into a basin, ... I will not take anything from upon the banks of your ponds, I will not depart upside down for you.

Overleaf: ***Spells 185 and 186*** *On the left, in a shrine topped by a falcon head and a frieze of cobras, stands the falcon-headed, mummiform funerary god Sokar-Osiris holding crook, flail and was-sceptre (Spell 185). To the right, behind a heaped offering-table, stands the hippopotamus-goddess Opet wearing horns and disc, resting on a sa-amulet, a sign of protection, and offering life and a flame to the deceased (see Spell 137в). Behind her Hathor as a cow wearing a menat-collar emerges from the Western Mountain, on whose slopes is Ani's pyramid-capped tomb chapel, into the clumps of papyrus which fringe the Nile Valley (Spell 186). 10470/37*

Thus says that one who cannot count: 'What will you live on in this land to which you have come so that you may be a spirit?'

'I will live on bread of black barley and beer of white emmer, four loaves being in the Field of Offerings, for I am more distinguished than any god. I will have four loaves daily and four portions of roast meat in Heliopolis, for I am more distinguished than any god.'

Thus says that one who cannot count: 'Who will bring it to you, and where will you eat?'

'Upon that pure river-bank on the day when I have brightened my teeth with myrrh.'

Thus says that one who cannot count: 'What will you live on in this land to which you have come so that you may be a spirit ?'

'I will live on those seven loaves; four loaves are brought from the house of Horus and three loaves from the house of Thoth.'

Thus says that one who cannot count: 'Who will bring them to you?'

'A nurse from the house of the Great One and a stewardess from Heliopolis.'

'Where will you eat them?'

'Under the branches of the djebat-nefret tree beside ... to which I have been taken.'

Thus says that one who cannot count: 'Will you live on someone else's goods every day?'

I say to him: 'I plough the lands which are in the Field of Rushes.'

Thus says that one who cannot count: 'Who will guard them for you?'

I say to him: 'It is the twin children of the King of Lower Egypt who will look after them.'

'Who will plough them for you?'

'The greatest of the gods of the sky and of the gods of the earth. Men will thresh for me as for the Apis-bull who presides over Sais, men will reap for me as for Seth, Lord of the Northern Sky.'

O you who turn back the ished-tree on your own account, who uproot falsehood, whose faces are pure, shall I be with the confederates of Seth on the mountain of Bakhu? I will dwell with those potent noble dead in order to excavate the pool of Osiris and to rub (his) heart, and there shall be no accusation against me, N, by any living person.

# GLOSSARY

ABYDOS: ancient town in Upper Egypt, especially sacred to Osiris.

ABYSS: the primeval chaos before creation, thought of as a waste of waters.

AKER: earth-god represented as a pair of lions or sphinxes back to back.

AMMIT: hybrid monster present at the Weighing of the Heart, ready to gobble up those hearts weighed down with sin.

AMUN: Theban god who became state god of Egypt from the New Kingdom onwards.

ANDJET: 9th nome of Lower Egypt in the central Delta; ancient religious centre.

ANKH-TAWY: 'Life-of-the-Two-Lands': a name of Memphis.

ANUBIS: Jackal-god of embalming, closely associated with Osiris.

APEP: Serpent-demon, arch-enemy of the sun-god.

APIS: sacred bull worshipped at Memphis, earthly manifestation of Ptah.

AQEN: god associated with the celestial ferryman.

AROURA: area of land, about two-thirds of an acre.

ASH: Libyan god closely associated with Seth.

ASYUT: ancient town in Middle Egypt.

ATEF: tall white crown flanked with ostrich feathers and horns, worn especially by Osiris.

ATUM: primeval sun-god worshipped at Heliopolis; also the aged sun at its setting.

BABAI: minor deity, usually malevolent but also connected with the crowns of Egypt.

BAH: heron-god symbolic of abundance and plenty.

BAKHU: eastern mountain where the sun rises.

BASTET: cat-goddess of festivity and fertility with cult-centre at Bubastis.

BATY: a minor bull-god.

BES: benevolent dwarf-demon with lion-like features.

BLACK LAND: the fertile Nile Valley as opposed to the flanking Red Land; Egypt.

BUBASTIS: cult-city of Bastet in the eastern Delta.

BUSIRIS: city in the central Delta sacred to Osiris.

BUTO: city in the northern Delta sacred to the serpent-goddess Wadjet.

CHAOS-GODS: deities of the primeval chaos.

CHEMMIS: the hidden place in the Delta where Isis hid from Seth and brought up the infant Horus.

CHILDREN OF IMPOTENCE: opprobrious epithet of evil spirits.

CONCLAVES: assemblies of the gods, one of Upper Egypt and one of Lower Egypt.

COPTOS: town of Upper Egypt, centre of the worship of Min.

CROCODILOPOLIS: cult-centre in the Faiyum of the crocodile-god Sobk.

CUBIT: measure of 20.6 in.

DAY-BARK: boat in which the sun-god crosses the sky above the earth.

DEP: one of the two towns (with Pe) which, united, formed the Delta city of Buto, predynastic capital of Lower Egypt.

DJAFY: minor deity, son of Hathor.

DJED-PILLAR: cult object resembling a tree trunk with lopped-off horizontal branches, sacred to Osiris, Ptah and Sokar.

DISMEMBERED ONE: the dead Osiris before resurrection.

DOUBLE LION: form of the sun-god as two lions back to back.

DUAMUTEF: jackal-headed Canopic deity, one of the Four Sons of Horus.

EDFU: cult-centre of Horus in Upper Egypt.

ELEPHANTINE: island at the First Cataract; southernmost border of Egypt proper; source of the Nile in Egypt.

ENNEAD: company of Nine Gods.

EYE OF HORUS: torn out by Seth, restored by Thoth, symbolic of everything good, beneficial and pleasant.

FAIYUM: inland lake and marsh area west of the Nile in Middle Egypt, centre of the worship of the crocodile-god Sobk.

FENKHU: people of Syria.

FIELD OF OFFERINGS, FIELD OF RUSHES: Egyptian equivalent of the Elysian Fields.

FIVE GODS: gods of the five epagomenal days at the end of the 360-day year, namely Osiris, Horus, Seth, Isis and Nephthys.

FLAIL: whip-like part of the royal insignia.

FOREMOST OF THE WESTERNERS: an epithet of Osiris.

GEB: earth-god, consort of Nut; one of the Ennead of Heliopolis.

GOD'S FATHER: priestly rank.

GREAT CACKLER: epithet of the creator-god when in the form of a goose.

HA: god of the West.

HAPI: god of the Nile, symbolic of abundance.

HAPY: ape-headed Canopic deity, one of the Four Sons of Horus.

HATHOR: cow-goddess of love; patroness of the West.

HELIOPOLIS: ancient centre of the sun-cult, now part of modern Cairo.

HEMEN: falcon-god worshipped near Esna in Upper Egypt.

HENU: the Sacred Bark of Sokar; Sokar himself.

HERACLEOPOLIS: a religious and political centre on the west bank in Middle Egypt near the Faiyum.

HERMOPOLIS: ancient religious centre of Middle Egypt, especially associated with Thoth.

HOGGING-BEAM: beam running the length of a vessel at deck level to lend rigidity to the hull.

HORAKHTY: 'Horus-of-the-Horizon': sun-god, usually falcon-headed; often combined with Re as Re-Horakhty.

HORDEDEF: son of King Khufu (Cheops) of the Fourth Dynasty who built the Great Pyramid; later revered as a wise man.

HORUS: falcon-god: ancient creator-god; opponent of Seth; son of Osiris (and Isis) and his successor to the kingship of Egypt.

HOTEP: god personifying the Elysian Fields.

HU: authority personified as a god.


IGAU: another name for Anubis.

IHET: sky-cow who gave birth to the sun.

IMAU: cult-place in the western Delta.

IMPERISHABLE STARS: the circumpolar stars.

IMSETY: human-headed Canopic deity, one of the Four Sons of Horus.

INERT ONE: the dead Osiris before resurrection.

ISDES: form of the god Thoth.

ISIS: mother-goddess, sister and wife of Osiris, mother of the young Horus.


KA: the vital life-force or genius of a person, born with him and resembling him exactly. Attendant on him in life and especially death.

KHEPRI: scarab or dung beetle representing the young sun.

KHERAHA: religious centre south of modern Cairo.

KHNUM: ram-god who created man on a potter's wheel.

KHONS: Theban moon-god.

KITES, THE TWO: Isis and Nephthys as birds lamenting the death of Osiris.


LAKE OF THE TWO KNIVES: sacred water at Hermopolis where the sun-god came into being.

LETOPOLIS: religious centre at the apex of the Delta, cult-place of Horus.

LIMP ONE: the dead Osiris, before resurrection.


MAAT: goddess of truth, justice and cosmic order; often depicted as a small seated figure with an ostrich feather on her head being presented to a god by a worshipper.

MAFDET: protective goddess, killer of snakes, in the form of a civet or ocelot.

MANSION OF THE PRINCE: palace at Heliopolis where divine justice is dispensed.

MANSION OF THE PYRAMIDION: temple of the sun-god in Heliopolis.

MANU: western mountain where the sun sets.

MASTER CRAFTSMAN: title of the High-Priest of Ptah at Memphis.

MEMPHIS: first capital of Dynastic Egypt; cult-centre of Ptah; almost opposite modern Cairo.

MENDES: religious centre in the central Delta.

MENQET: goddess of beer.

MIN: ithyphallic fertility god of Coptos.

MNEVIS: bull sacred to the sun-god, worshipped at Heliopolis.

MONT: falcon-headed Theban war-god.

MOUNDS: the 14 mounds or regions of the Elysian Fields.

MUT: vulture mother-goddess of Thebes; consort of Amun.


N: name of the deceased person, whosoever he might be.

NAREF: necropolis near Heracleopolis associated with the Osiris myth.

NEDIT: place near Abydos where Osiris was murdered.

NEDJEFET: place in the region of Asyut.

NEFERTUM: god of the lotus, son of Ptah.

NEHEBKAU: serpent-god, a form of Re.

NEITH: ancient creator-goddess, worshipped especially at Sais in the Delta.

NEKHEN: ancient capital of Upper Egypt, cult-centre of Horus.

NEPHTHYS: sister of Isis and Osiris, consort of Seth, mother of Anubis.

NESHMET-BARK: Sacred Bark of Osiris.

NETJERU: ancient town in the 12th Lower Egyptian nome, in the northern central Delta.

NIGHT-BARK: boat in which the sun-god sails through the Netherworld.

NOME: one of the 42 administrative and religious districts into which Egypt was divided, 22 in Upper Egypt, 20 in Lower Egypt.

NUN: the primeval watery Abyss personified as a god.

NUBIA: the land south of Egypt proper; the area between the First and Second Cataracts.

NUT: sky-goddess whose arched body formed the vault of heaven, consort of the earth-god Geb; one of the Heliopolitan Ennead.


OMBITE: He of the Upper Egyptian town of Ombos: epithet of Seth.

OSIRIS: God of the dead; legendary primeval king of Egypt slain by his brother Seth; also a title commonly prefixed to the name of the deceased who thus became identified with the god.


PAKHET: lioness-goddess of Middle Egypt.

PE: one of the two towns (with Dep) which, united, formed the Delta city of Buto, predynastic capital of Lower Egypt.

PELICAN: as goddess, advocate of the dead, mother of the dead or even the deceased himself.

PER-NESER: national shrine of Lower Egypt.

PER-WER: national shrine of Upper Egypt.

PILLAR-OF-HIS-MOTHER: i.e. her sole support, god of the Thinite nome and a grade of funerary priest.

PTAH: human-form creator-god of Memphis.

PUNT: also called God's Land, source of aromatic resins for incense, probably in the region of modern Somalia.

QEBEHSENUEF: falcon-headed Canopic deity, one of the four Sons of Horus.

RE: form of the sun-god at his noon-day strength, often falcon-headed.

RED CROWN: distinctive royal crown of the kingdom of Lower Egypt.

RED LAND: the desert flanking Egypt, as opposed to the Black Land of Egypt proper.

RENENUTET: harvest-goddess and nurse in serpent-form.

RIVALS, THE: Horus and Seth when they contended for the kingship of Egypt after the murder of Osiris.

ROD: measure of 100 cubits = approximately 172 ft.

ROSETJAU: name of the Necropolis of Giza or Memphis, later extended to mean the Other World in general.

SACRED EYE: eye of Horus torn out by Seth and restored by Thoth, symbolic for everything good, beneficial and pleasant. Also the eye of the sun-god symbolising the sun's destructive power.

SACRED LAND: the necropolis.

SAIS: ancient city in the northern central Delta, cult-centre of Neith.

SAKHMET: lioness-goddess symbolic of destructive power, consort of Ptah at Memphis.

SATIS: goddess of Elephantine associated with Khnum.

SEBEG: the planet Mercury as god.

SEKHAT-HOR: 'She-who-remembered-Horus': cow-goddess.

SELKET: scorpion-goddess, protectress of the dead.

SEM-PRIEST: funerary priest; supervisor of the burial rites.

SEPA: town in the Heliopolitan nome sacred to Anubis.

SESHAT: goddess of writing and reckoning.

SETH: god of storms and the desert; brother and murderer of Osiris and rival of Horus; also the god who guards the sun-god Re from the evil serpent Apep.

SHABTI: magical figurine, servant of the deceased, which will carry out on behalf of its dead master all the hard work required of him in the Other Life.

SHESMETET: lioness-goddess, personification of divine power.

SHESMU: god of the wine-press.

SHETYT-SHRINE: sanctuary of Sokar at Memphis.

SHORES OF REKHTY: place in the extreme north of Egypt.

SHU: god of the air, consort of Tefnut; one of the Heliopolitan Ennead.

SIA: intelligence personified as a god.

SILENT LAND: realm of the dead.

SISTRUM-PLAYER: musician-priest of Hathor (a sistrum is the Egyptian rattle); also the name of the goddess' young son.

SOBK: crocodile-god, son of Neith.

SOKAR: falcon-headed god of the dead in the Memphite area; often combined with Ptah as Ptah-Sokar.

SOPD: god of the eastern Delta.

SOTHIS: Sirius the Dog-star as goddess; sometimes takes the role of Isis.

SUPPORTS OF SHU: the columns of air supporting the sky at the four cardinal points.

TATENEN: Memphite creation-god assimilated to Ptah.

TAYT: goddess of weaving.

TEFNUT: lioness-goddess, consort of Shu; one of the Heliopolitan Ennead.

THINIS, THINITE NOME: religious centre of Upper Egypt where Osiris was worshipped; also the district of which it was the capital.

THOTH: scribe of the gods, god of wisdom and learning represented as an ibis or a baboon; mediator between Seth and Horus; restorer of the Sacred Eye to Horus.

TJEBU: ancient town in the 10th Upper Egyptian nome.

TJEKEM: name of the sun-god.

TJENENET-SHRINE: originally the holy-of-holies at Memphis.

TJENMYT: goddess of beer.

TWO BANKS, TWO LANDS: name for Egypt.

TWO FLEDGLINGS: Horus the Protector of his father and Horus the Eyeless.

UNWEARYING STARS: stars which rise and set.

URAEUS: upreared cobra, symbol of royalty.

WADJET: serpent-goddess worshipped at Buto; protectress of Lower Egypt.

WENES: ancient town in the 19th Upper Egyptian nome, on the west bank in Middle Egypt.

WENNEFER: name of Osiris.

WENTI: name of the sun-god.

WENU, WENUT: religious centre near Hermopolis and its hare-form goddess.

WEPWAWET: 'Opener-of-the-paths': wolf-god of Asyut, closely connected with Osiris.

WERERET: a name of the white crown of Upper Egypt.

WEST: the region where the sun set, hence the land of the dead.

WESTERNERS: the dead.

WHITE CROWN: the crown of Upper Egypt.

XOIS: religious centre in the central Delta.